ACT OF DESPERATION

ARTHUR RICHTER

Copyright @2021 by Arthur Richter

All rights reserved. No part of this book may be reproduced in any form or by any electronic or mechanical means, including information storage and retrieval systems, without permission in writing from the publisher, except by reviewers, who may quote brief passages in a review.

This publication contains the opinions and ideas of its author. It is intended to provide helpful and informative material on the subjects addressed in the publication. The author and publisher specifically disclaim all responsibility for any liability, loss or risk, personal or otherwise, which is incurred as a consequence, directly or indirectly, of the use and application of any of the contents of this book.

WORKBOOK PRESS LLC
187 E Warm Springs Rd,
Suite B285, Las Vegas, NV 89119, USA

Website:	https://workbookpress.com/
Hotline:	1-888-818-4856
Email:	admin@workbookpress.com

Ordering Information:
Quantity sales. Special discounts are available on quantity purchases by corporations, associations, and others.
For details, contact the publisher at the address above.

ISBN-13:   978-1-955459-33-4 (Paperback Version)
           978-1-955459-34-1 (Digital Version)

REV. DATE: 13/05/2021

Act of Desperation

By: Mr. Arthur Richter

Chapter 1

It was a warm August evening Ma and us kids were sitting having a good old time talking about everything, and nothing and just what came to our minds, on the front steps of the apartment house we lived in.

My mother Mary, with my older sister Pat who was going on fifteen. Along with my other older sister Christ, who was thirteen, then there was my older brother Paul, who was twelve, and myself Art who was the youngest going on ten years old.

My mother Mary was in her thirties. Where seeing her from my eyes. She was a very attractive woman. Where yet one wouldn't know it just by just looking at her, by the way she was dress herself.

Where at the time, we were living on welfare? In a rundown apartment building all wearing hand me down clothes. From the church, and the Goodwill. Do to our father Frank. Inability to be able to prove for his family. Being the family drunk, and we all had to suffer because of his dependency on alcohol.

When Christ alarmingly shouted out! Getting everyone attention but, knowing just by the way she said it. If had to be her seeing dad coming home.

" Oh, no... Not again..."

"What is it Christ?" We all asked at the same time looking at her.

"Look..." She pointed in the direction, down the street across from where we were sitting.

Where we all stared in the direction she was pointing her finger. To see what she was so alarmed about. Where it didn't take us long to discover the reason behind her outburst.

Where our eyes locked onto three, figures that were approaching us, from across the street. Where sure enough it was dad. Being dragged home again, stinking drunk again by two, other men holding him up between them.

The three, of them were all stumbling over each other while walking towards us. Where they then preceded to push, and shove their way through us. As we all rose to let them pass, as they stumbled dragging dad along with themselves up the steps. Into the front door of the apartment building.

Paranoiac fear ran ramped through are minds! Knowing just how mean, and cruel dad becomes when he's drunk, where he would eventually always winds up yelling, and beating on us.

"Ma, why can't we just leave him?" I asked as we all sat back down on the steps. Not wanting to follow dad and his friends up to are apartment.

" He would only come after us no matter where we were we would go dear."

"What are we to do Ma?" I nervously asked." You know how he is when he's drunk."

"Wait honey, he's slowly drinking himself to death. Judging from the way he's going at it lately. It's not going to take too much longer."

"Ma, why don't we go to the police?" Christ ask

"What good would that do us? They would only release him when he sobered up, and we would find ourselves worse off than we are now."

"Mary...!" Frank yelled down. Sticking his head out of the kitchen window, yelling out to her.

" You better get all you assess up here right now! All of you...!"

"Oh, Ma...?!" Paul panicky cried out to her." I'm so scared ...! Please Ma, do we've to go up there?!"

"Yes, we've to Paul, now we better get upstairs before we really get him mad. You all go to your bedroom, and stay out of sight, and let me handle him. Now remember don't say or do anything that might provoke him."

Ma, Lead the way. Leading us all up the steps into the door of the apartment building. Then up the steps to the second floor. Where she stood inhaling a deep breath, before opening the door. To lead all us kids inside, into kitchen where we all came upon, and his two drinking partners. Sitting around the kitchen table, drinking still more beer as we entered.

"Well, it's about time you got you assess up here..." Dad slobbered yelled out. Wiping off the deer drooling down his chin, with the back of his hand. As the 3 of them sat around the table in T-shirts. As we all gathered up around Ma, hoping that he would ignore us.

Dad was gone for two, days. Out on one of his drinking binges. Where all 3 of them stunk from a reeking beer odor, where they all looked like they slept in the gutter.

"Well, don't just stand they gawking...!" Dad annoyingly shouted out." Close the damn door Mary, and as for you brats. All of you get your assess into the bedroom, and stay there out of my sight. If you know what's good for you.. Now move it!" He dementedly shouted.

Where I slammed the kitchen door shut for mom, Then followed the others running literally terrified out of the kitchen behind them, and into the one bedroom, that we all shared together.

As if the devil himself was chasing after me.

Being the last one, of make it into the bedroom. Where fearfully closed the door behind me but, purposely leaving it slightly ajar. In order to hear what was going on in the kitchen.

Using it as a warning precautions to let us know if he was coming into are room, and the mood he was in.

Where at time we would all gather up behind to listen in on what was going on in the kitchen. While hoping, and praying he wasn't losing his temper, or getting himself upset. To where he would lash out at Ma, for some reason or another.

"As for you!" Frank yelled out at Mary." Get me some more beer out of the ice box, and don't tell me there isn't any. We brought some with us, now move it!"

"Say Frank how's about a game of cards?" The fat beer belly guy sitting to the right side of Frank asked.

"Sure why the hell not but, what will we play for?"

"Pennies I guess that's all we've left between us." He replied back. Slyly looking over in Mary's direction. Getting an insidious grin upon his face while answering Frank.

"Mary bring me the cards!" Frank demandingly yelled out at her." And where in the hell are those fucken beer?!"

* * * *

Us kids where sitting in the dark whispering amongst ourselves, on Pat's bed. Listening to everything that was going on in the kitchen, while talking amongst ourselves.

Listening to them boosting and bragging about what great lovers they were. Trying to outdo the other. Acting in a vulgar, revolting manner. While Ma, waited on them, bringing them more beer.

"Pat I'm scared...!" Christ nervously cried saying." He's getting even more drunker than when he came home with those two, drunken friends of his.

What if he might decide to come in here and hurt us again... After those two, other guy finally leave?!"

"Not me he's not. Not this time!" I angrily whispered out saying."

He doesn't scare me! I'm going to sleep with my baseball bat right alongside me tonight. If he so much as touches me! I'll hit him right on his big fat drunken head with it!"

"Shut up Art." Pat alarmingly spoke up saying." You sawed off little shrimp! That's just stupid talk. By the time you could even attempt to grab that bat.

Dad, would have his hands around your neck, and would most likely be beating you over your stupid silly head with it himself.

Ma, is right. There's nothing any of us can do to him but, wait until he drinks himself to death. So let's just stop talking stupid, trying to scare everyone in the process. About what we are going to do, if he comes in here. When there's nothing anyone of us can do...!

If it happens, it happens and we'll just have to endure whatever he wants to do to us. Where hopefully it won't be as bad as it was the last time. When that judge told him what he will do if he h\ears about him beating up on us kids again.

Let's just hope that he passes out again from drinking too much. Now let's all shut up before he really does come in here, and beats the living hell out of us, again.

Ma knows how to handle Dad. If anything happens we'll know about it. All of us just stay away from that door and keep quite. We don't want to draw attention to any of us."

* * * *

"Mary!" Frank authoritatively shouted out at her. "Bring us more beer, and hurry up about it! We all want another beer now dammit, right now...!"

"It's coming Frank." She hurriedly went to the icebox taking out three, more beers carrying them over to the table. Sitting them down before Frank.

"There's your beer." She hastily said. Turning to walk away from the table, to go out into the living room.

When Frank got up from the table, and staggeringly walked towards her. Catching up with her before she walked through the doorway, into the living room.

Where Mary startlingly felt his arms wrapping about her waist. Forcefully turning her around to face the table. Where the other two, where sitting. So that they could watching as he pulled her back against him. Now holding her about her waist.

Where Mary could do nothing but just stand being forced to face those two, guys. In a state of shock. Totally bewildered, and confused. Not believing what was happening to her right in front of those two, other drunken slobs. As her own husband stood behind her. Actually attempting to physically impose his will upon her.

While putting her on display before them in a degrading grotesque manner. Alarmingly placing her in the position of frantically thinking to herself.

'That her temporary embarrassment wasn't worth risking arousing Franks rotten temper.' Where she submitted to his demands of rubbing himself against her behind, as she stood staring diligently directly at the other two, men sitting at the table. Watching with transfixed interest saying to herself.

'All their talk about their masculinity wasn't degrading enough. Now to be subjected to be put on display by my own husband.'

Looking over towards the kid's bedroom door, hoping that they weren't bearing witness to what she was being subjected to.

"Damn, Frank you have yourself one hot women there." The tall skinny guy sitting across the table, from the fat one, jeeringly intently. Spoke out saying.

"Yes, I do don't I." Frank arrogantly replied sliding his hands up her sides.

Until Mary startlingly felt his hands moving up upon the sides of her breasts. Where immediately a horrifying thought flashed into her besieged mind.!

'Was his boastful attempt to prove himself as the man of the house, or was he attempting to taunt, tease, or arouse those other two, men's sexual desires, or just trying to prove that he's something he's not?!'

The thought prompted her to panic at first. Where the thought of them touching her. Made her skin crawl, as if millions of ants were walking upon her skin. Provoking the fear of her situation to become far more perilous.

Where just as she was on the verge of breaking free form Frank's demeaning hands. The tall slinky guy jumped up from his chair annoyingly speaking out.

" I can't stand it anymore...!" As he came staggering over to where Frank was holding onto the sides of Mary's breasts, bending her towards slightly. Keeping her behind pinned back against him.

Where the other man came up to stand before her rotating, grinding his hits before her. Simulating that her was fraternizing himself upon her genital region. As he slobbered is words speaking out.

" Oh, yes. That feels so good..."

"Yeah, alright it does...!" Frank yelled out." Just remember everything has its price..."

"No! No...!" Mary panicky cried out. Frantically struggling to break free from Franks restraining hold. Looking over that the children bedroom." My, God Frank...! No!"

"Shut up you slut!" Frank angrily demanded. Giving her breasts a painful besieging squeeze.

" I'll break your fucken neck right here, and now...!"

"Damn you Frank! Do you want the kids to see what you are doing out here?!" Mary defiantly yelled out.

Knowing that he meant every word he said. Knowing that she had no have alternative but, to submit to being violated. As Frank held her pinned back against him.

Mary's fear for herself was not her major concern. Where it was for her children. That were in their bedroom. Where they would be subjected to baring witness to Frank allowing those other men violate her.

Finding herself praying to God, that they would all be asleep, and wasn't seeing what was going on.

Where her hatred, and vindictiveness for Frank. Made her contempt, and loathing for him become, so enraged.

That all she could think about, was enduring her hopeless situation. So that she could get her revenge.

"I'm sorry Mary but, I was breaking, and it's not as if you're a virgin.

Where, knowing how you love it so much. Where you are always complaining about the way I neglect you. Where beer doesn't come cheap. You best get used to it my love, because you are going to start paying your way around here.

You see, now didn't I tell you she would do anything for me...?"

Frank spoke out to the man amorously holding onto her hips continuing his aggressive assault taking advantage of her vulnerability.

" All I had to do was to ask her in the right way. Just remember, you pay more, you get more. You are getting a barging as it is."

Mary stared diligently towards the kid's bedroom door. As the last of the two, men stumbled over to join his friend. Standing beside him. As Frank released his restraining hold upon Mary's breasts.

Allowing her to stand freely. Walking back over to the kitchen table. To sit down facing the three, of them, speaking out.

"Now I owe either of you nothing. You are owning me now. Now if you want more than to stand there admiring her. You damn will best start paying up until you come up with a reasonable price you best not touch her, if you know what's is good for you.

As for you Mary, you get us another beer, right now...! I don't need you undermining my price by scaring the hell out of them."

He demandingly spoke out ordering her. Smugly grinning at her, as she stood staring at him with enraged contempt, and disgust in her eyes for him.

"Forget it Mary." He challengingly stared back at her saying." You wouldn't stand a chance in hell. Besides there's nothing you could do about it."

He implied staring at the kid's room." You know I wouldn't stop with just you. Besides you know as well as I do. You are just as much to blame as I am, for the way things are around here. Seeing how it was you that brought it about. Now move it!"

Mary went to the icebox opening it to find it empty." Your out of beer

Frank...!" She slammed the door angrily replying back. Walking away from the icebox towards the kid's bedroom door. To check if they have been witnessing what was going on.

"Shit...!" Frank shouted out." Damn it woman...! I had it.! Is it too fucken much, to ask to have a few damn beers...?! God knows I give you enough money to pay for it...! Come you guys let's go. She's not going anywhere."

He angrily rose from the table walking towards the kitchen door. Stopping to turn around to face her as he opened it.

"Don't think that this is over. It's far from over. In fact, it's just now beginning. From now on Bitch! I'm going to start getting something more out of you besides nothing. You got it, and I'm getting nothing out of it but, having to support it, and I'm going to do just that! Come on guys let's get the hell out of here!"

He said leading them out of the door out into the hallway. Slamming the door shut behind him.

* * * *

"Damn Frank." The tall skinny guy spoke out to him as he leads them down the stairs reluctantly wanting to lead.

" That's sure some woman you've there. She's worth every penny of the 5 bucks. Which I might add you still owe us seeing how it wasn't worth for what I did get"

"She sure was Frank." The other guy spoke up saying as well." How much would it cost with her panties down, and us out of ours?"

"$10 bucks but, it's going to cost double to go up inside. I'm not just going to give it away. Now let's go and get something to drink. I'm starting to sober up"

"$20 bucks, what do you say?" The tall one ask." Give me credit until next week and I'll come up with it?"

"You have to be kidding...?" Frank lead them out of the building saying." By next week she could be worth $30 bucks easy. You best come up with it while the cheap offers are still cheap.

It's a business I'm dealing with here. That it's a matter of supply and demand, and I've the monopoly on the goods I'm proving. Plus, I have two, others as well. That are going to cost far more than my wife is going to be going for."

"You mean those daughters of yours?" The fat one asked.

"If the price is right I'll sale my own mother... You know, now that I think about it. Nah... She's to fucken old.

She's most likely all dried up inside any ways. Besides I'll have enough to deal with, with those fucken brats, and that bitch I call a wife."

* * * *

'Oh, my God...!' Mary sat at the kitchen table saying to herself. Nervously crying her eyes out, not knowing what to do.... Looking over towards the kid's bedroom door.

' Thank God, the children didn't see what was happening out in the living room...' Literally hating Frank more than I ever did. Knowing that I was going to have to do something, before he actually follows through with what he threatened he was going to do.

'What am I going to do...? I can't call the police, and have them all arrested for what they did to me?

If I did that they would take Frank away from me?! I can't let that happen... I just can't...! I'll be taken off welfare, and the kids, and I will have no place to live... He's are only means of support...

I hate him worse now... More than I ever did, for what he did to me tonight. What hurts me even worse. Is that he sold me like a common whore. I'm not going to let him whore myself for him, or any man...'

Mary bewilderingly rose up onto her feet. Staring vengefully at the kitchen door once again thinking to herself.

' Alright Frank I'll handle you in my own way... This has gone too far, and it's going to stop right here and now..'

Mary went to shower, and toss out her underpants. Then went to sat down in her rocking chair in the living room.

Vengefully waiting for Frank to return home. Knowing in her mind what she would have to do when he did return. Hiding a carving knife behind her back.

Chapter 2

It was 2:30 in the morning when Frank came walking into the kitchen door. Drunk on his ass, walking into the living room. To using the door jamb to brace himself up from falling on his face. As Mary sat calmly struggling to hold back her contemptible rage, she was harboring wanting to lash out at him.

"Hi, love I'm home..." He solemnly spoke out. Waving his hand, blinking his eyes. As if trying to focus his eyes to see clearly.

"So I see, and alone this time I hope?" Mary sarcastically replied.

"Yes alone... so what's eating you?"

"Other than you, and your drunken friends nothing!" She argumentatively rebutted with loathing, and contempt in her tone of voice.

"Don't be getting on me now woman, I'm in no mood! You loved it, and you damn will know it! So come on let 's go to bed..."

"Listen to me your drunken bastard! If you ever dare do anything like that to me again. I'll make you regret the day you were born!"

"Are you threatening me?!"

"No! I'm promising you! That I swear I'll kill you with my bare hands...! You decrypted moron! How dare you do such a vowel, contemptible, outrageous thing to me...! Just where do you get the gall to lower, and demean me to the level of a slut?!"

"You will do what ...?!" He infuriatingly challenged her, in a threatening manner." Why I ought to...!" He stopped saying. Staggeringly walking towards her with an enraged clenched fist.

Mary retaliated by raising up onto her feet. Clutching the craving knife in her hand.

" Come on you drunken Bastard...!! I'll cut you up into dog meat...! Take one more step towards me, and I'll cut your disgusting heart out!"

Frank stopped abruptly, nearly stumbling over but, catching himself. To unsteadily stand his ground. Becoming panicky stricken swaying from side to side, struggling to maintain his balance.

"Alright, Mary so I made a mistake...! No one was hurt by it... Now, just put the knife down..."

He nervously spoke cried out. Staring diligently at the blade of the knife. Knowing that she was capable of carrying out her threat.

"Alright Frank." She replied backing away from him.

" I'll put it down. Just remember I can always get another one, and that I've had it with you... and it's going to stop right here, and now...!

I swear Frank! If you ever so much as lay a hand on me, or the children, or try to put me through what you did this night. I'll kill you sadistically...! inch by inch!

Knowing you will come back, just like you always do. Where I'll be waiting for you to fall to sleep. From which you will only wake up to suffer an excruciatingly horrifying death from which you will carry straight into hell with you! Now get your drunken ass to bed...!"

Mary vengefully spoke out at him. Asserting her position where he was concern. authoritatively saying.

" You had your fling, now get the hell out of my sight!"

"Yes, dear..." He pessimistically replied." Are you coming?"

"Maybe...!" She derogatorily replied." But remember this. I might be your wife but, I'm no longer your woman. You sold me...! Don't you dare ever touch me again, unless I want you too!"

"Yes dear." He forlornly replied. Dragging himself grudgingly off towards their bedroom door. As if he was a man without purpose. Undermining himself in his defeat as one.

* * * *

Frank was a good man. He was once a proud enthusiastic man, with high hopes, and ideals. When Mary first met him. He could think of nothing but, about her.

Frank was young prestigious, and very domineering nuclear physicist. Considered to be an utter genius, in his own right.

Who wound up losing his identity, and the recognition of his gender. By denouncing himself as a man, and as a human being. Over the lustful want of Mary's strives for recognition.

Mary knew of his suffering, and that she was the cause behind his downfall. Who cause Frank starting to drank, to forget. Where in doing so he also lost his self-esteem.

The only thing that mattered to him was Mary, Where he struggled so to become the man, and the person she wanted him to be. Where he blamed himself for failing doing so.

Which was the main cause behind what he did to her. Forcing her to submit the way he did, was his way of exerting his retribution. For all those he remorsefully sent to their deaths.

Known only onto Mary, and him, himself the true reason that caused it, and why Frank was so down on himself.

Frank became a fugitive from justice. Who took on an alias identity name to hide. Rather than to have to be forced to kill again. Knowing if his new identity was ever discovered he would be forced into killing all over again.

There was no other renowned scientist like Frank. What he had in his head was incomprehensible but, yet he did nothing with it.

* * * *

Mary stood watching the figure of a man disappearing into the darkness of their bedroom. A man that wanted to forget but, couldn't. Yet a man who had it in his ability to totally destroy all life in a blink of an eye.

Who was still being sought after for over the past 15 years. When he suddenly upped and vanished. To assume the role in life that he was forced to live in along with his family. Where only Mary know why.

As Mary entered their bedroom, sliding in under the covers. With her back to him. Knowing in her heart that her love for him would never diminish.

"Honey…" Frank mournfully spoke to her." I'm sorry… I don't know what could have come over me."

"I do, now go to sleep."

"Mary please forgive me… You know I love you."

"Frank do you have any idea how degrading it was for me? Allowing you make me out as if I was a slut. I can never forgive you for that.

I'm here because I do love you, and I know you for who, and what you once were but, you obviously don't care why I have put myself, and our children through all I have.

Those men violated me but, what was even more infuriating. Was you aiding them by letting them maul me as far as you did. Not knowing how far you were willing to let them go. Just sitting there watching.

Do you have any idea how grotesquely infuriating it was for me having to let them violating me in the way you allowed them too."

She stopped abruptly not wanting to recall the contempt she felt. Having to submit herself to feeling those drunken bastard touching her.

" It's getting out of control Frank. Maybe you should go back."

"No!" He panicky shouted out." You can't let them do it to me again! Mary please I bag of you don't let them find me…! I promise that I'll never do it again…! Please Mary please…Forgive me. I just can't go through it again, I just can't…!"

"Alright honey." She rolled over to face him. Taking him into her arms, consolingly hugging him up against here. I'm here, and yes, I do so love you, I won't let them ever find you."

"Oh, Mary..." He cowered up against her. Slumbering off to sleep, as she held him in her arms.

Mary held him in her compassionate arms until she was sure he was fast asleep. Then rolled out of bed to go to the bathroom.

Upon returning from the bathroom. She seems Art standing beside the bed. Holding a carving knife in his hands. On the verge of plunging it into Frank's chest. As he laid in a deep sleep upon the bed.

"No...!" She panicky whispered. Rushed up to Art, grabbing his hand. Just in time with the point of the knife just inches from Frank's chest.

Dragging him out of the bedroom, by his wrist into the living room. While holding her other hand over his mouth. Tossing him down on the sofa, panicky taking the knife out of his hand.

"No! Art No...! That's isn't the way...! He's not worth wasting your life over." She hostilely spoke out. Going to close the bedroom door. Then walking back over to him.

"Now young man! Just you sit right where you are! and relax. There be no killing in my house, do you hear me...?"

"But Ma...he has to die...! I can't live like this any longer he's going to kill all of us."

"Not by your hands he's not."

"Ma, he doesn't deserve to live...!"

"Honey I'm your mother. I happen to love you very much. I'm not going to attempt to make excuses for your father action. Where I can't allow you to destroy your life from out of hatred of him.

Vengeance is mine smith the lord. It's my place, not yours to decide your fathers fate. He'll be punished severely for his transgressions but, it will be I alone that will have determined his punishment, while he and I are alive, not you.

Honey you are only ten, years old. You are too young to understand the reasoning behind why people do the things they do, to other people. Where it's not for you to take it upon yourself to lay judgement upon anyone.

When you yourself are without rational reasoning to be able to stand in judgement over anyone to such an extreme as you were going to inflect upon your father.

Such an act of brutality isn't worth, having to live with the anguish of what you did. For the rest of your life.

Its cruel, and inhumane treatment to inflict upon yourself, over someone who wasn't worth such as sacrifice to begin with."

"Ma, I see you as a person filled with love, compassion, and warmth. I also see loneliness, fear and bewilderment I see a person divided between herself and her inhibitions."

Mary startlingly discovering at that precise moment that Arthur was truly his father's son. Noticing that his father's intelligence was beginning to emerge.

As astonishing as it was for her to startlingly discover, as well as also except. She knew Arthur's genius was becoming to advance for his adolescence mind. That it had to be enhanced slowly, if to prevent the same downfall that inflected his father to befall him as well.

"Arthur wherever have you learned to talk like that? Those word are not of a mind of a ten, year old boy but, of a well-educated thought process."

"I don't know? I see, and I feel, and I can articulate on my thoughts as they just come out. I see to comprehend what it is I'm saying but, I'm not always certain. That I'm saying what I'm trying to relate."

"Art do you understand what you're saying now?"

"Yes, but the diction, seems of very little importance. Compared to the interpretation to the content with my words I'm attempting to relate to.

They don't seem to be getting across the way I want them to mean at times but, I guess that one doesn't need definition. When the complexities don't expressively project the concept of one's feelings that seem to complicate my reasoning at time and I lose control over my actions. It's confusing at time I'll say that.

Like now where it appears that neither of us are getting through to the other. Me despise for my father isn't diminishing but, are only suppressing my impulses to react irrationally, while not caring."

" Art you have aged so much in some regards but, yet you are still so impressionable, that your mind takes on its own interpretations.

You were willing to sacrifice yourself for me by killing your father, why? Could it be because you lack the ability to understand yourself, or are you just allowing your feelings to surpass your intelligence is telling you?

You were going to kill to relieve your pain, and suffering. that you feel that your father has brought upon you, where it was in face upon me.

Was it out of fear, or not being able to deal with. That which you can't understand about your father, or yourself for that matter. Unknowingly being oblivious to the consequences of not using your better judgement regard right and wrong?

You're only ten, years old. Don't attempt to surpass your intelligence to comprehend what you are feeling, until you're mentally aware of the consequences of your actions. Which means that if you are in doubt, or confused, ask.

I'm talking to you now addressing your intelligence to reason intellectually. Only that which you can understand, and to react with the curiosity of uncertainty to ask about which you don't understand. Where you well refrain from reacting until you are fully aware of your actions.

Art I want you to understand what I'm going to say to you is going to be harsh but, it has to be said.

It's not your place but, mine to reprimand your father. Even though I grant you, that in your eyes he doesn't deserve to live because his actions might have appalled you.

Whereas you know nothing of him, or why he's the way he is, where as I do. It's the indifference that you share with him that are also causing you to react irrationally toward s him.

Honey I admire your intellect as astonishing as it is. Its far above your capability to comprehend the words that you speak. Let alone the meaning behind them, and even then. I alone must ripe my own retribution. Seeing I was the one affronted, who was being imposed upon.

I do fully understand the repulsive indignation, and the reprehensible indecencies. That he has brought upon this house.

Where you must understand that I'm also speaking to you on the level. I'm hoping that you can comprehend. Where just speaking words alone, don't make them understandable, or right. Which makes them meaningless and unwarranted to begin with if one doesn't have the intelligence to apply the right words to relate to what the conversation is all about."

"Ma, I can't help but, to find myself bewildered?"

"Now that's very understandable but, in which way might I ask?"

" Ma, you are so beautiful but, yet I feel that you are hiding yourself behind so many uncertainties, and fears, and I don't see it that it's because of us kids.

Which leads me to think. That maybe if it wasn't for us kids holding you back. You wouldn't have to put up with him? It's obvious that he hates us, and you for having us."

"Honey listen to me; you are as much a part of me as I'm of myself. I gave your life, I feed you from my breast, and I changed your dirty diapers.

I was never ashamed of you, nor have I ever felt imposed upon by you, or any of my children...Come here honey..."

She called out to him extending her open arms to him to come to her. Offering him the consoling arms of her composing him as just being a ten, year old upset little boy.

"Oh, mommy..." I cried out. Hastily going into her loving arms. Breaking down emotionally crying as she hugged him against her.

"Yes, honey." She consolingly whispered." I know... Cry it all out ... Get it all out of your system. I want you cleansed, and pure of heart, to become free from the burden that is torments you so." She spoke out to him holding him in her arms. Until he cried his last tear.

"Honey I want you to promise me that you will let me handle your father, and that you will never attempt to do such a horrible thing again. Now promise me."

"Yes, I promise." I solemnly replied. Cowering up against her. Hugging her with all his strength.

"Now that's my big boy." She passively spoke. Breaking his constricting embrace, aiding him to rise up onto his feet to stand before her.

" Now it's off to bed with you."

"Yes, mommy." I replied walking out of her hands. That were holding me upon my sides walking towards the bedroom door.

"Honey." May called out to Art. Stopping him just before the bedroom door. Causing him to turn around to look back at her.

"Yes, what is it mother?"

"It was nothing..." She evasively replied back, having a change of mind over what she wanted to tell him." Just go to bed now, and have nothing but, sweet dreams."

"Yes, mother." I entered the bedroom closing the door behind me.

Chapter 3

Days went by without anyone mentioning anything about what happened. However, that didn't stop us kids from not forgetting about it.

It was Friday, the first day of December. We were all sitting around outside on the steps impatiently waiting for the welfare check to arrive in the mail.

Only to watch the postman come, and leave. Without placing anything in our mail box. Where we all forlornly went back up to are apartment. Thinking that it would come tomorrow. Where in its place came a knock upon the kitchen door.

Where again we unexpectedly discovered, that we were receiving an unexpected visit from the welfare counselor instead. By a women whose name of Miss Connors.

Where we also unexpectedly discovered, that her purpose for coming was to inform dad. That he wouldn't be receiving anymore welfare checks. Unless he would be willing to go work on one of the newly funded state work projects.

She told him, that if he wasn't able to work, and wanted to be exempt from the project. He would have to get a doctor's excuse. In writing, stating why he wasn't able to work.

Dad became infuriated as hell over the new unforeseen devolvement. The last thing he wanted to do, was work. Where he didn't have any choice in the matter other than to agree.

She instructed him to report to work on Monday, morning. Then while upon leaving she handed him the check we were expecting.

Stressing upon him. That he wouldn't be receiving another unless he reported to work every day. Before she left, being lead out the door out into the hallway by Ma.

Without uttering a word dad, stuck the check into his pocket, and went storming out of the apartment. Leaving us without anything to eat, and no money to buy anything.

However unknown onto us kid's ma, already foreseen what Frank would do. Prior to escorting the welfare worker out into the hallway. Where she was handed ma, another check.

The check came through, due to Ma's collaboration with the welfare department. That cause dad to be placed onto one, of the state projects.

Where thankfully the day didn't turn out to be a total disaster as we thought it was going to be. For the first time in days we went to bed with a full stomach. As usual Pat, and Christ slept in one, bed. As Paul and I slept in the other.

That night however. I was alarmingly awakening with dad standing beside my bedside. Stinking drunk shouting out incoherently.

Striking out at Paul lying beside me. Hitting and beating on him. Hitting him unjustly upon his head and face. Taking it upon himself to virtually yank, him out of the bed. By his hair. Down onto the floor beside the bed. Then turned his attention on me. To brutally start in on beating me with his fists.

Ma, came charging into the bedroom to see what was going on. When she saw Frank profusely hitting on Art with his fists. She panicky charged towards him! Attempting to stop him.

When dad hit her, with a clenched fist, with such a force. That the force from blow sent her hurtling back against the wall beside the open door. Where she unconsciously plopped down face first onto the floor, and just laid there in a lifeless state.

As dad stormed out of the bedroom stepping over Ma, laying on the floor before the open door. Leaving Paul and I crying in pain from his brutal attack.

Where I managed to crawl out of bed. Down onto the floor, and crawled towards the bedroom door. Grudgingly hopping to get help. Where I was pulled to a halting stop. Just before reaching the doorway, by Paul grabbing my foot.

"No, Art you'll never make it. He'll kill you if he catches you."

I laid motionless panicky looking out the door. To see dad come charging back into the room to grab Pat by her hair.

Yanking her out of her bed, out of Christies hugging arms. Holding his hand over her mouth, muffling her screams of utter terror. Shouting at her as he drug her out the door.

"I said that I would teach you the hard facts of life! and now is as good as time as any for you to learn just how hard life can really get!"

Christ laid panicked stricken cowering up against the head board of the bed. To terrified to move, or even dare to scream out. Knowing that dad wouldn't hesitate from coming after her.

Where Paul and I laid cowering upon the floor beside are bed. Also not daring to scream out. Knowing that dad would come back to continue to beat us, Worse than he had been already.

Ma, started to move. She crawled towards Paul and I. Them laid motionless between us. Bleeding profusely from her nose unable to do anything but, watching, and listening to what dad was saying to Pat. As he stood holding her helpless. To protect herself in the middle of the kitchen.

"Ma, are you alright?" I painstakingly whispered out. Being riddled with pain all over my body

"Yes, Now all of you. Don't any of you so much as utter a sound."

"But ma, what is he going to do to Pat?!" Paul fearfully ask

"Nothing I hope. How are you two doing?"

"Not so go ma," I grated my teeth replying. Struggling to endure the pain I was in form my chest, and stomach. Where dad was brutally hitting me with his fist.

"Paul what about you?" I'm hurting pretty bad as well..."

"Ma, we've to get help...! He's going to kill all of us...!" Christ whispered out. So terrified to move from where she was.

"He hasn't yet. Christ go find someplace to hide, and stay hiding... Don't come out for anything. Unless I tell you to. It's Pat that I'm worrying about ...

Now I'm going to try to get up and get to the phone to call the police. You two, boys just stay put, and try not to move."

"No! Ma...!" Paul panicky cried out trying to stop her from doing anything foolish, panicky whispered out to her.

" He'll kill you for sure...! I can't let you do that... Ma, there's nothing we can do...!

You said it yourself that we must survive the best we can. Where none of us are in any condition to stop him.

"Ma, Paul's right. We don't stand a chance in hell of getting away from him...!"

"I can't allow this madness to continue. I warned him what I would do. The next time he ever dared to lay a hand on me or you kids ... I should have killed him them..."

Ma, remorsefully spoke out conceding to the boy's fears. Knowing that they were right about what they were fearing might happen. Where none of us were in any position to help ourselves let alone Pat

Where all we could do was lie there, and watch, and listen to what was happening to Pat as he stood holding her by her throat.

Asking her how old she was. Swinging her above the floor on the tips of her toes. Watching her face became all distorted from lack of oxygen. With the look of death defying terror upon her face. As she struggled to inhale enough air to breath.

"Daddy... please.... Please daddy you're hurting me..." She besieging pleaded with him to release her.

"Am I now...?!" He sinisterly replied. Squeezing her neck even harder. Causing her to almost pass out.

"You Son-of-a- Bitch...!" Ma, screamed out at the top of her lungs at him." I'll kill you...! Leave her alone Goddamn you...!"

"One more word out of your revolting mouth, and I'll ring her fucken neck right here and now...!"

He turned his depraved eyes attention towards ma, saying. Squeezing his constricting fingers harder against her neck.

"Please... Daddy...." Pat gasped choking out, mercifully crying out to him." Please daddy... Don't hurt me... Daddy you're drunk... You don't realize what you're doing."

"Who's drunk...?! I'm as sober as a dime standing on its end..."

"Why doesn't she just shut me...?!" I nervously whispered out to Paul." She's only going to make her situation that much worse. How can she be so stupid...?!"

"Hush both of you..." Ma, nervously whispered out." Don't make a sound either of you. We can't risk invoking his anger anymore that it is already."

"Please daddy you're hurting me... I'll do anything... Please let me go..."

" Shut up damn you...! Shut up...! How dare you defy your father...? Now get down on your knees, and show me your repentance! For being disobedient to your father...!"

He authoritatively yelled out at her. Shoving her down upon her knees before him. Still holding onto her throat.

"Mother we've to do something...!" I fearfully cried out to her." Damn him...!" I infuriatingly blurted out." I'll kill that bastard...! For what he's was forcefully putting Pat though... I swear I'll kill him.

"Alright you little bitch!" Dad yelled out at Pat. Pushing her backwards down onto her knees upon the floor.

" Let this be a lessen to you! I'll tolerate no deception, or defiance from anyone in my family. I brought you into this world.

You are mind to do whatever I want to with! Don't you ever forget it

... Now get your ass back to bed. Move it ...! "He demandingly shouted.

Pat crawled on her hands and knees towards the bedroom door. As dad stood looking over at the three, of us laying in the doorway. Then came staggering walking over towards us.

Aggressively uplifting ma, up onto her feet, by her hair. Shoved her back against the door Pinning her and the open door back against the wall behind it. Holding her up by her throat for Paul and I to see, as Pat crawled under her bed hoping to hide from dad.

"Now you listen to me...!" He engagingly yelled out at her." I'm not about to forget your threat. If you ever think about caring it out. I'll ring your kids heads off, and shove them down you revolting throat!"

He aggressively pushed her head back against the door yelling out at her." I'm dead already, so don't talk about it. Just fucken do it...!"

He released her stepping back from her. Letting her drop down upon her knees choking for air to breath. To go storming out of the bedroom, them though the kitchen. Slamming the kitchen door behind him, as he went storming out of the door.

"Boys are you alright." Ma, asked. As she grudgingly pushed herself up onto her feet. Rubbing her throat. Walking over towards where we were lying about the floor. Kneeling down between us.

" Now don't either of you move until I check you over..."

Mary examined Paul first. Determining that Paul only sustained a few bruises on his face.

" Alright Paul you'll be alright. I'll get you some aspirin shortly, now go climb back into bed."

Where she helped Paul's pain stricken body got up onto his feet then aided him to get back in bed. Where she covered him up again. Making sure to hug him, to insure him that he will be alright. While examining his head one, more time. Just to make sure there wasn't any blood in his eyes.

Which could indicate he could have suffered a concussion. Where she would have to take to the hospital. Seeing that his eyes were clear.

Where she them went to check on Art. Worrying more so about him because he was smaller than Paul.

" Alright young man, now let's have a look at you Art."

"Ma, I'm alright…" I spoke out saying as she went about examining me.

"Sure you are … You are so alright; I should take you to the hospital… I don't think there's any broken bones though but, you sure took one hell of a beating on your head, and chest. I want you to sit up awhile, so that I can keep a close eye on you. Come on now I'll help you get up."

Mary aided Art up onto his feet, then out into the living room. Where she then aided him to just sit-down upon the sofa. Where she sat down beside him.

"Ma, really I'm alright. You best go check on Pat and Christ. Pat took one hell of a beating herself."

"Alright but, don't you move until I get back." She walked towards the bedroom. Looking inside the dimly lit room before entering. Seeing Pat now laying on the bed. Crying her eyes out as she entered.

"My god Ma…" Pat terrifically cried out. Hugging her mother to herself." I was so scared that he was going to kill me. It was so horrible…"

"Yes, honey I know… Pat honey you must listen to me. I don't know what to do about what happened. What I do know is that I have to get you kids out of this house, before he kills one, or all of you.

He's gone too far this time… He has to be stopped. Where I'm the only one, who can do it but, I can't until I know that you kids are safe.

He nearly killed Art. That's how badly he beat him up this time. I'll never forgive him for what he did to you but, you must.

You can't live with the thought of what he did, or what he might have done." You mustn't ever forget what he is capable of doing but, you can't live in fear of it. Not all men are like your father was.

"Ma, he really hurt me… I'm still bleeding from my mouth, and nose…"

"I know honey. Now you just lay back, and relax, and let your head lean back over your pillow, until the bleeding stops."

Mary consolingly puffed up, and positioned the pillow under her neck, so that she could lean her head back.

Reaching into her dress pocket pulling out her handkerchief applying it to her nose." Now hold onto this. It should stop the bleeding."

"Oh! my God...! ma...!" Christ pathetically unneeded cried out. As she emerged from the closet. Coming to stand beside the bed.

Seeing Pat lying upon it, looking down upon her face. Seeing it all back, and blue with her lips all puffed up and still bleeding.

"That revolting Bastard...!" She hysterically gasped out from horrified disbelief.

"Shut up Christ!" Mary yelled at her." Don't you start getting panicky on me now! Go get me some warm water and a cloth.... Don't just stand there... Do what I told you..."

"Yes, Alright." Christ nervously replied. Running out of the bedroom towards the bathroom down the hall from the bedroom.

Hastily returning running back into the bedroom. Handing Mary a pan full of water, with a wash cloth socking in it.

" Here. ma, what are you going to do about this...?! I'm going to be next aren't I...?!" Christ paradoxically cried out saying.

"Stop it! Just stop it Christ...!" Mary frustratingly shouted out at her." Getting hysterical isn't going to solve anything, now just calm down."

Mary place the damp cloth on Pat's swollen nose removing her handkerchief " Just hold onto the clothe Pat. You are going to be just fine.

It doesn't look like he did any real major damage but, you will have to say home from school until the bruises go away."

"Ma, what if he returns?"

"When he does Pat. I'll be waiting for him this time! He's never going to lay a hand on you kids again. That I promise you but, let's get one thing understood right here and now.

No one is going to do anything, or say anything about what's been happening in this house. Do I make myself clear to both of you?"

"Yes, mother." Christ reluctantly answered." Yes, we hear you mother but, I don't know how much more of this I can stand...

This is a mad house, and it's driving me crazy...! If he so much as touches me I swear I'll run away, and never come back!"

"I understand Christ, and I couldn't blame you if you tried but, it will get you nowhere but, right back here. Don't you think I myself thought of running away?

Your father is all are problem, and the time has come where I must resolve it. Now climb into bed beside your sister, and go to sleep."

Mary rose saying, walking towards the door." I need to go check on Art." Mary walked out the door closing it behind her. Going back into the living room to check on Art as he was now sloughing half laying upon the sofa.

Sitting down beside him. She pulled him up his T-shirt to visually examining his chest, and stomach. Physically feeling about with her hands this time." Frank really hurt you this time, didn't he?"

"I'll live ma; I'll live long enough to see him rot in hell! He hurt me ma but, he hurt me more than he ever could physically by hurting you! The day will come when I'll make him pay dearly for hurting you."

"Hush now ." Mary laid him down beside her on the sofa, hugging him to her." Honey I love you so much." She slumber wept, hugging him against her. Trying to keep him from noticing.

" Honey, no mother could ever be so blessed as I. To have such a son like you, now you rest and I'll do the same."

"Ma, are you sure you're alright?"

"Yes, honey I'm just fine, now go to sleep." She consolingly spoke out to him. Hiding her sorrowful face above his head. So that he couldn't see the ugliness on her spiteful face. That was so distorted from animosity towards Frank. Over what he did to her children.

As she held Art's battered body compressed against here's. Feeling the pain that was inflicted upon him. Being absorbed into her, as he slumbered off to sleep in her arms.

Knowing that his mind would never forget the hell he was forced to live in because of her. Causing Mary to think back in her mind. Knowing why Frank hated Art mores then the others.

* * * *

It all started when Frank got it into his head that Art wasn't son. Which cause Frank from never stop doubting the fact that he was.

Where he would never tell Mary how he came to think that he wasn't. Where he was always harboring the lingering doubt of uncertainty. Where when he comforted Mary with is concern. Mary left lingering doubt in his mind that she wasn't telling him the truth. Where in his eyes. Mary was the one, who knew who Art's real father was.

When unknown even onto Mary herself. She herself wasn't all that sure if he was. Due to certain extenuating circumstances that transpired.

Where she had no intentions in substantiate Franks concerns. Whereby used any method she could too refused to do what was needed to be done. Because there was no way anyone knew for certain.

That she could have compromised her morals, and her love for Frank. Where her main concern was for Art's safety was her primary concern. Knowing that she might have rescinded her own scruples knowingly.

While having to deal with Frank as he descended deeper, and deeper into his own suffering. Being denied the certainty that he needed to be assured about.

Knowing that it wasn't her who was destroying Frank by turning a highly educated man into the lowest from of human being, that ever walked upon the face of the earth where the rest of his family was concerned.

Where his own government who he worked for exploited his advance intelligence, to satisfy their own greed for power to adamancy their obsession to conquer over any odds, to maintain their superior supremacy in the world standing.

Where in Mary's mine. It was the government who was the main cause behind Frank dragging.

His entire family into hiding because of what they extracted from that genius mind of his.

Where he was subjecting his entire family not only living with him but, also slowly watching himself becoming a disgusting low life degenerate

That he claims he was force to do something so deplorable against his will. That he's not mentally able to handle what they made him do.

Which he also claims, caused him to have to scrutinize Mary's own principles. That generated the thought of deception where Art being his son was concern. As well as her in regards her royalty to her own country, and the government that he worked for.

With her knowing how it could have been her influence upon him. That implicated her in which brought about the deaths of thousands.

With total disregard for those victimized in the process. While only caring about what concerned herself.

When even unknowingly had a part in bringing about unfortunate turn of events, that would be defined as non-reversible event of genocide.

Where afterwards Frank starting to drank to forget, where Mary couldn't be having to take care of her family.

Where since the day Art was born. He brought into this world with him nothing be hardship, despair, and misery upon her, and the rest of the family. Where Frank was no longer the gentle, caring, and compassionate man she first married but, a despicable, contemptible human being who was cruel, and heartlessly uncaring.

How Mary hated those years. That brought about the end, and the uncertainty of any new beginning. Where due to its failure to just accept what is. He allowed his uncertainty to effected his entire family already secure way of life.

Where it was compiled with Franks inability to accept the consequences for his ignorance. Thereby due to his obsessions, caused his mind to go astray from his responsibilities to his family, and to all that he prized so highly. In spite of his determination to rectify the wrong that he's done, and is doing by not will to accept his responsibility of being a father to his children.

Mary Know that her threat was meaningless. Where he also knew it as well. Even though Mary had possession of several envelopes one, of five. That she had two, other copies of. Whereas if was ever mailed, would cause the others to be send out as well. To others who would love nothing more to find out the truth about a certain event that took place.

Mary was to the point where she literally had it with Frank, and the horrible life her, and her children were having to live. Wanting to get back to living a moral life again. Seriously considering about ending the way of life she was being compelled to live.

She rolled off the sofa leaving Art sleeping, and went into the kitchen. Reaching behind the refrigerator pulling out an envelope. Placing it on the kitchen table so that Frank could see it when he came back home.

Walking back into the living room she laid back down on the sofa cuddling up against Art slumbering off to sleep.

* * * *

In the weeks that followed life went on as usual with nothing much happening other than with Ma, and Pat having a lot of private conversation together. That they wouldn't let anyone hear.

Dad came home two days after the last incident. Where it took Pat more, and more stressful time to become relaxed around dad. To where she would dare turn her back on him. Until all was suppress, and soon was back to moral again.

Out of curiosity Paul, and Art went to ask Pat about what her and Ma, were talking about that they were keeping such a well-kept secret. Wanting to find out why it was that she didn't no longer hate dad for what he did to her. Her reply was.

We weren't old enough to understand, and that dad had a great many problems, that we weren't aware of.

"Pat he's nothing but, a drunken bum!" I resentfully replied." I hate him for what he does to us…He's a bastard…!"

Ma, is always sticking up for dad but, go ahead. Deceive yourself into believing that he's going to miraculously stop tormenting us…!" I disbelievingly disagreed with what she was saying, Replying back to her.

" He doesn't love you, or even respect you. He doesn't need an excuse. Other than he's a lush, and a sadistic bastard as well.

I don't know what Ma, is telling you about that bastard. Where you damn well better believe in what I'm thinking about that, rotten excuse for a man as well as a father. That is, he's nothing more than a cold unscrupulous, masochist!

The next time he takes it upon himself to get disgustingly drunk. Where nothing, or nobody is ever going to stop him from doing it again, or maybe most likely something even worse. Like really hurting, or even killing someone like one, of us.

Pat he almost killed you the last time. What's going to stop him from doing it next time? You know as well as I do. When he's drunk, he's got no conscious, or concern about anyone but, himself. When it comes to taking out his hatred for himself, on anyone who isn't capable of taking care of themselves."

" Art I can see how you feel the way you do about dad but, we have our own lives to think about. We can't let what's happening in our lives now ruin the rest of our lives for us."

"I heard enough of this malarkey." Paul spoke up." How old did you say you are? I can't believe I'm hearing what I'm hearing coming out of that obnoxious mouth of yours…" Paul disconcertingly spoke out substantiating her ignorance.

"You two, can talk until your faces fall off for all I care. I'm leaving… Girls, they are gullible enough to believe anything…" He walked out of the bedroom disbelievingly saying.

"Who the hell cares what he thinks about girls! He's a jerk anyway, you understand don't you Art?"

"Pat what I can't understand is why you let ma, change your mind about dad."

"Alright Art I'll tell you but, only if you promise me that what I tell you goes no further than between us."

" Sure I promise let's hear it."

"Art what I'm going to tell you is nothing to the likes of what you ever heard before. Damn...!"

Pat frustratingly blurted out hearing something going on out in the kitchen. Startlingly thinking that ma, or dad just came home, and comforted Paul doing something.

"Come on Art let's go out and see what's going on, we'll have to finish is talk later." She rose up from her bed, walking out of the bedroom door into the kitchen. To join the rest of the family with Art following behind her.

"Kids I'm glad to see you all together I want to talk to Paul alone. I want everyone else to go outside, and to stay out. Until I call you in for lunch. Now go on.

As for you Paul you follow me." Ma, walked out of the kitchen with Paul following her into the living room.

The second we got out side. Christ went running off down the street leaving Pat and I alone.

"Art I'll be right back I forget something." Pat said, running back into the apartment building. Leaving me standing at the foot of the front steps asking myself.

' I wondering what Ma, wanted to talk to Paul about." Then thinking 'What could Pat have forgotten...?'

Deciding to sneak back into the apartment to see what was going on. To discover when I walked into the unlocked, and partially open kitchen door. Pat kneeling before Ma's bedroom door, looking through the keyhole.

Pat must have heard me coming in. Where before I could take another step inside. She raised her head and turned it towards me. Holding her fingers across her lips, as if telling me to be quite.   Waving me him over to the door to join her. Inquisitively I went to stand behind her whispering." What are you doing?"

"Would you like to see what Ma, and Paul are doing?" She whispered back to me saying.

"Yeah, sure." I curiously replied. Kneeling down beside her, in front of the door so I could peer inside the key hole. To see what was going on.

" You must be very quiet..." Pat moved aside from the keyhole making room for me to look into the key hole.

Where out of curiosity I placed my eye against the keyhole. To see Ma, sitting on the edge of her bed with Paul kneeling before her, hearing her saying.

"What am I going to do with you Paul...? Damn you boy...! What is it going to take for me to change your disgusting ways? This is the third, time in three, months I'd to go to school because of your revolting behavior!"

"Hey Art." Pat whispered out to me. Tapping me on my shoulder, as I watched on with intensified interest at Ma, and Paul. Straining my ears to hear why ma, was speaking so angrily out at him. While shaking her finger at him as if she was reprimanding him. Trying to get him to what listen to what she was saying to him.

"Paul you're going to become a man, if it kills you. If I ever hear of you doing anything unmanly again. I'll turn you into a bitch myself! Now look up at me

"Yes, mother..." Paul looked up towards her with his sorrowful eyes

" Paul I really don't know what to say to you about what you are doing."

"Ma, I really am trying but, I just can't seem to help myself."

" Paul this has to come to a stop, before it gets too far out of control.

Where I won't be able to help you. You were born to become a man someday. I don't know what more I can do to stress that to you."

"Ma, I know that you are trying to help me but, it doesn't seem to be doing any good. I guess that I'm just a hopeless case."

"Paul you are going on Thirteen, years old. You should be by now experiencing some form of masculinity urges. That will start you showing some interest in girls no other boys.

Do you've any idea what you are doing to yourself, and this family. Mostly me? I don't want to go to school again, and have to be subjected to your degrading flirtations."

"Ma, I'm sorry I guess it's just not in me to feel any form of emotion when it comes to girls."

"Paul when you grew breasts, and can conceive a baby. Then you can have all the boys you want but, until then. You are going to be the man that the good lord intended you to be."

"Come on Art we better be leaving before someone comes in, and catches us in here. We best get out of here now."

Pat whispered out saying, raising up into a standing position beside him. Impatiently waiting for me to raise up and join her.

Where she anxiously lead me back out of the apartment and back outside. Where we both stood at the foot of the steps. While I ignorantly attempted to figure out what ma, was yelling at Paul about.

Looking at Pat with a confused expression upon my face. From not being able to relate to what was being said between ma, and Paul. Where I ignorantly spoke out asking.

"Pat I wonder what Paul's problem is?"

"Stop wondering so much but, if you ask my opinion he's beyond help, and don't ask me why I said that either. Its none of my concern.

However, I'll say one thing about you Art. You're not at all like Paul you are all boy... Now where is that damn Christ?"

"Pat I've been hearing the boys in the neighborhood talking about Christ."

"I know Art, so have I. I just hope for her sake. That nothing we have been hearing is true. She's only going on Fourteen. She's far too young to be letting every boy in the neighborhood use her like."

Pat abruptly stopped. Not wanting to say anymore that might corrupt the way I thought about my sister.

"Pat have you...? I mean you are the oldest. Surely you must have had a few boyfriends."

"Art I don't know how to answer that, other than to say I rather not. Where besides you are too young to be thinking about such things.

Where I can see that you and I are going to have a long talk. Where you are going to tell me just what you think. I might be referring to where Christ is concern. Then I want to learn just how you heard about such things. Now let's go find Christ."

She reprimanded him saying, leading me off down the street. Into the direction Christ ran off in. Not wanting to speak any more about Christ, and boys.

"Pat I might be young but, I'm not blind. You are a very beautiful girl. Where I didn't mean to embarrass, or offend you either by asking. I was only carious that's all."

"What do you mean by not being blind?" She inquisitively asks apprehensively.

"Pat some nights I lie in my bed watching you sleeping. When the light from the sign from across the street. Reflects into the window where I see you in a totally different light.

I want to reach out to you but, I'm so fearful of doing so.

Where I see, and feel strange things, and I try to understand but, how can I. When I don't even understand what's going on inside me. Is that natural Pat?"

"Like I said before Art you are all boy. I admit somewhat prematurely because of all of us having to sleep in the same room. Where I can't stop you from looking.

Where you are about to see things that you shouldn't be seeing, where girls are concern. However I never want become frightened by what you see where girls are concern, and remember that girls are nothing to be fearful of. They are only physically different from boys.

You know Art I'm glad that you told me. All we have is each other where the closeness we share together goes beyond a brother, a sister relationship.

Where I'm sure you are very curious about a lot of things that are different between us. Where now that I know, you're taking not only notice but, interest as well.

I think it's time the two, of us are going to have some very serious talks but, not right now. Where I seriously want to answered your questions as best as I can. Where the answer to your first question is.

Yes, Art I've let boys get close to me. I had no way of knowing what was happening out of ignorance. Because Ma, never talked to me about such things.

Where all I can say for myself as an excuse is. That it all happened so fast that I didn't even realize what was happening.

We were just kissing, and before I knew it. I was laying on the grass with him on top of me. I thought it was the natural things to do. I was that naive and gullible at twelve.

Where in your case now that I know, what is going on inside you. I'll help you all I can but, you must keep it our secret."

"Pat what do you mean?"

"I mean, who better to learn the facts of life from than from one, who loves you. You are very impressionable not to mention susceptible. Where for boys could be very dangerous in a lot of ways, where girls are concern.

One, bad experience could become life shattering to you. I'll not have you turn out like Paul did. Not if I can do anything about it, you're not."

"I don't understand Pat?"

"You will Art, you will…. Now let 's find Christ and get her back home."

Chapter 4

Things at home weren't perfect but, a lot better than they use to be. Dad wasn't drinking as much as he did before.

I guess it was because he had to report to work every day, or lose the days earnings. Where he had no choice but, to stay somewhat sober during the week.

Where now it was only on the weekends that he went out drinking. What was somewhat a relief if one, would consider sitting on a time bomb, not knowing when it was going to go off. Could be considered a relief.

It was Friday we all come home from school for lunch. We were sitting around the kitchen table eating popcorn, and sugar-bread that ma, made for us. When a knock came upon the kitchen door.

"Well just don't sit there." Ma, look at us sitting around the table spoke up saying." Someone go answer the door."

"Yes, Ma..." I answered her. Getting up from the table, going to answer the door. Opening it. To startlingly see my Uncle Bill standing before it.

"Uncle Bill...!" I ecstatically blurted out." Is that you...?! Hey everyone...! It's Uncle Bill!" I excitedly shouted out, bolting out the door into his open arms.

"Well... Hello there little man." He joyously said hugging me to him." You're getting awful big, and fat for just being only ten, now is it?"

"Well I'll be...?" Ma, came to the door saying. As the others gathered up behind her. Standing just inside the door.

"Could this be the house where I last seem all those little tots running about wearing diapers...?" Bill jokingly asked.

"Hello Bill." Mary warmly greeted him. Walking up to him, giving him a welcoming hug as he held Art in his other arm.

"Come on Mary surely you can do better that." He asks, giving her a passionate kiss while grabbing, then gropingly rubbing her behind.

"Now that's what I call a hardly welcome…! He boastfully commented." Getting somewhat on the pudgy side, are you Mary?"

"Really Bill must you in front of the children?"

She stepped back for him saying. Stepping back into the kitchen door saying." Come on in." Leading him into the living room. Making a point to comment on his inappropriate behavior.

" Just remember to behave yourself, and keep your hands to yourself…" In a condescending tone of voice.

We were all siting around in the living room. When dad came home, and saw Uncle Bill sitting on the sofa.

Taking a noticeable objection to his being there. By standing gawking at him with a certain amount of objectionable disregard to his presence, by the facial expressions he was giving Bill.

Uncle Bill was a man in his early 50's. Who was a fancy dresser, a bit to obviously dressing on the female side? With all the jewelry reflecting his feminine nature.

Especially in keeping himself looking in immaculately physical condition, and cosmetically for his age.

Keeping himself looking slender built while maintaining a muscular structured physique.

Mary's resented Bill for serval reasons. One, was Bill was a scientist just like Frank was. In fact, it was Bill who helped Frank to disappear. That only Frank and her know about besides one other. That being he was also Art's godfather.

The one, that infuriated Mary the most, was him always commenting on. How uncanny it was that Art looked so much like him, every time he saw Art.

That also went for Frank as well, when every time he would see them together. Where Frank never stopped making insinuating comments on his comparison to Art as well. As to how much the two, of them looked so much alike.

Where neither Bill, or Frank looked nowhere close to looking anything a like. Even without the makeup Bill was wearing.

As it turned out. We all sat around for hours listening to dad and Bill reminiscing about old times. Until gradually we all started to get bored, and one by one eventually got up and left, until it was only dad and Bill.

Where they eventually went out into the kitchen, to sit around the kitchen table. To continue their reminiscing back, and forth between each other.

Pat and I were in the bedroom, while Paul and Christ sat listening to the radio, back out in the living room. As ma, was going about nonchalantly straightening up the place after everyone.

"Art I want to talk to you about something very important." Pat spoke out saying uneasily to him. As they sat together on her bed.

Nervously looking back towards the half open door out towards Bill, and dad sitting at the kitchen table.

"What it is Pat is, there something wrong… I haven't done something to upset you have I?"

"No you didn't do anything to upset me." She annoyingly replied." Now just stop asking so many damn questions, and just listen." She annoyingly snapped back, from being interrupted from what she was about to tell Art.

"I want to tell you something about Uncle Bill, and I'm only doing so to warn you. So just shut up and listen dammit!

Now what I'm about to tell you must remain are secret. It's about something that happened when Paul and I went to visit Uncle Bill two, years ago. When Paul was just over ten, the same age you're right now.

When we arrived at Uncle Bill's. For the first week we had all kinds of things to talk about, and places to go, and things to see. Where after we them began to get on his nerves.

Just a little at first, then a lot.

Then gradually we all really began to get on each other's nerves. Do mainly to Uncle Bill's being prohibited from indulging himself. In his perverted way of life.

Art the only reason I'm telling you now, is so that you don't do what Paul did for him. You are all boy, and soon you will become a man. Not something like Uncle Bill, and Paul are, because of Bills influence over Paul.

Bill's last person I ever wanted to see showing up here but, he's here Where I'm not about to let all we shared together go to waste, because he came here.

Art you know how men like to do things to girls. You should by now. How that's the way it was intended to be between boys, and girls. Where it's not that way with Uncle Bill, or for Paul no longer now, because of Bill.

It wasn't until one, night a week after we arrived. Paul and I were sitting on Bills legs as he sat in his favorite easy chair. With his hands wrapped around are waists.

We were talking about all the things we did that day. When he started bouncing us up and down upon his legs.

I wasn't thinking anything of it until I felt something strange growing against the side of my leg. As he kept jerking us up and down rubbing himself against the side of my leg.

Bill knew exactly what he was doing. How I knew. He looked directly at me and said. "There now don't be afraid that's only my creeping Charley.

He's not going to do any harm, he's just trying to be friendly that's all but, he's very bashful around girls...

Pat dear maybe you wouldn't mind leaving for a while. While Paul here and I get to know each other a little better. You know, boy talk that sort of thing."

"Sure alright." I slid down from his leg, and went into the bedroom but, I didn't close the door all the way. I left it open just enough so that I could see out into the living room.

Art I seem what Bill referred to as his Creeping Charley to Paul. I wasn't so young, or naive not to know about what I was seeing.

However, my own curiosity got the best of me. As to why Bill was exposing himself to Paul the way he was. I mean they were both boys. So why should there be any difference right?

I couldn't hear a word that they were saying. However, I could see Paul shaking his head "Yes"

That's when Bill took Paul's hand and placed it down upon himself. Glided his hand. As if showing Paul how to get personal with his Charley.

I wanted to go out, and say something but, I became frighten. That something might drastically happen to both Paul and I.

I knew of Uncle Bill but, nothing really about him other than he had this outgoing personality about him.

So I decided to wait, and see before doing anything stupid. The last thing I wanted was for him to attack me. Like daddy does us kids now at home.

I watched as Bill released his hand, and said something to Paul. Paul had this look of shocking dismay upon his face.

Then his dismay diminished, and he became excited. Actually smiling becoming more enthusiastic about what he was doing to Bill's, Charley, with his hand

That's when I decided to put a stop to what was going on, I went back out into the living room, and walked right up to them.

Bill was so shocked that he turned twenty, different colors right before my eyes. Not knowing what to say. Where however Paul didn't seem to pay me any mind to my presence while continuing what he was doing. But, instead he just faces me, and said.

"Hi, sis. Look Charley and I are becoming friendly. He likes me so much that he's going to give me ice-cream."

"Ice cream...?" I snapped back at him, asking him

"Yes, but it's a very special ice cream its meant only for boys." Paul ignorantly replied back saying.

All the while Uncle Bill just sat there without saying a single word. As if in a state of shock, and disbelief. Letting Paul explain about his Charley. As Paul vigorously continued to appease his Charley, right in front of me.

I knew about what went on between a boy and a girl. Where I never knew it went on between two guys. Where something told me. That something wasn't right about what Bill was having Paul do to him.

Bill's facial expression changed drastically. Giving me the same look dad would give me when he was about to lash out at me.

He was virtually scaring the holy hell right out of me. When he spoke out with a threatening tone in his voice.

"This is guy business. You best stay the hell out of it. If you know what's good for you! Mention a word of any of this to anyone, and I'll rip out you fucken tongue, and shove it up your ass. Now get the hell out of are sight, and let your brother and I be!"

I stood in utter shock as Paul totally ignored what was going on between Bill and I. Becoming more engrossed in what he was doing.

As Bill pulled his head towards him and started kissing Paul neck, then licked on his ear. Tickling him, encouraging him not to stop.

I just knew that someday he would show up again and would carry out his threat. If I ever told anyone about what went on between him and Paul.

The last week we were there with Bill. Paul and him would do all sort of guy, on guy things totally ignoring my presence.

Art that's why Paul is the way he is. Uncle Bill made him the way he is, and I'm not going to let him do it to you.

So now you know why ma, is trying to convert Paul into being a man he's supposed to become by know where girls are concern.

Even though I thought what the two of them was grotesque and would never allow myself do, or let any boy do to me. Paul showed no resentment as I would have.

"But how does ma, know? You didn't tell her did you?"

"No, Paul did. He had no choice but, to after the principal at school had ma, come to school. However, dad doesn't know.

Art, Paul likes other boys. If Ma, does manage to pull him through this. Maybe he'll turn out to be alright. However, if she doesn't, he'll nerve become a man but, a man's women for a man.

He'll become an outcast. He'll become confused, and disorientate between his masculinity, and femininity just like Uncle Bill is.

Do you understand what I'm saying to you? Bill wants to have sex only with other men not women.

Ma, once told me, that men as well as women have certain responsibilities in life. One of which is to live up to what's expected of them. Women are warm, compassionate, and loving. That's their nature.

Man on the other hand are strong, and masculine. The two must unite in order to from a solid bond of unity. It's the nature of things as it's supposed to be, and as god intended it to be.

Not man onto man, where a woman was born to be man's counterpart. Where the essence of their combined unity. Is what structures those that are conceive from their joining.

Art the essence of who we are, is what brings man and women together. The sensation that men, and women feel when they are together. Is what establishing the bond of togetherness between each other.

It's the indifference between them, that creates life as we know exists as human beings. You can't turn from yourself now. I won't let you…! You must promise me that you'll never stop being the boy that you are. Where I'll promise you, I'll help you grew up to become the man that every woman would come to admire. As the man you were born to be."

"I won't Pat I promise you. through I'm but, a mere boy now. I know that I will become enriched by your sincerity.

I'm no longer blinded with doubts, and aspirations, or uncertainties thanks to you. I know who, and what I am again thanks to you.

Where I also know that I have infringed upon you. While taking advantage of my position as your brother, and your love for me to learn from you."

"Please Art don't feel that way. You mustn't feel that way. If I felt apprehensive about my doing what I have done. I would be harboring remorse over doing so. I feel no regret, or remorse.

Because I know you will use all I taught you to make some girl feel very special when the time comes to shear some, or all that you have not yet learnt.

You've no idea how you make me feel about myself… To be the one who freed you form all those inhibitions. That might have had inhibit you to do honor onto yourself. So that you can now be just yourself and grew maturely normal.

Art we have been sharing something wonderful together. That could have been shared by only us, and the love we share for each other.

For that I harbor no regrets, only admiration for us both, and the girl who's going to be the recipient when the time comes.

Art honey I speak to you now, not as you sister but, as a girl. Don't ever forsake me. To do so would be demeaning yourself, and the man I've brought forth from within you. "

"Sis I want to reach out to you but, I fear to do so. Not because I'm so close but, yet so far in years but, of what's beyond that door.

Sis I am still a mere boy. A boy with desires that surpass my abilities to express them. Is it wrong of me to love you but, not as a sister but, as someone so beautifully desirable?

This isn't right, and we both know it but, never have I ever wanted so much to soar in years. To lavish you as a man onto a woman.

"Please Art... Please don't say no more. When your words have taken possession of me far more than you could physically.

You are right. That door is all that stands between us. Where all I can say is, thank god, for that. For the growing girl in me is only waiting on the man you will soon become. Where you are right. Now is not the time for us.

Art I do so want you to feel the flame of a longing, loving, desirous women but, not of a sister...

Where I know not what are we going to do that? "

She bewildering spoke out, not as a mere girls but, of that of an obsessed women. Finding herself swooning over a mere ten-year-old boy. Knowing what I bestowed upon you all that I desired for you to know selfishly.

I looked up into her gorgeous sparkling blue eyes. Never loving, admiring, or respecting anyone as much as I did her.

"Pat you have giving me your all, along with all that make you so majestically divine, and all I can do, is take. Not being able to give nothing in return. When I want to bestow upon you the revelations that you are so richly deserving of..."

"Art damn you...! Pat frustratingly gasped out. "You have to be the devil himself . The word you speak are not those of a ten-year-old brat kid, dammit! As insane as this is becoming I find myself wanting to ravel in the infernal of hell itself with you."

"Pat I want you too..." Once again skeptically looking towards the door. "But I'll not demean you anymore than I already have."

* * * *

"Damn you Art...!" She annoyingly gasped out. "You are right! We can't risk getting caught together... However, you are not going to get away with this. That's for damn sure! Like it, or not. It's going to happen so set your mind to that!"

Pat frustratingly replied covering up her expose thighs, hand pressing her dress. Looking over towards the half open door.

" Alright go...! Get the hell out of here, now... I'll be out shortly. I should have known better than to have listen to all you said. When I had the devil himself by his pointy tail.

Your right, what is going on between isn't normal?! Because you yourselves aren't anywhere near being normal yourself...

What ten year old brat has the ability to manipulate people like you do...? You aggravate the hell out of me...! Now get dammit...! I want to be alone."

"I'll go but, my hearts not in it, and its more for your sake than mind that I am. Just remember. That if I had it in my power I wouldn't be leaving."

I slid off the bed walking towards the door. Going out it leaving Pat sitting on the bed alone. To go walking into the living room.

* * * *

"So there your young man." Ma, spoke out to me as I emerged entering the living room. Noticing the sorrowful look on his face. "Why such a sorrowful look on your face dear?"

"Ma." I spoke out to her walking over to her sitting on the sofa, to stand before her.

" Why is life so hard...?"

"Life...?" What are you talking about?"

"Growing up ma. I'm finding it so confusing. Not to mention difficult, and to say the least nerve-racking..."

"What's the matter dear...? Mary sympathetically asked me. Holding her open arms out to me." Come here honey, and sit down, and tell me all about it. You can tell your mother what's troubling you."

I walked into her consoling open arms, and stood looking into her loving blue eyes." Ma, it's really nothing but, yet everything, and it frightens me so."

"So what's happening in here...?" Uncle Bill entered the living room asking seeing Ma, and I together.

"Nothing Bill, Arts just a little bit upset about something, I'll handle it. Why don't you go back out into the kitchen, and talk with Frank some more?"

"I will Mary in a minute." He replied walking over to sit down in the easy chair beside the sofa." Come here boy, and tell me all about it. Us men have to stick together, we can't let the females know are secrets, now can we?"

"That isn't necessary Bill. I'm his mother I'll handle what's bothering him." Mary defiantly replied in a reprimanding tone of voice.

"I was only trying to help Mary."

"I realize that Bill but, he's my son your yours. I've to live with his problems each, and every day. You don't! and I'll advise him not you.

I'm the one that's going to have to live with your advice after you are gone, and I rather not. She sharply snapped back reprimanding him"

"Mary you have become a very hard woman. Would you mind telling me why?"

"No! I don't mind if I do. As a matter of fact, I have long been waiting for the opportunity to tell you straight out why!" She argumentatively replied.

" You come, and you go. Where you becoming involved in any of our personal problems for the short time that you are here. Is an infringement upon us?

Whereas you have involved yourself enough with this family. I don't need any more of your personal conviction, or opinions interfering in the way I handle, or advice my children."

"Well, that's putting your position bluntly. May I have asked why you are so antagonistic towards me?"

"I was hoping that wouldn't have asked that but, seeing now you did. I don't like what you did to this family. Where if wouldn't be for the fact that you are Franks brother. Where I once had some respect for you. You wouldn't be sitting across from me right now. Where you know damn well, what I'm talking about!

Your so called advice, and guidance has placed a burden upon my family! Why you on the other hand... No she blunted out."

Mary stopped abruptly, catching herself before she really let her contempt for him really come out. Knowing it wouldn't do anyone any good.

That the damage he inflicted on Paul took to deep a root to stop what he done. Where it would only damage her attempts to correct what little bit of the damage she has thus far been able to **emend.

"Alright, Mary you made my position very clear. Maybe I best go back into the kitchen where I would be out of your way? He rose from the chair saying.

"Yes, I think that's a very good idea..." Mary snapped back defensively watching him walking back toward the kitchen.

"Ma, what was all that about?"

"Nothing dear, nothing for you to worry your head about. It's just something between your Uncle Bill, and me that's all."

"Mary." Frank called out to her raised up from the kitchen table. "We're going out for a couple of beers, we'll see you later."

"Yeah, sure. Just don't come home drunk. I haven't forgotten the last time you did, and you better not. I mean it Frank I've copies, don't ever forget that I will use them if I have to..."

"Yeah sure I here you." He yelled back, walking towards the kitchen door." Come on Bill lets go." He called out to Bill opening the door. Leading him out into the hallway. C closing it behind him.

Christ, Pat and Paul all came into the living room to join ma, and I anxious to hear why ma, was so down on Uncle Bill.

"Good I'm glad to see you all here together. I want the three, of you to get yourselves a change of clothing, and some pajamas. Then go down the block to the Fries.

That's where you're going to spend the night. Art and I will be along shortly, we've a few things to discuss first, now go on."

They all went to gather up their things then returned back into the living room to find Mary and Art still sitting on the sofa.

"We're ready Ma." Pat spoke up speaking for the others.

"Well go on them, and do what I told you to do. And Pat, make sure they don't get out of hand. You two, better listen to her now. Now go on."

They left leaving Ma, and I alone in the apartment. I wanted to tell her about what was upsetting me but, I couldn't.

I felt certain that Ma, would never understand about my feelings for Pat, or what we were sharing together.

So as we talked. I used a name that I knew at school to direct my frustrations on. Whereas ma, as usual attentively listened with the utmost diligence to what I was saying.

Letting it become known to her. That I was all boy but, a bit too young to be able to cope with my frustrations concerning girls, and their demeanor.

"Honey listen to me." She consolingly spoke out to me." I can't tell you what to do, or what not to do. You yourself can only do that.

However, I'm in the position to give you some insight as how to make dealing with girls a little bit less frustrating. Seeing how I once was a young girl just like the ones you are getting yourself all frustrated about.

You sit beside me as a boy of ten but, yet so much a man. That I can't speak to you as a mother in this matter but, as a woman who was a young girl once herself.

You see, and hear, and you are obliviously curious about girls, as they're about boys. All I can say is. That girls are girls that are women in younger bodies, and that they don't know any more than you do about what's going on inside them.

Look at me dear, and you'll see what they will become. It's the indifference that's going to very, and become very more noticeable in so many ways but, not only in their appearance.

Right now you see, and might have even touched. However, you must also look beyond your curiosity, and your feelings, towards what you see and feel.

You must look into her mind for the reason why she's allowing you to get close to her, allowing you to do so.

Dear, it's only natural that you should feel the way you do now. You're only ten, years old. You must give yourself a few more years before you will even begin to understand their reactions towards you.

Honey, knowing that I will help you all I can. That I will only be able to do that if you to open up to me, like you are now. Otherwise I won't be able to help you."

"I will Ma, but, what am I to do when you are not around to help me?"

"Just do what comes naturally. Then come tell me. However, if you feel uncertain about yourself, remember this.

Girls are as timid, and as sly as you are. Challenge them, even go so far as to exercise authority. However, do so with respect, and they won't back away from you. Believe me dear, I to was a young girl once myself. I know what I'm talking about.

Females young, or old, like aggressive guys. It shows them that you have confidence in yourself. Which will arouse their curiosity to want to find out more about you.

It's been said that the pen is mightier than the sword. The person who said that doesn't know how right he was. When it come to the way girl as well as women think.

Where the man thinks of brute force the women uses her brains, and her wisdom to overcome. Never forget that.

Honey if you ever dare to repeat what I'm about to tell you I'll deny it.

If a girl approaches you, or permits herself to satisfying your curiosity. Do so, and learn from her generosity to enhance your confidence. They want to learn from you as much as you want to learn from them.

Only through them will you establish the characteristics that will become necessary to your status in life, but never mistreat, abuse, or denounce them.

Always honor, and respect then as a person, and never make them your enemy but, as your friend. A vindictive female is the last person you ever want to have to deal with. We are unscrupulous in nature."

"Ma, I think I understand what you're trying to tell me. You must love dad very much to put yourself through so much because of him…?"

"Why your sly little devil you…?" She startlingly reprimanded him replying." Why you have been using your frustrations to work something out of me.

Now that's a lowdown underhanded sneaky trick I must say but, your ingenuity is commendable… I can see how that I have to keep reminding myself to look beyond your youth to your intelligence."

"Ma, my intelligence has nothing to do with my ignorance. When it's put at an imposition of becoming obvious such as it is now. I can't no longer ignore.

I don't like not knowing how to direct my intelligence. I've so much going on in my life, that it surpasses my intelligence to reason. I'm trying to understand but, how can I under these stressful circumstances? I've no use for girls in my life right now. Where they are becoming a very important part in it, whether I like it, or not."

"Honey, don't try to understand that which is not ready for your mind to comprehend. Just go alone with it, and try to learn from it. For when the time is right for you to know how, or when to apply it, you will know.

It's a part of growing up. Take advantage of it while you can. You will be surprised just how much it will benefit you in your life.

Some learning doesn't come from going to school. It comes from learning from others, and dealing with everyday life.

Of course education comes first. It prepares you to provide for yourself, and bale's you to support yourself but, that's only one, of many parts that comes with having to grow up.

One, has to develop the wisdom to know when to apply what you learned from others, and when dealing with others as well.

It is accentual when it comes to understand the other people, who we all have to live with, and that's where the wit, and the knowledge comes in. It aids you in dealing with one's life crises when they arise.

"Ma." I sit here looking at you, and all I can see is that you are so beautiful. You have the face of an angle, and the body of a divine Goddess.

Yet you hide your beauty, and you torment yourself in hopeless absolution, and suffering. Your solidarity is degrading to your splendor."

"Damn you Art!" She frustratingly replied. "You're only ten don't forget that. Just where do you get off talking to me like this?"

"I'm sorry mother. I didn't mean to upset you..." I suddenly became alarmed by my mother's tone of voice. Frightfully wanting to change the subject.

" Ma, why are girls so different than boys...?"

"Mary was not only startled but, also confused by Art's sudden transition but, back to one of adolescence where she knew in her own mind that he was mentally prepared for a challenge of wits when comforted aggressively.

Where she knows that his mind was just like his fathers. That his mind would emerge above the others. To where eventually it was going to be hard for him to maintain a conversation on one subject at a time for too long. That it was his minds way of relating, by jumping from one subject to another while using the change to analyze the previous one he was having. Thereby by keeping an objective mind so that he could associate with the others train of thought,.

Art 's mind was that of his fathers. That's why the two, of them collided so much. It was due to their way of coping, and comprehending to reflect back.

Where in his mind every question deserves an answer and until it derives at one. He would continue to keep changing the subject.

The only other man that Mary ever loved, and admired beside Frank. Was the man who was behind Frank's disappearance.

Who offered Frank a new life. Where as it turned out. It was Frank who couldn't deal with the mental anguishes. That he left behind in his previous life.

Mary went to him out of desperation because of Frank's drinking. Ruining his second chance at a new life. The letter that she placed on the kitchen table was address to that very person.

Where Frank knew that if she ever mailed it. He would be spending the rest of his life in a top security facility for the hopelessly insane. Too atone for what he done.

"Art you have an uncanny way of changing a subject. However, to answer your question would even frustrate you even more. So yes, I'll allow you to ask your new question. What was that again…? Oh, yes we are back on girls again. You sure do have a one, track train of through about girls…?

Chapter 5

As it turned out Ma, and I never did join the others that night. Ma, made diner then we went out for a walked doing very little talking, just enjoying each other's company.. Then returned back home after startlingly realizing how late it was. Where upon doing so. We fell to asleep laying together on the sofa watching the TV.

Ma, assured me that she wasn't about to let me sleep alone. Not knowing if Frank was going to come back home, or not. Where as it turned out. Neither Bill, and dad never did return home that evening.

Ma, was feeding me breakfast when the other kids returned back home from spending the night with the Fries. With Christy asking Ma, where we were all night.

When Bill and dad came walking in the door. Appearing somewhat hangover, with dad asking ma, to make them some coffee, as they sat down to join all us kids already sitting at the table.

* * * *

Where things went somewhat normally around the house with even Bill settling into the humdrum routine around the house. Spending the following week with us.

Then the weekend came again. Whereas though everything seemed to be somewhat normal. The tension continued to build, as each day got closer towards the weekend until the finally dreaded came down to Friday night, after dad came home.

Where to everyone, shocking dismay. Bill and dad startlingly decided that instead of going out they would stayed home, and enjoy each other's company.

Where I wanted to remember a lot more. As it turned out, that was the first time I ever remembered seeing dad sober on a Saturday morning. As

I came walking out following the others out of the bedroom. Seeing ma, serving up coffee to dad sitting at the table. Along with Bill sitting beside him at the table.

As we all gathered up around Pat, with me hiding behind her. Nervously trying to keep out of his sight. Not knowing what to expect. I was finding it that stressfully astonished by the sight of dad being congenially sociable to anyone of us kid, or for that fact mom, especially in the morning.

"Ma."

"Yes, what is it Pat?"

"Ma, is it alright with you if we go to the park? I'm sure that you grownups want to be alone."

"I guess it will be alright but, be back before suppertime."

" Sure thing Ma, come on you guys let's leave the adults alone." Pat spoke out leading us out the door.

Where as it turned out. The second we arrived at the park Paul and Christ ran off, leaving Pat and I sitting together on a park bench.

"Art I haven't been able to stop thinking about Bill. I want to get him good for what he did to Paul, and I don't want him to ever forget who got him. For the rest of his life!

I've been thinking, and there is a way I can show him for what he really is. All I would need is someone to attest to what sort of degenerate he really is.

Ma, knows what he did to Paul but, dad doesn't. I've got to get that moron out of my system once, and for all, and I'm going to need your help to do it.

Art will you please help me...? I've it all planed out, and it will only take a little effort on your part."

"Alright I'll help, as you knew I would. You just tell me what you want me to do, and I'll do it."

Pat told me of her plan as we walked around the park. With me acting childishly as usual. While the more Pat told me of her plan, the more fearful I became about her involvement in it.

"Pat what you are attempting to do is begriming to appear very dangerous. Exposing him for what he is, is one thing but, exposing yourself to him. Could place you in a great deal of jeopardy.

"Not really you will be there to ensure that nothing will happen to me. Then there's dad, and ma. If he dares to lay a hand on me. If dad doesn't make him regret it ma, sure as hell will. You just make sure that you hold up your end, and I will handle the rest, look Art."

She pointed towards the playground at Christ and Paul running towards them. As they sat down on the bench waiting for them to catch up to them.

"Hi, you two." Christ spoke up, stopping to join Pat and I waiting for Paul to catch up to her." We best be going home now I'm striving…" Christ walked away from the bench saying heading towards home.

* * * *

That night after supper Ma, and dad, went out for the first time in years. To visit one of their old

friends. Leaving Bill to watch us kids until they got back. Just as Pat said they would. While the two, of us were out in the kitchen drying the dishes.

"Art this is our only chance to put my plan into action. So far it's working out perfectly. Now listen to me, this is what I want you to do.

I want you to keep Paul and Christ out of the living room until I do this." She took her nose in her fingers and twisted it.

"Then I want you to send Christ out, and keep Paul occupied until I get Bill into Ma's bedroom. Where I'll leave the door open halfway.

Where you can bring Paul up to be able to see inside. Then when you are in position just. Tap on the wall, to let me know you are there, and I'll take it from there.

Art if anything happens out of what we were talking about. I want you to run out of the house as fast as you can, and call the police."

"Pat are you sure that you want to do this?"

"Yes, I'm sure he's going to regret what he did to Paul. Now get going and do what I told you to do."

I walked towards the bedroom, and stood by the door. Calling out to Paul to get his attention where he was sitting on the sofa with Bill.

" Hey, Paul." I called out to him. Getting Paul's attention along with Christies at the same time. Who was not sitting on the other side of Bill on the sofa..

"Yeah, what is it?' Paul turned towards me standing in the bedroom doorway. Yelling back at me.

"Come here, and bring Christ with you I need to talk with the two, of you about something important."

"Can't it wait?" Paul reluctantly rose up from the sofa discouraging asking?" Not waiting for a replied back, turn his attention on Christ, annoyingly saying.

"Come on Christ let 's see what Art wants. We'll be right back Bill." Paul lead Christ towards the bedroom door."

"Take your time kids Bill uncomfortably spoke out saying sarcastically." I'm not going anywhere."

"Say Bill." Pat spoke out to him. Emerging from the kitchen door walking towards him sitting down beside him on the sofa. Wiping her damp hands off on her dress.

" I've been meaning to talk to you about something for quite some time now."

"Oh, you have, have you. About what?"

"Mainly the way you are mistreating me again. Favoring Paul over me."

"Have I been doing that? I'm sure that it wasn't intentional."

"Yes, it was, and we both know why, now don't we?"

* * * *

"Christ, Paul, Ma told me to tell you. That she wants you to go spend the night with the Fries again."

"Thanks a lot Art." Christ sarcastically replied back. "I really do appreciate you finally telling me... I swear Art you have no memory at all." She frustratingly replied, going to her dresser to pack some things to take with her.

"Well I told you now didn't I?"

"Yeah, you did...!" She tossed her pajamas in her overnight case. Dashing out of the bedroom heading towards the kitchen door, not waiting for Paul to follow her behind her.

"Hold it right their young lady." Bill yelled out at her. Stopping her at the kitchen door." Just where do you think you are going?"

"Ma, said that I could spend the night with the Fries down the block. Bye now..." She answered him back yanking the door open. Darting out, slamming it behind her.

"Hey...!" Bill confusingly shouted out." Come back here...Shit...! I swear that girl is sloppier that a grassy pig..."

"Oh, let her go she'll be alright at the Fries. Besides that's just one less to worry about."

"Worry about?" Bill skeptically asked

"Yes, you and me are going to have to come to an understanding right here and now. If we don't I'm going to have to tell dad, about what you and Paul did while we were visiting you."

" Pat you're not attempting to extort something from me are you? If you are, you are going to find out. That I'm not all that easily intimidated, and let's not forget. It's your word against mine. Where I also know a few things about what's been going on between you, and boys."

"That only goes to show just how stupid you are. Do that, and ma, is going to ask. Now you came to know what you are talking about. Good luck explaining that. As for Paul he already told ma."

"So that's why...?"

"Why what?"

"Nothing that concerns you just what is it that you want?"

"Why you of course."

"Me...?!"

"Yes, you." Pat twisted her nose saying. Signaling Art to bring Paul where he could witness what was going on between Bill and her.

"Why you little..." Bill angrily started to say. Stopping abruptly, spotting Paul and I coming out of the bedroom walking towards him.

"What in the hell are you two, doing out here?!" Bill disturbingly shouted at them stopping them form coming closer to him." Get back into your bedroom and don't come out until I tell you too! Now move it dammit...! Now!"

We went running back into our bedroom. Where I partially closed the door to stand beside the door jam. So that Paul and I could see back out into the living room, without being seen by Bill or Pat.

"My god, Art. What's the matter with Bill?! Something sure got him angry?"

"I don't know but, I'm not about to go out there, and ask him. I'm going to stay right here out of his way, and so are you if you know what's good for you.

Just keep quite. Beside we can pretty much see, and hear what's going on between them. The last thing we need is trouble. Besides it's Pat's thing not ours. I'm not stupid. I learnt from living with dad. Go ahead if you want I'm staying right here."

* * * *

"Bill let's face it you treated me wrong, and we both know it. I'm much older now. Where I didn't really know what you and Paul were doing back then but, I sure as hell do now!

I don't want to discuss this out here when someone might be able to hear. Why don't we go discus this in ma's bedroom?"

Pat said, not taking no for an answer. Walking towards ma's, bedroom. With Bill following behind her.

That was Art's clue to put the next phase of Pat's plan in action.

"Paul I wasn't going to tell you this but, I heard Bill talking to dad, about Pat. Bill was saying something about wanting to have a good time with her tonight. Maybe that's why dad took ma, out.

I just seen them going into ma's bedroom. What do you say we go have a look see if we can hear, and maybe even seeing what's going on? Let's go, and find out what is going on between the two, of them? What do you say, what to go and maybe have a look see? I know I do?"

"You damn right I want to...!" Paul angrily replied back." And you better not be ling to me... Now let's go...

"Now just calm down and relax here. I don't know what's getting you upset. But, can hear it in your voice, that you're upset about something. Paul I don't need any trouble with either Bill, or dad. So don't go pulling anything stupid that going to involve me."

"I'm calm down damn it! Now let's go...! Beside I'm older than you are. I can handle things better than you can. Now let's get going."

"Alright we are going..." I reluctantly lead him out of the bedroom. Up to the partially open door of ma's bedroom.

" Look we got lucky>" I whispered out pointing to the partially open door. "We best be really quite now. If we don't want to get caught spying on them."

We positioned ourselves so that we could see through partially open door. With me kneeling down, and Paul standing up behind, and above me.

Just in time to see Pat standing before Bill, unbuckling his belt. When

I tapped on the wall beside the door to let her know we were in position.

Watching Pat reaching up under her dress removing her underpants. Handing them to Bill, them went to pull down one of the shoulder straps of her dress.

Exposing her bra covered breast, as Bill let his pants drop down about his ankles still holding onto her underpants.

"Damn him...!" Paul angrily spoke out." He promised me...! He's not going to get away with this...!"

As he irately went charging into ma's, bedroom. Where he literally shoved Pat away from Bill with such a force. That he sent her flying back against the wall beside the bed. Sending her plopping down on her butt, with her back against the wall.

Shouting, and raving at Bill. "You...! You lied to me...! How could you...?! After all you said to me...?!" Totally ignoring Pat laying slouched down against the wall beside him standing before Bill.

"No, Paul...! It was all her fault... You have to believe me...She was going to tell your father about us! If I didn't submit to her demands...!"

He defensively attempted to explain holding Paul's hand by their wrists, so that he couldn't strike out at him.

" Why would I let her have her way. Knowing that you were in the next room unless I'd no choice?! Now just calm down, and let me find out what she's up to dammit...!"

"Well, alright...? I guess so...?! But, don't you ever let me catch you ever pulling such a despicable thing again, or I'll tell him myself...!

As for you Pat! If I ever catch you touching him again, I'll rip you heart out!" Paul irately yelled out. Threatening her as she laid propped up leaning back against the wall, with her legs stretched out on the floor, and Bill still holding onto her panties.

My staring became so diligent that I didn't even hear Ma, and dad, coming home. Until I heard mon's voices coming from the kitchen behind me.

"So where is everyone...?" Ma, asked me. Catching me standing before her bedroom door. While placing her purse down on the kitchen table. Standing looking about the apartment.

"Who the hell cares I'm going to get myself a beer." Frank walked over toward the icebox. As mom walked towards me, standing before her bedroom door.

"Where are you going?" Frank spoke out asking her opening himself a bottle of beer standing before the icebox.

"I'm going to get this blasted girdle off that's where." Mary replied walking down the hallway towards the bedroom door and me.

As I panicky stood not knowing what in the hell to do. Knowing what she was going to see once she looked inside her bedroom. With me so utterly shock I couldn't ever stutter out a single word to warn anyone in the bedroom.

Where ma, came to an alarming halt frozen in a state of utter shock! Before the open door standing behind me.

Seeing Pat sprawled stretched out upon he floors fully exposed slouching back against it against the wall beside her bed.

With Bill holding what could only be Pat's underpants in his hand sitting down at the edge of the foot of her bed with Paul standing before him with Bill's pants down about his ankles

With Paul darting forth hugging himself up against Bill panicky looking back at ma, standing behind me.

Frantically struggling to compose herself from going totally berserk over the despicable appalling sight she was being force to bear witness too! Irately shouting out.

"Oh! My God...!" Mary horrifically yelled out." What's going on here...?! Bill what are you doing with my daughter Paul...?! Why you perverted Bats rad...!" She irately yelled out at him. Staring on with utter disbelief.

" I'll kill you...! "She insanely creamed out...! Charging pass me by shoving me aside of her as she charged through the door at him. Being brought to a jerking halt by Franks grabbing hands grabbing her about her waist. Pulling her back outside the doorway.

"No Mary...!" Frank yelled out at her." Stop you hysterics..." He held her around her waist preventing her for entering the bedroom." Getting irate isn't going to solve anything..."

"Thanks Frank." Bill gasped out a sigh with relief.

"Don't thank me you Fucker...! You're not going to get away with this! That's for damn sure!"

"Frank you don't understand...?!"

"What's there to understand other than what I'm seeing with my own eyes... I'm broad minded but, only to a point! Just what in the hell are you doing with my son, and daughter?!"

"Damn you Frank...! Let me go...!!" Mary irately yelled out. Struggling to break free from his restraining arms holding onto her." Goddamn you Frank...! Do something...! Kill that son-of-a -Bitch...!"

"Will you shut up damn you!" Frank defiantly yelled back at her." Alright damn you...! I'll do something."

He aggressively shouted at her. Physically shoving her back against the door jamb irately yelling.

" Shut the fuck up! Or you'll be wearing your big mouth down about her ass and let me think damn you...!"

"Let me go damn you...!" Mary aggressively shouted out at the top of her lungs. Making a desperate attempt to break free, to lash out with her long finger nails to get at his throat.

Where Frank grabbed her by her throat instead. Pinning her head back against the door jamb shouting out insidiously." Knock it off damn you...!"

"Hey... what's going on here...?" Christ entered the apartment, hearing all the hysterical shouting going on. Coming upon Frank clutching Ma, by the throat, pinning her head against the door jamb of their bedroom doorway.

"Ma...!" Christ frantically screamed out, running towards her. Furiously beating on Frank's back, and sides. To get Frank to let her go.

Only to alarmingly stop! Spotting Pat lying on the floor against ma's bedroom wall fully exposing herself naked from the waist down. With her dress up above her waist. While noticing Paul hugging himself up against Bill who was sitting with his pants down about his ankles on the edge of the mattress.

"Oh...! My god...!" She paradoxically screamed out. Running towards the kitchen door and out of the apartment. Screaming out in utter terror ranting and ragingly frilling her hand about head like a raving maniac.

"My God...! Frank...! go after her...!" Mary panicky cried out to him. While clutching her hands about his waists. Struggling to pull his hands away from about her throat but, he was too strong for her.

"Hell! Bitch! Let her go...!" He disconcertingly spoke out, maintaining his chocking grab around her throat. Looking towards the kitchen door. "She'll be back as soon, when she calms down."

"I hate you...! You depraved moron...! I hate you...! Mary frantically screamed out at Frank! No longer fearful of dying." Come on you creep...! Kill me damn you...! Or I swear I'll Kill me...!"

"What was that you called me...?!" Frank release one of his hand from around her neck, to raise his hand. To strike her. Shouting back at her.

"Go ahead hit me...!" Mary defiantly challenging him. Staring him directly in his enraged eyes." But, you better damn well kill me ...!

If you don't You better not ever close your eye around me! I'll surely kill you if you dare to hit me! Your drunken son-of a Bitch...! I have had it with you...! You're going to pay for his...! Come on kill me damn you...! Do it... Do it ...!"

"You...!" Frank insanely shouted out. stopping short of hitting her. To stare at Bill and Paul. With Paul holding onto him. With the look of utter terror in his face.

"You...!" Frank infuriatingly shouted out at Bill. Still restraining himself from hitting Mary." It's all you damn fault...! Get the hell away from my son damn you...!"

"Alright Frank I'm getting..." Bill fearfully panicky, shoved Paul away from him pathetically speaking out. Holding his hands up protectively.

" Frank it's not my fault ... You have to believe me... She's the one that started all this trouble." He pointed an incriminating trembling finger at Pat. Still spread out on the floor against the wall." She's nothing but, a rotten Whore...!"

"Go to hell you perverted child molester...!" Pat definitely shouted back at Bill. Using the wall to get back up onto her feet." He's lying through his revolting teeth!

I was sitting on Ma's bed minding my own business when he came in and asked me if I would like to meet his Charley. Holding himself in his hand through his pants on his Charley. Them Paul came storming in and shoved me against the wall."

"That's a lie...!!" Paul shouted out." I see her... She had her hand inside his pants...! It's mine not here's ... Uncle Bill promise me that it would always be mine...Charley is mine not here's It's mine... It's mine...! "Paul hysterically ranted.

"Why your little slut...!" Frank irately shouted out at Paul." As for you Pat I'll tend to you later ... I always knew that you were a tramp...!"

"Fuck you Dad!" Pat defiantly rebelled shouting back standing her ground against him." Now get your disgusting hands off mother, or you will have more than her to deal with...!"

"Why your defiant little trollop...! I'll beat you black and blue..." He insidiously shoved Mary aside, and started walking towards Pat.

"Like hell you will...!" Pat rebelliously replied walking away from the wall trying to stay out of his reach." I'll tell this time... I'll tell the police if you dare to touch me."

"You will what?!" He threateningly shouted out. Abruptly stopped his approach towards her contemplating her threat.

"You heard me...!" She authoritatively stopped backing away from him to stand her ground. Shouting back at him.

" I'll have you thrown in jail, and you Bill behind bars... Come on big bad Daddy... Come beat on me. I dare you to touch me...!

I've a witness this time. You will have to kill us all. Come on damn you! What are you waiting for ...?! Do you damn revolting thing...!

As for you dear Uncle Bill... I've you good! If the cops don't get you. Once I tell them about you, and what you are. You will never be going to be able to stop running. So you best start your running now!"

"Alright let's just all settle down here and get to the bottom of what's going on here." Frank spoke out composing himself now. Thinking to patronize the situation before it got any worse than it was already..

" Just what are you up to girl? It's obvious that you set this whole thing up."

"Independence Dad. You've been infringing upon us enough! I must admit I never expected it to work out this well but, now I'm glad it did.

You're not going to hurt anyone in this house ever again. Your also no longer going to torment, or terrorized this family. You are dealing with me now! Not, Mom.

As for you Bill you're going to get all that's coming to you for what you did to Paul but, to show you I'm fair mined I'll give you two, days before I call the police. Good-bye Bill."

"Now Pat I'm sure we can work something out." He nervously spoke out." Pat you can't do this to me I'll do anything just don't call the police."

"I'll think about it but, I don't want to ever see your face again, and before you leave I want you to tell Dad what you did to Paul.

Come on Ma let's get out of this cesspool." Pat walked past Frank and then me and ma, walking out of the bedroom with Ma, and I following behind her.

"Pat dear, I don't care about Bill but, you just can't have your father arrested."

"Ma, you have to stop protecting him. He's a mentally deranged person, who has to be stopped. You can't control him, and we both know that none of what just happened is going to change anything. He's never going to change."

"Pat I hope for all are sakes that you are not right your father. But, your father is no ordinary person. you see him for what he's become. Where I know him for what he really was."

"Ma, tell me why it is that you are protecting him."

"I can't Pat I just can't."

"Surely Ma, it couldn't be anything worse than this hell. We all have been forced to live in because of him."

"Yes, it can and it's for that very reason I can't tell you now. Where it's not for me why I can't. It's for you kids who are going to be the one's who're going to have to live with it. Now please let me be alone with my thoughts."

" Alright Ma, but, I'm very serious. If dad so much as touches anyone of us I will carry out my threat. As for Bill he's got two, days."

Chapter 6

Unknown to Art what took place with their Uncle Bill is going to bring about the turning point in his life to where his fate was going to lead him to eventually meet a woman who would become the defining link in his life that's going to have a devastating effect on both their lives.

* * * *

While all the bickering, shouting, and auguring was going on. I snuck away from ma's bedroom door, and went to sneak back into my room.

Hoping to wait out all the commotions until it died down. Not wanting to get involved unless Pat called upon me to come to her aid. Thinking to myself.

'I better be getting out of here before someone discovers me and gets me involved in all the chaos. Thinking I best get away myself just like Christ did.

While sneaking to my bedroom I exposed myself to ma, sitting at the kitchen table. Where she caught sight of me turning to close my bedroom door. Instantly speaking out to me to get my attention.

"My, Arthur dear..." Ma, startlingly said, spotting me on the verge of closing my door. Trying to hide in my bedroom.

" Whatever are you doing trying to hide in your bedroom? I was wondering what could have happened to you while all the shouting, yelling was going on.

I really never paid your whereabouts any mind until I just saws you sneaking in your bedroom trying to hide from it all..."

"I was trying hide ma, not wanting to get myself involved in all that was going on..." I nervously answered her. Frightfully looking over towards ma's bedroom door.

" Ma, I couldn't take another beating like dad gave me the last time. Ma, I was never more horrified in all my life because of what went on!

I just wanted to run away, and hide I was that terrified. So I snuck away to hide in my bedroom.

I didn't realize that you did the same thing.

Ma, I wasn't about to risk trying to come out until everything was over. That's how terrified I was, and still an... Thinking that I would go hide under my bed, until I thought it was safe to come out. Then I was going to make a mad dash like Christ did."

"Come here dear...." Mary sympathetically called out to me. Opening her arms to me. As I went running into her protective arms. Cowering into them, hugging myself against her. As she sat hugging me to her. With my entire body trembling profusely shaking against her.

"Honey we must talk but, not now. All you need to know right now is that your mother is here with you, there's, and there's nothing to be frightened of. You have my promise of that.

Now I want you to go into bedroom and try to relax, and try to get some rest. I'm sure all you heard has been hard on you but, you must try not to let it affect you. You have nothing to be fearful of.

Honey I must go out and look for Christ. Just stay in your room and you will be just fine. I don't want you to be frightened all the fighting is over for now. As for your father, and Bill. They will be becoming with me, so you have nothing to fear from them.

As for Pat, she will be just fine. It's best that she be left alone for her to think about everything that's happened. So just leave her be sitting out in the living room"

"Mother I'll go, and stay in my bedroom. Just find Christ, and bring her home." I nervously stepped back out of her arms.

Skeptically looking around, being frightened. That dad would suddenly up, and jump out at me, to grab hold of me, and start beating on me.

When a demanding knock came upon the kitchen door.

"Now who can that be...?' Mary rose up from the table speaking out, walking towards the door. Stopping before it before opening it to speak out through the door saying.

"Yes, who is it...?" She asked before opening it.

"It's the police..." An authoritative voice replied." Open the door lady..."

"Yes, immediately..." Mary nervously replied. Opening the door just ajar to look out into the hallway saying." Yes, what is it officer...?

Mary evasively asked standing behind the ajar door. Open just far enough for her to peer out, at two officers standing on the other side of it.

"Is your mane Mary lady, and do you have a daughter by the name of Christ?" The officer standing facing the door asked.

"Why yes, I'm Mary, and yes, I do have a daughter Christ. Is she in some sort of trouble?"

"No, she's quite safe now. He condescendingly snapped back." She's at County General Hospital."

"The Hospital...?!" Mary panicky replied." My God...! What happened to my darling Christ...?!"

"Cut it lady!" The officers sarcastically snapped back." She told us what she seen. Now open the door lady!

"He authoritatively demanded!" Holding the flat of his hand against the door preventing her from closing it. Along with using his foot against it. To jam it. Getting ready to forcefully shove it open, if she attempted to slam it shut.

"Yes, of course..." Mary nervously replied. Opening the door allowing the police to enter, stepping aside for them to enter.

As they barged their way inside. Shoving Mary back inside as they barged their way inside. Stopping before the kitchen table looking about. With the one initially speaking to Mary demandingly asking.

"Where's this Uncle Bill...?"

"I'm Bill..." Bill entered the kitchen. Entering the kitchen coming from out of Mary's bedroom by himself. Startlingly coming upon the police standing in the kitchen.

"You mister are under arrest!" The other officers immediately grabbed hold of him placing him in handcuffs." In fact all of your under arrest...!"

"Under arrest...? What in the for ...?!" Frank came walking into the kitchen just seconds behind Bill. Acting Ignorant asking.

Also being taken into custody immediately by still another officer." Hey...! What's going on here...?! What's the charges ...? You can't arrest me...! without cause...!"

"How's child abuse, and sexual molestation of a minor for starters...!" The arresting officer. Aggressively applied the handcuffs around Franks wrists, answering his question.

While still another officer entered the apartment, and stood behind Mary. Who stood in a state of shock, and dismay. Over what was happening. Not being able to comprehend any of what was happening. Panicky asking.

" What about my children...! You can't arrest them! They didn't do anything wrong?!

There be no one here to take care of them...?!"

"Now's not the time to start worrying about them lady. We will be taking care of them... We are placing the children into protective custody. Until such a time that this matter is settled."

"There must be some mistake officer...? Mary dumbfounding gasped out.

"Tell it to your daughter lady, who's lying in the hospital in a state of shock, repeating all that she seen taking place here. Then the judge

There's more officers waiting outside. Now where the other two, children? I see you already have one. right here.

It's alright son, everything is going to be just fine. We are here now too protecting you. Be a nice boy, and just come quietly, no one is here to harm you. Now come along now...."

"No....!" I paradoxically shouted out running to my mother's aid. Standing before her. Protecting her with his body.

"No...! You can't arrest my mother...! I won't let you!" I frantically yelled out at the officer standing before me.

Aggressively shoving him back away from us. Frantically turning to hug myself up against her. While cowering up against ma's leg. Clutching my locking fingers about the back of her legs refusing to let he go...!

"Sorry son but, it's the law. You're going to have to come with us..." The third officer forcefully pulled me off Ma. Dragging me away from her, as frantically struggled against him. Wanting to go back to my mother kicking, shouting, and screaming in defiance. Not wanting to be taken away from her.

"It was them...!" I panicky pointed towards Dad and Bill." Not my mother... Them...! It was Them...!

Ma, tried to stop it but, dad hold her by her throat threatening to kill her...! You can't arrest my mother...! I won't let you...!"

I frantically struggled to get back to her. Screaming out struggling to shove the cop out of my way as he blocked me from getting to her.

Where out of desperation I ran towards the kitchen drawer. Pulling out a carving knife. To stand threateningly. Holding the knife ready to strike out at the cop standing before ma." Let her go or I'll kill you...!"

"Now son just put the knife down..." The officer spoke out calmly to me. Speaking very slowly while stepping towards me. Reaching out his hand to me. Forcing me to back up against the cabinets behind. Where it causes me to look behind me just for a second. When the officer shouted out.

" Damn you...!" Charging towards me attempting to grab the knife out of my hand. As I attempted to slash out with the knife cutting his hand from becoming panicked. Over him shocking me by surprise.

" You cut me...!"

As the officer drew his revolver and pointed in a state of rage directly at me. Shouting out threateningly." Hold it right their kid!

Don't you dare move a muscle or I'll blow you head off...! Drop the knife kid...! I'm not fooling around here. I'll kill you were you stand...! Now drop the fucken knife damn it...!"

I panicky dropped the knife, from out of utter shock. Of looking down the barrel of the gun the officer was pointing at me. As still more officers came charging into the kitchen.

When the one holding the gun on me grabbed hold of his me to jerk me away from the knife lying on the floor. Then shoved me into another officer's hands.

"Get him the hell out of here now...!"

Where I was aggressively pulled out of the apartment. While the officers gathered up Paul, and Pat and dragged them out of the apartment building behind me, and placed us all into a waiting police car. Parked out in front of it. Shoving us all into the back seat together.

"Now all you kid just sit still..." An officer annoyingly shouted out, slamming the car door. Locking us inside.

Where all we could do was just sit there, watching the police bringing out Ma, Dad, and Uncle Bill. Shoving them into a paddy wagon. Where the paddy wagon pulled out form the curve speeding off right past us.

The look in Art's eyes as he pointed out the side window of the car. Watching that paddy wagon speeding past him. Was one, that Pat would never forget as long as she lived. As Art screamed out.

" Ma...! Come back...! Come back... Don't leave me...!"

"Stop it Art!" Pat yelled out at him. Pulling him away from the side widow as two, officers climbed into the front seat of the car. As Pat constringed me hugged me against her. Trying to console me through my anguish.

"Well they Are gone." The officer sitting next to the driver turned his head towards us sitting in the back seat together. "Saying as the officer pulled away from the curve.

" They can't hurt you kids anymore. Now you can tell us what's been happening now so we can make sure they will never be able to again."

"We have nothing to say to you." Pat defiantly replied." No one is going to say anything to you. Unless are mother tells us to."

"Young lady I don't think you understand that we are trying to help, and protect you kids. It's are job to protect little kids from being abused. You would think that you would be grateful."

"Let it go Steve. There's juvenile hall now. They will know how to get the answers that we need out of them."

"Look you two." Pat whispered to Paul and I." Say nothing to nobody about anything. Ma's in serious trouble because of what Dad, and Bill were doing to us kids.

Now listen to me both of you. They'll must likely split us up, and talk to each of us alone. Don't believe anything they might tell you. Now both of you promise me that you won't tell them anything about what happened tonight."

"We promise don't we Paul?"

"Yeah, I promise."

"I mean it Paul…"

"I heard you Pat." Paul annoyingly replied. Going back to look out the side window as the car pulled to a stop.

Before a dark gray four, story building. Where the officers climbed out of the car to opened the back doors. Allowing us to climb out

"Alright kids come on let's go. This is going to be your new home for a while." The one, who was driving the car spoke up saying.

As we all climbed out of the car. Then were lead into the building. Where the three, of us were lead up to separate doors. Me being the last to stand before a closed door.

"Yes, come in." Donna a young social worker called out. Hearing someone knocking on her office door.

Where the officer opened the door. Leading Art inside the office, up to the desk where some strange women were sitting behind.

"Well hello their young man." She greeted me saying smiling." My mane is Donna please do sit down, and make yourself comfortable. No one is going to hurt you here."

"Alright! I'll sit...!" I rebelliously replied sat down in the wooden chair before her desk.

" But, I'm not going to say anything!" I defiantly stared at her as she sat calm, and composed smiling at me." Will you go get my sister now?"

"No, not just yet. Not until you are totally relaxed, and when you show me that I could leave you alone to go get her.

I can't leave my office knowing that you might do something impulsive, because you are feeling hurt, and frightened.

Young man I can understand, and sympathize with you. As to why you could be upset. I would be myself. You have just gone through a horrifying ordeal.

However you must understand that you are only making it worse on yourself emotionally, acting the way you are doing. When you've nothing to fear from me. Now please for both are sakes just relax, so that we can become better acquainted."

"Why?"

"Why? So I can better understand you, and it will be a sign that you are beginning to feel at ease. You did say that you wanted to see your sister didn't you?"

"Yes."

" Well then let's say we start by you giving me your name."

"It's Art."

"Well Art I'm indeed honored to have the pleasure of meeting you ... Now you see that wasn't so very hard now was it...? We are already beginning to like each other aren't we?

You do like me don't you Art? I know I like you very much...

" She smilingly said using her young beautiful facial expression to project an aura about her of trust, and compassion. Softening me up hoping to gain my trust.

Her red lips, and blue submissive eyes reminded me so much of my mother. Where with her long blond hair hanging down enveloping the sides of her face like veiling strands of gold. Like my mother's looked when she wanted it to make her hair look nice .

Made her resemble so much like mom. Just sitting across from her looking at her was enough to soften me up to the point where I wanted to run into her arms and cry my heart out.

I was missing her so terribly much, wanting to be with her. I felt so all alone and scared I needed someone so desperately just to hold me...

"Well, I guess so...?" I uneasily replied, as her enchanting eyes kept my eyes engrossed onto her face." Maybe just a little."

"Art I'm not here to harm you in any way. Don't friends try to help out each other? That's all I'm trying to do for you. Art please let me help you... Where I can't help the person that I like so very much, if you don't let me help you."

"What do you mean lady?" I defiantly replied. Breaking free form her bewitching smile." I don't need any help... What are you trying to do take advantage of me?!"

"No, Art I wouldn't impose upon are friendship like that. What I really was trying to do was to see if you could help me." She replied, instinctively changing her approach. Saying to herself.

'This is no ordinary impressionable boy. He's not stupid by any means...'
"Art I know that you are more than capable of taking care of yourself."

"You said help you. How?"

"Wait just one second." She turned her eyes attention from Art to look towards the officer standing inside the closed door of her office.

" That's alright officer you can go now. My friend and I've something to discus in private if you don't mind we would like to be alone."

"Sure thing." He replied, turning to open the door." I'll be waiting right outside."

"That won't be necessary officer, just close the door on your way out."

"Well, alright if you are sure…?" He replied, going out the door closing it behind him.

"He's gone now Art we can talk between ourselves now. "

She sounded so damn sincerely sympathetic I couldn't help to feel I could confide in her. By removing the police officer so that we could talk just between us.

It never once occurred to me that she would still use what we talked about against my parents. That's how good she was at manipulating me.

"Art now I want you to first promise me that you won't tell a soul about what I'm going to tell you. Will you promise me…?"

"Well. Alright I promise but, I don't see how I could possibly help you anyway?"

"You just listen to me, and you will see. I know why you were brought here I was reading about your case when you came into my office. However, the report only says that you were having sexual relationships with your parents."

"No! I wasn't…! That's a lie…! I wasn't! I'm telling you… I wasn't…!"

"Art now calm down. You didn't give me a chance to finish what I was going to say to you. Now just calm down, and hear me out.

At first I want to tell you. That I too have a son, about your own age. That's why I asked for you to be assigned to me.

Art I do like you very much. You are far too nice of a boy for me to bring any hardships upon. The questions I'm going to ask you. Are for my own personal reasons, and seeing how we became such good friends.

I thought that if I were to ask you to tell me some secrets. That are keeping you from trusting in me. That you would help me remove any and all doubts between us concerning your present home life. That I might better my own relationship with my own son.

Where in return in you confide in me. Just maybe I could return the favor by maybe figuring out a way I could go about helping you get you back home with your parents.

Art I to love my son very much. Just as your own mother loves you I'm sure. However, the reason I'm ask you us is because my son has no one-else but, me. His father is dead, and I'm not always there when he needs me.

Where if you don't want to help me. I'll understand. Where in any case. I just want you to know that you will always remain my very dearest friend."

"I don't know how I can help you?"

"Just tell me all about all you seen, and done at home that might help me get you back home to your parents, say within the past month. So I can maybe use something so that I can approach my son with some new ideas.

All I need is information; I can do the rest from there on. I promise you that all that you tell me will only go as far as this office, and me along with my appreciation for your help."

I just sat looking into her eyes.' Thinking to myself about all she said to me. Wondering if I could believe her.' She did sound so believable but, remembering what Pat said to me about, not believing in anything they would say to get me to believe I can trust them.'

"Art I know what's troubling you. It's not that you don't believe me. It's that you don't trust me. That's it, isn't it?

Art if I confided in you. Why shouldn't you trust me? I trusted in you by telling you all I did.

Look at me Art. Do I look like that sort of person that would lie to you...?

I'm just as human as anyone-else. I'm a woman alone who's in love with her son. I want to reach out to him, but I don't know how..."

She was actually pleading with him, hoping to break down that wall that stood between us. By placing him in the position of authority. Making herself appear ignorant but, yet receptive to anything I could tell her.

"Alight..." I conceded to her persevering manner. Lowering my wall of resistance, unknowing falling victim to her conniving tactics." Alright I'll tell you what you want to know."

"Oh, thank you...!" She joyously replied." Thank you ever so much Art, I do so really appreciate this... You are going to make me so very happy .

Would you mind if I wrote down what you tell me? My memory isn't all that good, and I don't want to forget any of the important things."

"I guess it's alright. As long as nobody else see's it."

"Oh, no... they won't. I promise you..." She enthusiastically picked up her pencil saying.

"So where would you like me to start?"

"Oh, I don't know...?" She bewilderingly pondered not wanting to appear to be too anxious." Now let's see... I know... Why don't you start by telling me about your home life, then go on from there..."?

As I talked she wrote. I told her all about being on welfare, and how my father was nothing more than a worthless drunk, and how he would come home and beat up on everyone.

Once I got started I just couldn't stop. It just kept coming out only to come to a sudden stop. suddenly realizing that I was telling her about what I didn't want to tell.

"What's the matter Art?!" She startlingly looked up from the paper she was writing on nervously asking." Art why did you stop?"

"I don't know...? I just did that's all. I don't know if I should tell you anymore?"

"Art you told me so much about yourself, and your family already. There's nothing you could possibly have to say, that could be more horrifying than what I've already heard.

That father of yours really put you through hell. As for you mother, nothing you've said shows me that your mother did only what she had to do to protect you. My only concern is why didn't she have him arrested?"

"I don't know. She kept telling us kids that it wouldn't do any good. That when he got out. He would only come after us, and maybe kill us all.

She really did do all in her power to protect us. I didn't mind the beatings so much. It was those other things that he did, that I hated him for doing. I swear when I grew up I'll make him pay for what he did to my mother..."

" Art how do I know that you're not telling me the truth about all this?"

"You don't. Just like I don't know if you were telling me the truth." I skeptically replied.

Staring back at her, directly into her eyes.

'Damn it!' She frustratingly reprimanded herself.' I'm losing him... Somehow I've to break down that damn wall he's putting up between us again..

I've to regain his trust, and confidence. In order to get the information, I need, to obtain the evidence against his parents. That I'm so damn close to getting...'

"Art if it upsets you to talk about what you and your mother might have shared together. I don't want it to upset you.

However, you must realize that I need to know all you are feeling about your relationship with her. So that I can better understand what I'll be sharing with my own son.

I'm just as frightened as you are but, I've opened myself up to you. You can't stop now, leaving me without not knowing..."

Donna had no choice but, to pray on his sympathy. Knowing it was the only way to get him to open up to her.

"Art I need your reassurance that I'm doing the right thing. If you are feeling ashamed and frightened now. How do you think it makes me feel?

Art when one loves another. One doesn't care about anything else but, being with them, and showing them how much. They love then regardless of the consequences.

You are my friend. I feel that I can confide in you. You are also one very incredible young man. One that I'm proud to call my friend..."

She suggestively spoke up. Rising up from behind her desk. Walking around to lean back. Sitting partially on top of the desk before him. Bracing herself up on the flat of her hands.

" Art you're not kidding me. Your eyes give you away. I see by the way you are looking at me. Your eyes don't look upon me as those of a boy of ten, years old.

They ogle, and emanate desirous passion as someone twice your age. With exploitation intent, as well as without apprehension of what they see before them.

Art it's time for the truth, and nothing but, the truth. It's obvious that you have shared something very personal with you mother, haven't you?"

"No...!" I defensively rebutted." I love my mother ... I don't know what you are referring to but, yes, of course we do share a lot of things together. She's my mother...?"

"Do what things Art?" She challengingly asked." Why are you becoming so defensive when I ask you about your mother?

Alright them. If not only with your mother with who them? Your sister Pat perhaps...? Just what do you share with your older sister?"

She became aggressive attempting to insight him to emotionally breakdown from out of fear, if nothing else. Applying child psychology on him.

Only to be stunned by the reacting he comforted her with. That totally shocked her off balance, not knowing how to react against a mere ten, year old boy.

"Why don't you go ask her?! I don't know what you are talking about."

"I'm sure you do know what I'm implying. You just don't know to describe it in detail. Like I said before. It's time to tell the truth. If not for yourself than for your mother. Now I want to know everything.

What you don't realize is that your mother is in very serious trouble. Where I alone can get her out of it. Where I can't unless I know everything that went on up until now, and I mean everything.

I'm not going to stick my neck out not knowing how far I've to stretch it. I don't want to find out later on that you have been making a fool out of me. How is that going to make me look with you only being ten years old?

Your eyes, as well as your mannerisms tell me you know a lot more than the average ten, year old where females are concern. If you want to be able to get back home with your parents. You best start telling me just what has been going on in your family.

Believe me Art. I'm very sincere about wanting to help your mother. I'm a mother myself. Now give me something to help her out of this mess your father, and that Uncle Bill has gotten her into.

"If you are so sincere, why is it that you yourself would be willing to intervene for someone you don't even know?

You have been lying to me all along. Why should I believe you now…? I know once I leave this room I'll never see you again.

The reason I'm staring at you so diligently is because I want to remember you. You can't keep me here of ever. Someday I promise you we will meet again! Where I'm not one, who easily forgets. Where I have been told by serval people that I have a photographic memory"

"Art you can't blame me for what happened to you, and wanting to find out just what has been going on with you and the rest of your family."

"No, I can't! But, I will for trying to use me to hurt my mother. I'll tell you what you want to know. But, if any harm befalls my mother because of it. I'll hold you entirely responsible. Now go sit down and take up you damn pencil, and remember this day, for it might not be the last time we share what transpires from this day hence." I sort of used a threatening tone to my voice when I made that comment...

Wanting to let her know that when it came to my mother. I meant what I said. Which started the clock in my head **tick- tucking hoping that it would be the last time we saw each other.

I dictated as she wrote. Picking up where I left off. Telling her about my brother Paul, and how Pat attempted to get her revenge on Uncle Bill.

That lead up to everything that transpired up to the time we came together, and brought about my parents and Uncle Bill being arrested.

Donna's heart went out to Art, as she sat writing down what he was telling her.

She was finding herself hating herself for having had to lie to him. Not liking what she had to do but, discovering while talking to him. That in level of intelligence was extremely advanced for a mere ten, year old boy.

Where against her own better judgement found herself not being able help herself from becoming smitten by him. Because he had this charisma about him that put her at odd with her own feelings that she almost instantly from the second she laid her eyes on him that she found herself developing. Where she herself couldn't even put some sort of logic to that would make any sense for her to be feeling towards him.

As she sat behind her desk placing her pencil down staring at Art actually doting on her own thoughts about him. As he sat before her desk, deeply engrossed in his minds tormenting thoughts.

"Art what is really troubling you about all this?"

"A great many things. You for one, and myself for another. I sit here looking upon you knowing that I divulged my entire life to you.

As horrid as it was. I honestly feel relieved that I did now. However, I've to look upon you in a different light now. As the one who holds the lives of many in your hands. Including my own."

"Art I'm sorry but, being sorry won't change anything. I still want to be your friend I promised you I'll do all I can for your mother.

I wish there was something I could say, or do for you. That would insure you of my sincerity..." She rose form her desk, walking around in front of it to sit leaning back on are arms once again.

"There is..." I looked up into her eyes saying. Raising up to stand before her." Just hug me for one second..." I sorrowfully said.

"Oh, Art..." She sympathetically opened her arms to me. Hugging me against her, with nothing but, compassion for me, as I wept burying his face against her.

Donna held me compressed against her Opening her heart to his anguish, as he squeezed constricting arms about her waist hugging himself up against her.

Donna in all her twenty-Three, years. Never felt so unemotionally unstable towards anyone. Most of all a mere boy of ten, years old boy.

Where in the two years she served as a counselor at juvenile hall, she dealt with a great many kids but, none like Art. Where he was far from being considered an ordinary kid. But, there was something else about him. Like an inner fear about the anguish he was yet going to have to endure , and a feeling about him being able to do us.

Knowing that Art was a highly intelligent person. Who was however entrapped in a boy's body, With whom she was finding herself emotionally struggling with, not wanting to become emotionally involved with. Where there she was submissively doing so.

Allowing herself to adsorb overpowering sympathy for him. As his tears of sorrow, and despair seeped through her blouse onto her flesh. From the socking material of her blouse becoming saturated and absorbed upon her nurturing breast. As she held his flooding eyes against her, running her fingers through his brown hair.

"Art." She softly called out to him." I don't honestly know how to relate to you. I want to in so many ways, but I can't."

"I'm sorry too..." I released my constricting embrace from about her waist. Stepping back out of her arms. Wiping my tear filled eyes with the back of my hands.

Standing drying my eyes to see clearly. To see her observing eyes, staring down at me. Filled with the expression of confusion, and bewilderment.

"My mother told me that a girl is only a young women trying to grow up, where a women is only the young girl trying to recapture her youth. That were pre-established from convictions that now frustrating them.

Because they can't accept the imposition placed upon them, when it come to their feelings. That they came to suppress while having to grew up, and can't allow themselves to feel again as women. Because they have to adhere to other levels of moralities.

Am I not a person with feelings? Are you not also a person with feelings? Are we not both sharing the same feelings of frustrations that restrict us both from responding to them?

Age being the detrimental factor. Where age in itself doesn't suppress, or separate but, segregates us from us being who we are.

As well as are feelings, that are within all of us young, or old. Regardless if or are gender.

Where neither you, or I are not impervious to the aspirations that divides, and hinder us from reaching out to another. Because one is denying what they are feeling while the other is frustrated, and confused because they don't know what, or why they are feeling what they are."

"Art how can I contradict, or dispute all that you have said? When you said it all in a way one, can, what restrains us from acting upon are impulses... Just who are you...?

The emissary of the devil himself. That came upon me to embellish, and, or persecute me. For all that I might be feeling right now. Just what are you expecting of me...?"

"I expect nothing. You stand before me reflecting being distraught. Distorting your beauty, making yourself look ugly, and grotesque, but yet it changes nothing when it comes to you personally.

Where you are only trying to put on appearances... You can't hide yourself form yourself, or me. The one who looks upon you seeing what is going on inside of you.

Denying yourself for being receptive to your feelings that have become erupted within you.

Your right I'm not like any other kid. Where the only crime I commented, was wanting to be loved, and excepted, and was never given the chance to be a kid.

Where you are knowing in your heart, and mind. That I don't deserve the fate that awaits me. Knowing that I'm placing my life in your hands. Where your decision from this point can influence my destiny as to what lies ahead of me.

Where I could tell you. That I could walk out that door, and never give you a second thought but, I can't do that.

However, yet when I walk out that door. All that am will be going with me, but can you knowingly allow yourself to do that? If knowing by doing so, you will be denying yourself from acting upon your own feelings, knowingly denying yourself and dreading the thought, the rest of your life. Watching me walk out that door?"

I said daringly walking towards the door thinking of leaving. While I had the chance of hopefully escaping the uncertainty that I felt sure was awaiting me. If I didn't do something to prevent it.

"Oh, my God..." She gasped out submissively becoming totally mesmerized by the hypnotic effects he was having on me.

" You're not real... I can't let you do this ...? I need time to think ...Please Art I can't let you walk out that door.

I swear... That you're the devil himself. She nervously looked upon me just a few feet from her office door. Wanting to feel virtually helpless form letting him walk out it. While struggling with herself to find a reason to stop him from doing so. Knowing that the officer who brought him is standing on the other side of it.

Possible taking any chance I might have to help him. Out of my ability from doing so. Not wanting Art to follow the same fate that so many other have. Who have been denied the chance

to receive the help, they need. Instead of just being tossed into the legal system.

Where Art like so many others just get lost up in. Only to turn up standing being persecuted by the same system that was believe would help him.

"Art I will do what I can for your mother. However, once you walk out that door. Nothing that took place here between us and deter the outcome for what lies ahead for all those who were involved in what took place. Which I'm sorry to say also includes you as well."

"Donna can I still be your friend?" I asked contemplating just how far she allowed me to pursue my endeavor to walk out the door. Making it to the door. Where I stopped hesitatingly to open it.

"Please Art. Just come back and sit back down. You don't want to do that. Now come back and sit back down so that we can finish what needs to be done."

I reluctantly went to sit back down before her desk saying." Yes, let's talk. The question is. What more is there to say that we haven't already covered?"

"Art until this matter is cleared up. You will have to remain here, along with your brother and sister. Where what you need right now is a good night's sleep. As for me I don't know just yet how I'm going to deal with all this." She got up walking towards the door opening it.

" Come on Art let's get you settled in for the night." She stood before the open door saying.

Where again I reluctantly rose, and followed her out into the hallway. Where upon as I stepped out into the hallway I spotted Pat, and Paul sitting on a bench. With guilty looks upon their faces.

As Donna lead me up to the bench they were sitting on, where she told me to and wait with them.

"So what's the matter with you two?" I asked, upon sitting down in between them on the bench joining them. Where Donna left the three, of us sit. As that same officer who brought us in. Remained standing beside the bench.

"I told them everything Art." Paul nervously spoke out saying." They tricked me..."

"So did I, Art." Pat remorsefully spoke out saying." What about you?"

"So did I Pat. Pat what's going to happened to us now...?"

"I don't know Art. I guess we'll just have to wait, and find out."

"Alright you three, come along." A heavy set women approached us saying. Being followed by two, other men.

"Where are you taking us?" Pat nervously asked the women.

"Just follow us, and shut up." She reprimanded her replying. As we rose following her down the hall. Then up a flight of stairs, and down another corridor. Before coming to a stop standing before another open door.

"You two, boys follow those two men. As for your young lady you follow me." She leads Pat down the corridor. As we followed the two, men inside the door. Where we discovered that we were standing before of a dormitory filled with beds, and other kids all sleeping soundly on bunk beds

"Alright you two." One, of the men said." Find yourselves a bunk and get to sleep. Breakfast is at 6 AM."

"Yes, sir." Paul replied. Leading me down the aisle towards two, empty bunks, that were already made up. Where he took it upon himself to plop down stretching himself out. As I went to sit on the other bunk next to his.

"Ha...," Paul gasped out. I never thought a bed could be so comfortable..."

Chapter 7

Several days later Paul, Pat, and I were taken from the juvenile hall, and driven to the courthouse. Then lead into a courtroom.

Where Ma, Dad, and Uncle Bill were lead in, and made to stand before the judge, sitting upon his bench. As the three, of us sat in the jury box. Where Christ was brought in to join us.

"Hi, brat." Christ sat down beside me saying." How have you been without me?'

"Hush, sis." Paul whispered out to her." The judge is going to say something."

"I have read the charges being brought against the defendants. Where due to the complexity of the complications that have arisen in regards to the father.

I'm going to recommend him placed into custody of the Provo-Marshals until such a time that he'll be expected to appear. Here before this court to stand trial for his conduct in regards to his wife and family.

As for the defendant Uncle Bill. I must at this time inform him. That this is only an arraignment hearing. Where he'll be asked to make his plea of guilty, or not guilty. If not guilty he had to option to trial by jury on the charges of which I'll now state.

Statutory rape, Child abuse, and battery. Inflicting bodily harm on the minor children within the residence he was staying in. How do you plead?"

"Not guilty your honor. I'm also requesting a trial by jury." Bill spoke out pleading his case. Knowing that he would never come to trail. Because of his involvement with Frank and his involvement with the government.

"Let his plead be doily entered. As for the mother Mary's involvement in this case. There's no evidence implicating her in any of the charge against the other two defendants. I'm however retaining her in custody. As a material witness, due to the extraordinary circumstances pertaining to her husband.

Now regarding the children. I can't allow them to be returned to the home because there is no home for them to return too. Seeing how all the defendants are being retain in custody at this time.

Therefore, for the interest of the children. I'm going to make them a ward of the court, and order. That they be placed in the state adoption center, until such time the court feels they can be returned back into the home environment.

To insure that the defendants known as Uncle Bill, and Mary the mother returns back into this court. I'm imposing the maximum on their bail for Uncle Bill. And retention of the mother Mary until such a time she will be released from material witness status.

Therefore, I'm setting the bail at $50,000 dollars for Uncle Bill. As for the date of his trail I'm setting it for November 10.

I realize it's three, months away but, due to the mitigating circumstances involved in this case. The father's pervious matter retains top priority Where his date will remain pending. This court is adjoined."

"Alright folks come with me." The security officer spoke out to them. Leading them out of the courtroom.

"Where are you taking them...?!" I jumped up onto my feet shouting out." Ma...!" I panicky screamed out to her. Attempting to run to her but, being held back by another officer. As they were being lead out of the courtroom. With me shouting out.

" Ma...! Ma. Come back...! Let me go...!" As I frantically screamed out. Struggling to break free of the guards restraining arms. As the officer held me up from off the floor. As I continuously kept shouting and ranting. "I hate you...! Let me go damn you...!"

Little did I know that it was going to be the last time I was ever going to see my mother again. Where the image of seeing her disappearing out of my sight. As the door closed behind her was all I was going to have left to remember her by.

"Come on you little brats!" The officer angrily shouted out at Art. literally having to carry me around my waist. As I continued to viciously kick, and struggled to break free. Being carried out of the courtroom. Into a room behind the courtroom, with the others following in behind me. To be again guarded by still another officer.

Where I was shoved down into a wooden chair. Where beside it, stood a heavy set women wearing a uniform jacket, and a wrinkled dark blue skirt.

"Well here they're Miss Rain's." The officer said. Stepping back from me." They are all yours but, watch this one, he's a real kicker..."

The instant I saw her standing before me smiling. Something told me that she hated him right off.

"Hello kids." She greeted all of us saying, smiling with a smirking grin.

" My name is Miss Rains. You're going to be coming to live with me now for a while. Now come along, we must be getting home.

Your sister Christ just loves it there I'm sure you will also. Now the bus is just outside Now let's not bottle we have a long way to go."

"Maybe I should go with you to make sure that this one, doesn't take off." The officer asked the Miss Rains.

"That won't be necessary officer I'm sure he'll be a good boy, now won't your young man." She looked directly into Art's eyes. With her eyes threateningly terrorizing him.

"He'll be alright lady." Pat spoke out walking to take me by his arm." I'll look after him. Come on Art, we better do what she says. We have no other choice, we've nowhere else to go ... Don't worry we will all be back with Ma, very soon." Pat said leading us out of the courthouse into the waiting bus.

* * * *

As it turned out that little while turned out to be over 4 years. During which Pat turned eighteen, and left the adoption center. Where she continued to attempt to get Art released in her custody where the courts kept turning her down. Mainly because she had no real means of support to provide for me.

As for Christ. She didn't stay at the center very long. After a few months she was placed in a foster home where she was soon afterwards adopted. Where in any case. She never wrote, or came to visit anyone of us.

As for Paul. He didn't mind it too much, as long as he was able to keep up with what he was doing. Where he came to be the bested liked bitch amongst the other boys around the center.

As for myself I was going on fourteen, and was holding my own. Where I had Pat visiting me. Where however her visits were becoming fewer, and longer in between. Her last visit was over two, months ago.

The time in between her visits, were the hardest on me. I was without anyone. Whereas I couldn't be seen too much with Paul, because of his reputation. Where I was able to visit him I had to be isolate during my meetings with him. Over the concern that if I was seem consorting with him. Who knows what the other kids would think? Even though Paul still was my brother.

So I spent most of my time reading, and working on educating himself. While waiting for Pat to come visit me. However, for my good conduct I earned myself off ground privileges. Which meant that I could leave the grounds with a responsible adult person.

I never forgotten my mother. Even though during all the time I spent in the orphanage I never once heard from her, or even about her.

It was as if that she just ceased to exist. However, that wasn't stopping me from courting the days until I would turn eighteen, myself. Where I would be free to go out, and search for my mother on my own. I wasn't about to let her be forgotten...

I would be notified in advance when Pat was going to come visit me, on Sunday. It was Friday when Miss Rains informed me of Pat's appending visit.

It was 1 PM on Sunday, when Miss Rains entered my dorm informing me that my sister was down stairs. Where I virtually ran down to warmly greet her. Giving her a big hug.

"Hi, honey." Pat warmly greeted me. Hugging me back, as we stood before the front door." Let's say that we go someplace where we can be alone? I've your pass."

"Yeah, sure let's go." I joyously replied, following her out the door towards her car, parked out front. Where they both got in then Pat drove me out through the front gate.

" So tell me Art have you a girlfriend yet?" Pat turned to me asking.

"Forget them. You know I can't trust any of them. They would go running the head master, and tell him everything I said, or did. Even if I didn't attempt to do anything.

Where you know as well as I what he would do.

He would love nothing better than to send me to reform school. Like he did to all those others."

"Art you're going on fourteen, now. Where you are no longer a little boy. Art you're not becoming like Paul are you?"

"Hell no, I'm not! You know me better than that!"

"I'm glad to hear that but, I can't help to feel so sorry for you..." Pat pulled off the road into a wooded area. Where on one could see the car from the road. Shouting off the motor.

" There now Art we're all alone..." She turned sideways leaning back against the car door saying.

"Pat do I make you feel as if I'm imposing upon you?"

"What do you mean?"

"I mean it seems that the only reason you come to see me is because you feel that you are obligated to, because you are my sister and all I have left is you.

Pat you are my sister, and I love you but, I don't ever want you to feel that you have to come visit me. You too have your own life to live."

"Art I love you too. I thought that I couldn't be with you haunts me constantly... You have no idea how I long for the day. That we will be together permanently. However, that isn't possible right now.

Art honey, I wish that there was something more I could do for you. I mean something extra special that only I could do for you."

"Sis you have been doing that for years, and not just by coming to see me. There's nothing more that I could expect from you."

"Art I mean something that goes far beyond us just sharing a few hours together. There has to be something that you are feeling being denied. That I could do for you, or help you with?"

"I don't understand what you mean? You have already did more for me than I could ever hope for. Without your love. I wouldn't be here right now, to be able to see you, and hold you in my arms."

"Art I've been thinking what could a young man want more than anything else..." She suggestively placed her foot up upon the car seat. Taking up a relaxing position slouching down upon the seat. Making sure that I would notice what she intending on doing for me.

"Pat you can't be serous...?! I'm not a ten, year old boy anymore." I shyly commented embarrassingly attempting to drew her attention to the fact, that she was exposing her underpants.

" Why should I let that bother me, or feel uncomfortable when I'm with you. We are sister, and brother, and love each other, don't we? Where all we have ever had is each other, so why should I inhibit myself? Worrying about being prim, and proper.

Espccially when I'm out working having to be constantly on my guard about my modesty. Where I'm not able to be here with you as much I as want to be where I can sort of let my hair down.

Art I'm your sister I taught you all there was to know about girls. I see no shame in letting you see up under my dress.

You didn't mind it when you were ten, why should you now? Maybe I don't mind arousing the man in you. Where I have no doubt that you are having to suppress yourself from denying yourself to express yourself, like an ordinary growing boy should.

Art you've been coped up for over four, years of your life because of me. It was I who has been deprived you in so many ways. From experiencing the revelations of being with a girl...

It's not going to be any different than it was before, other than us being older.

Art I know what I'm doing if I didn't I wouldn't be doing this. You need to experience being yourself without fear of inhabitation.

Trust me Art I need you to be the man you want to be... I'll help you to follow your impulses. You don't know how it's been for me over you not being there for me.

Art I'm so all alone, and frightened. Nothings the same anymore, everything is changing so drastically.

I can deal with the change but, it's the nights... Those long lonely nights... You don't know what it's like to go home to four, walls. Sleeping in an unsafe empty bed, all alone. Only to have to get up the next morning. Having to struggle though it from one, day to the other... without the only person I need so badly to be with me.

I tried so hard, so very hard... I have even resorted to dating a few guys. Where all they care about is themselves. I need so desperately to be held and loved, and have someone to hold onto, and to love, and care about me. Like the two, of us were before I had to leave two, years ago.

Dammit Art! We belong together, and this God forsaken world is keeping us about... I love you so very much... All we ever had was each other's love...

I love you with all my heart, and soul! Where we are being forced to live in our own separate hell. When all we want is to be together, and left alone...

I've always been there for you. Where all you have to do is reach out to me. We need each other's strength in order to survive, if only for a fleeting moment..." She extended her open arms hoping to lure met to come into them.

* * * *

"Damn that boy...!" Miss Rains angrily shouted out from frustration. Looking at her watch reading 5:30. Pacing nervously about in her office. 'That boy is late again...!' She irately said to herself.

'He's out with that slut of a sister of his again. Doing only God know with her... With his own sister no less...!' She infuriatingly thought.' Speaking irrationally to herself...!

'He's going to screw up everything dammit...! I can't permit her to do that! I've a good thing going here, and I'll be damned if I'm going to let her spoil all my plans. Not when he is my last chance to make it big. Where I can finally get the hell out of here once, and for all!

I didn't bring her here to get her interested in him, so that whore of a sister of his can rob me from what I so rightfully deserve.

Not when I can make a small fortune, on selling what I would allow the two, of them to get away with while I'll be filming every detail.

Just one, time and I'll have them both under my control. Using the threat of sending them both to the reform school. I'll not only get possession of them both. I'll be able to dictate what they can and can't do. Which will be nothing, and everything as long I as I can film it... Where in the hell is he...?!"

* * * *

"Pat." I turned to her watching her hand pressing her skirt making herself look presentable.

"Yes, Art what is it?" She turned her eyes attention on him replying back.

"Why Pat."

"Why what?"

"Why did you? Don't you realize the consequence, and what it could do to both are lives?"

"Didn't you like it. Didn't it make you feel so much better knowing now...?"

"Sure it did. In fact, I never felt anything like it before. But, that doesn't change the fact that neither of us are prepared. If complication might have developed from what might have happened?

"Relax... It's nothing that wasn't destine to happen eventually anyway. I love you Art and where does it say I can't have you because you are my brother? Where even if there was. That still doesn't mean I can't have you if and when I want to. Where no one is going to tell me otherwise!

I say the hell with the what if's, and why not's especially when it comes to us who are the most deserving. Where it's too late now anyway to start concerning ourselves about anything, or one else but us."

"Pat I to feel the same way. You have no idea of how I'm feeling right at this very moment, and it's not because of what just transpired between us. Hell, I felt it even when I was just a kid.

Pat I can't go on like this... I just can't! I can't stand the thought of you being so alone. I don't want anything happening to you. Not now more than ever..."

"Art Stop it! Just stop it...!" She annoyingly spoke out at me." I can't bear to hear you talking like that. "I don't like it myself but, I'm no fool either.

You are doing something you shouldn't have to because you are in that horrid place! Otherwise it wouldn't have turned out the way it did. Where you weren't being honest with me leading me to believe that the old way was helping you when it wasn't.

By you not being honest with me upsets me to no end. When you could have come right out and told me. Where I could have been helping you all along. No wonder I have been constantly worrying about you.

Where now that I know you can be rest assured things are going to be diffidently changing between the two, of us from now."

"Pat I know you don't want to talk about what's going on in your life. You made is obvious that you don't seem to care anymore. Where I didn't want to ask what's been happening to you. That has been obviously behind the cause that was bringing about the change in you."

"Honey, I want to tell you. But, I just can't tell you not right now I just can't. Isn't are being together all that really matters? At least now that we have finally became totally together, and there's no longer any barriers between us"

"No, Pat it's made it worse. Suppose something should have happened to you. Where I might never be able to see you again. Where the thought alone now terrifies the hell out of me! I don't want to loss you not now... Not ever...! That's why I'm not going to go back."

" You're not what?!" Pat argumentatively shouted back at him.

"You heard me! I've been thinking about running away for some time now."

"You can't be serous...?! You're on fourteen! What will you do, where will you go, and how will you live? You have no means of supporting yourself. At least give yourself a couple more years where at least I can get settled in better than I am now, or be able to care for us both for a while."

"I'll come live with you."

"Me...?! Hey...! That's even more absurd than you running away now! I'm living off welfare, and working as a waitress. You can't come live with me, and you don't stand a chance in hell without an education on your own.

Besides I'll be the first person the authorities will come to, when you are reported not returning back when I came to visit you. I can't afford any more trouble than I'm already having to deal with.

Besides don't you dare ever attempt to think of running away. It's bad enough as it is having to worry about you where you are at now. Let alone not knowing where you're at. You will drive me mad just worrying about you... So you are just going to forget it...! Do you hear me?!

If you ever attempt to do such a thing. As much as I love you I'll find you, and ring your damn neck myself!"

"But, Pat..."

"But nothing! Now you listen to me! You are going back! Like it or not, and you are going to give me a chance to think of something.

Just give me some time to figure out a way for the both of us. You are not going to go off halfcocked, and do something stupid...! Not now you're not...!Your going back and stay there! Do you hear me!

Damn you Art...! You make me so damn mad at times... I don't want to hear another word about you running away. Do you hear me...?!"

"Yes, I hear you but, I'm not about to go waiting four, more years either. So you better come up with something soon."

"Don't threaten me! I'll do what I can! You know I will. Especially now that we are coming somewhat back together again. It's not going to be as hard as you are making it out to be but, mark my words.

If I even think that you are becoming anything like Paul. I'll make you regret the day you were born! You're going to turn out the way I want you to be. So you best set your mind to that fact. You, and your damn concern about what could happen isn't going to be a deterrent. The next time I come visit you.

You are staying right where you are at. You are getting free room, and board, and me beside. That should be enough to suffice until I can figure out something." She started the car saying, pulling back out onto the road.

" Let's say we stop for a cup of coffee before I take you back?"

" Sure I can't get in any more trouble than I'm already in. You know I was supposed to be back at 5 PM."

"Well you can't blame me for that. When it wasn't my fault. As I recall I wasn't the one, who was procrastinating taking forever. To get over all your damn apprehension instead of just acting like a moral fourteen, year old boy. Who would have taken advantage of the golden opportunity when it's presented to him to experience the wonders for himself? Instead of trying to figure out while it's happening asking questions no less.

"Sis you've no idea just how much I was mesmerized by your exquisiteness. I have always been astonished by your outer beauty. I had no idea of the splendor of your inner magnificence. That could only be described is that of a divining angle. I didn't want it to ever end.

Where even now just looking upon you. Makes me feel anointed captivated. ? Finding myself never wanting to come back to the realization of the living hell I'm being force to exist in.

I know what you were attempting to do but, it would only make matters unbearably worse on me. Your right I'm not ten, anymore. Where living with the haunting torment of what all we have shared, was never anything like I just experienced. Where now having to live with the loss of it until we see each other again. Not knowing when that would be, is only going to be even more unbearable for me to endure.

As much as I'm still reveling it the magnitude of enchantment of it all. I sort of wish that you let me revel in your splendor but, instead of just let me fantasized what it could have been like. Rather than knowing. Where I'm going to have to frantically struggle each passing intolerable day Trying to ad-live this moment over and over again.

Believe it or not. I harbor no shame, or regret. Whereas for my feelings towards you have become so overwhelming mesmerizing I'll never be able to look upon you as my sister any longer. But, that of a women who has capture my heart, and very soul."

"Thank you Art. You have no idea how I have longed for you to admire me in such high esteem. I was hoping that you wouldn't come to think of me as a whore, who seduced you.

I admit that I was blaming myself for denying you before I left and have been doing so up until know. I only did so out of fear that doing so would affect you, where not being satisfied just carrying on the way you were.

Believe me I know what I just did, and the serious repercussions of my doing so. Where I'm going to make it a point to not deny you any longer either.

For the time being I'm sure you will find it difficult to be satisfied but, you are going to have to. Where I'll try a lot harder to get to see you more often.

Art, now that you know. It's important that you keep it between only us, and don't attempt to do the same thing with any of the girls at the orphanage. If just one complains they will remove you and ruin are chances of being together. Where I would most likely never be able to see you again.

That was my foremost fear. That you might lose control over yourself with some girl. Where doing so will get you into serious trouble. You can't let that happen. Now promise me that you won't let that happen."

" Of course I promise but, it's not going to be easy by any means. I'm not immature anymore. I'm fully aware of any inappropriate actions on my part will lead me. Where I have to also admit. It's not going to be at all easy either.

Where when I was young I only sought to satisfy me curiosity. Where now thanks to you has developed a need that I'm not going to be able to satisfy when you're not around. So tell me. Just how are you going to be satisfying that insatiable need as well?"

" Art I believe you when you say you're not like Paul, when now I know for certain that you will never be become like him. You are going to have to accept certain facts of life. Where for right now that's all I'm going to say on the subject. Other than the fact that I'm here for you but, only if you retain control over yourself, and continue doing what you are doing for yourself.

If you screw this up. It's going to be your fault not mine. I dint do what I did for you to have you shipped off to some reform school.

Things will get better between us. I promise you but, until I can get you home with me. You are just going to have to settle for me, and the fact that you can trust me to keep what goes on between us, between us."

She pulled into an off the wall café. Located off the side of the road parking before it." Well come on let's go in. I need to use the lady's bathroom."

"Yeah sure." I climbed out of the car following her inside. Stopping behind her just inside the door.

"Art you go find us a table I've to go to the lady's room. I'll be right back ..." She walked away saying.

Where I went, and sat down in the first empty booth I came to, and waited for the waitress to come take my order.

*   *   *

The second I spotted him. An alarming, alarm went off in my head! As a young waitress by the name of Sue. Stood looking over at a young teenage boy, sitting staring out the window of the diner. Bearing a shocking resemblance to her nephew Tom While I was filling in for a friend.

Tom being the only one of all her relatives, who I loved with all my heart, and soul. Who I was still morning over him dying in tragic automobile accident. Along with his friend just a few months earlier.

The diner was one of my resent investments. Where I wanted to get a true prospective of its potential, so I took the opportunity when it came up. To see it firsthand just how profitable it might be for what I paid for it..

The charisma I felt was frightfully staggering. As I walked from behind the counter towards the booth where the young teenage boy was sitting at. Mindless looking out the window Getting closer, and closer to his uncanny facial reflection in the window pane as it become more descriptively visible, where I could focus in on what he might be looking like. Hoping, and praying that it wasn't Tom face I was going to be seeing Where everyone of his features uncomfortably resembles his.

Where the closer I got to approaching the booth. The more nervously I started shake until I came to a stop standing before it.

literally terrified to speak up. Out of utter fear it could be Tom himself. Coming back from the grave to show me that he was still alive. That's how horrified I was to speak out to him.

"Yes what will you have?" I nervously asked him. Standing before the table speaking out to get his attention.

Faintly hoping, and praying that it wasn't Tom with my heart beating like a slug hammer against my chest. Frantically hoping that he wouldn't turn his head to face me.

When the second he turned to face me, and the second his eyes made contact with mine. Every fiber of my being went into a chaotic state.

My nerves tingled as if thousands of prickly feet were walking on my flesh. Taunting me to the brink of swatting at the goose pimples. That his eyes were inflecting back into mind.

Causing the horrifying chills that were besieging my entire body. As I struggled to compose myself from fainting right there on the spot. Waiting for him to order something.

Going thought the traumatic mind boggling anxiety of becoming so overwhelming by who I was seeing. That the second I saw his entire shocking face.

I panicky found myself struggling to regain myself form what I was dreading the most. Dropping my order pad to sue the table to brace me up from collapsing right there on the spot.

With every fiber of my being was warning me to run! To run as fast as I could, the hell away from him! As my panic shaken mind became besieged. Literally captured on the exact image of Tom's reflection, staring back at me.

As I stood literally petrified with my feet frozen to the floor! Gasping in deep breathes bracing myself up using my hands pressing down upon the top of the table? Not believing what I was seeing.

"Oh, my Gosh...!" Art raspingly sighed out from disbelief. Becoming shocked by what was going on with the waitress standing before his table. Looking as though she was having a heart attack.

Becoming panicky by not knowing what to do to help her. Stuttering out. Miss are you alright…!?" As he frantically looked around the empty cafeteria, spotting no one to tell him what to do to help her.

"Just give me a second…" I raspingly gagged shockingly speaking out answering him. Struggling to regain my composure. Knowing in my mind that it couldn't possibly be Tommy

but, yet there he was! Sitting right before my eyes staring straight at me…!

Where somehow I miraculously fond the strength to stand up straight. Still utterly dismayed staring at him. Giving my eyes time to clear out the flickering stars flashing before them. Blindly struggling to say. While struggling frantically with me mind. Virtually denying who I was seeing

"I said that I was alright… So stop your damn staring dammit…!" I defensively attacked him. Trying to recuperate from the hallucination that was succumbing from.

"I'm sorry if I upset you. I was only doing so out of concern. You looked like you were having some sort of a problem standing…"

"I was, but I think I'm alright how… My god kid… You have no idea just how traumatic it is for me to be standing here waiting on you right now…! I disbelieving snapped out without realizing what I was saying. Catching myself, noticing the expression of shock. Coming upon his face.

"No Please don't take offence… It has nothing to do with you personally… Well it does but, them again it shouldn't… It's so uncanny… Do you have a twin brother by any chance…?"

" No, I do have an older brother but, we don't look all that much alike." Where I sat thinking to myself.

'Speaking of looks.' As Art himself found myself staring up into a set of two, sparkling blue eyes. In to the divining face of a Goddess, with a hovering halo shrouding over her glowing blond hair.

" Don't you think that you are a bit young to be looking at a grown women like you are doing. I take it your mother overlooked teaching you the proper behavior when you are in the company of a grown women." I reprimanded him for the offensive way he was staring at me so intently.

"I'm terribly sorry but, if you don't mind me saying this. That you appear to be projecting an aura of utter astonishment about you.

I've seen a great many replicas of the Goddess Venus, and there is a startling resemblance I must say."

"No, you may not say!" I annoyingly snapped back at him. Feeling imposed upon, from being admired so prestigiously by a mere teenage boy.

"Just tell me what you want to eat, and keep your thoughts to yourself."

"I... I don't know... I haven't gotten a chance to look at the menu yet... Coffee I guess ... My God but, you're beautiful...!"

"What was that you said?" I offensively asked again. Not expecting to hear those words coming out of his mouth.

Still struggling to gain control over the sensations I was being bombarded with. Dropping my pencil down on the floor, before the table.

Lowering myself down onto my trembling knees, using my hands to hold onto the top of the table.

"Oh, there it is..." I replied reaching out to retrieve it. Picking it up in my trembling fingers, rising to stand up before the table.

" Now what was that again, and just stick to what you want to order. If you don't mind...!"

Still denying the fact that it was none other than Tommy himself sitting before me. I snapped back at him.

Knowing that was the way he would always talk to me. Hoping to get me to respond to his cements in a receptive manner. So that I would padrone his flirtations by becoming smitten by what he would say to me.

" You're not from around here are you?" I rebelliously asked. Blatantly staring at him ignoring mouth attempting to take precedence over my decorum." What are you doing visiting a friend?"

" No." He replied " I've been living around here for a while now I live at the adoption center."

"At the adoption center?" I skeptically asked." Where are your parents?"

"I don't know. All I know is that they're still alive, I think...? But, someday I'll go out in search of them."

"Just how old are you?"

"I'm going on fifteen."

"Now that I'm finding hard to believe. By the way my name is Sue. The adoption center you say?

"Yes, why do you ask? I'm sorry if I offended My name is Art."

"Art is it? Well Art I was just wondering if there was any way that I might be able to come, and visit you?"

"Me...? Why would you want to come visit me...?"

"I've my reasons. Wouldn't you like me to come visit you? I must admit I've sort of taking a liking to you. I really would like to get to know you better."

"You must excuse me for appearing naive but, I fail to understand why?"

"I'm finding you somewhat interesting. Besides you remind me of someone I once knew, and established a fondness for. Where like I just said, you obviously have captured my interest. To a point where we might become close friends that's all. I'm sure that we have a lot in common with each other. I would like the chance to find out just how much."

I evasively answered him, not wanting to say too much. So that him might catch on to what was really going on in my mind.

Contemplating how I might be able to become rejoined with Tommy again. Knowing how ridiculous it was for me to even think about anything so absurd. Where I wanted to give myself time to think about even showing up but, still wanting the chance to be able to.

"I'll go get your order." I walked away from the table returning with a cup of coffee, and a specially made Sunday just for him.

"Why what's this...?" Art bewilderingly asked.

"Just something special just for you. By the way who was that women you came in with?"

"That's my sister Pat. She came to visit me today, and what a visit it was too."

"Speaking of visits when are you able to have them?"

"Sundays, and Wednesdays after supper but, all visits have to be okayed by Monday through Miss Rains. The assistant head master. However, I think I must tell you that the visits are restricted to family members only. So I don't think she'll let you come visit me but, thank you anyway."

"We'll see about that. Just maybe come Wednesday, you might have yourself a visitor. That is if you would like me to come visit you?"

"Sure I would. I would like that very much but, why would you want to go through all that trouble for me? You don't even know me."

"That young man you just might very well find out come Wednesday, night. For now, you just enjoy your Sunday." I walked away from his table going to patronize another patron who just came in.

"I see that you ordered yourself a Sunday." Pat joined Art at the table saying." Getting kind of exuberant are you?"

"It's already paid for."

"Oh, is it now…? And just where did you get the money to pay for it?"

"I didn't. The waitress paid for it her…" He pointed towards Sue standing behind the counter.

"Why?"

"How do I know, maybe she likes me…?"

"Art." Pat annoyingly spoke out to him. Looking directly at Sue. Feeling threatened by her majestic divines

" Art we are so great together, let's not spoil it with the likes of her. Can't you see that she's nothing more than an common whore? Just forget her.

I'm all the women you are ever going to need. As well as the only one, who would put up with your nonsense. Besides look at her..."

She has to be old enough to be your mother. Even if she is good looking, so stop pining over her. Nothing even going to come from wanting something you will never have. Now come on let's get out of here."

"But I'm no finished with my Sunday yet."

"Yes, you are. Now come on let's go..." She annoyingly laid $3.00 dollars down on the table saying." That should be more than enough to cover the bill..."

Rising up from the table walking towards the door. Hastily pulling Art behind her. Holding onto his hand dragging him out into the parking lot.

To shove him in the car, then climbing in after him. To drive out of the parking lot. Driving him back towards the adoption center. Stopping just outside the main iron gate turning off the headlights.

"Art I don't want to leave you here but, I've no choice for right now, or least ways until I can figure out a way to get you out permanently. Now are you sure that you don't need anything before I drive you in there, do you?"

"No, sis I'm alright."

"Are you sure...?" She suggestively asked taking her hand placing it upon his thigh." I hate the thought of leaving you like this. I want so much to do for you...

This is the part I hate the most when I've to bring you back. Having to leave you in that God forsaken hell hole.

You have no idea how it hurts me inside. I love you so very much that it tears me up inside...not being there for you"

Pat took him into her arms, hugging him against her. Kissing him lavishly about his face.

"Please Pat..." He cried out to her." Please no more... It's hard enough on me as it is. Don't make it even harder on me."

"I just can't help myself. If I didn't love you so very much I wouldn't be possessed so for the want of you, to always be with me…" She released her hugging embrace.

"Art we did have ourselves a fibrous day didn't we?"

"We sure did sis. One I'll never forget as long as I live. You best take me in now."

Art sorrowfully spoke out with a long withdrawn forlorn expression on his face. Struggling with himself from not reaching out to her. Not wanting her to ever leave him.

"Alright Art." Pat frustratingly replied driving through the iron gate. Pulling to a stop in front of the main doors.

Where Art climbed out of the car. Stopping to turn around to look upon Pat's face. Before closing the car door." Sis you have yourself a safe ride home now."

"I will honey, and never forget that I love you with all my heart. I'll try to come visit you again very soon."

"You do that sis." He reluctantly replied. Shutting the car door. Turning his back to her, walking towards the front door. Not daring to look back to see her driving off. Feeling his heart being kicked about below his feet.

As he forlornly neared the doors of the main entrance of the center. Only to stop before it pulling it open while gasping a deep breath before walking inside. To head directly towards the old cow's office to report in.

How Art hated that bitch. For all the dastardly things she did to him there at this place that he was forced to call his home.

Where he swore that someday he would pay her back for all she did, and had him do that he came to despise the ground she walked on. Recalling while walking towards her office the vowed he made to himself practically every day since Pat left.

' That sadistic bitch is going to get here's someday..' As he recalled saying to himself, entering her office. Finding her sitting behind her desk as he entered.

"Well!" She snapped saying speaking out the instant he entered her office." Have fun did you?! You do you realize that you are late?! You know that you are supposed to be back here before 5 PM. Where in the hell were you?!

No...! On second thought I don't want to hear your lies!" She reprimanded him, shouted at him. As he stood before her desk.

" You're just going to have to go to bed hungry that's all...! Now go upstairs, and get to bed! You haven't heard the last of this! You can be assured of that! Now get out before I really loss my temper...!"

"Yes, I'm going ..." Art replied waking out of her office, closing the door behind him. Going upstairs to his dorm.

Picking up his towel, and pajamas from off his bed, going into the bathroom to take himself a shower before going to bed for the night.

With Art remembered back over the first few years after his arrival, and the tormented hell that has put him through. Until Pat put a stop to it.

*   *   *

The times when she locked him down in the cellar, and turned off the lights. Telling him that if he dared to move a muscle. Venous snakes would bite and eat him. Just because she caught him sliding down the banister of the stairs.

Then the nights he spent scrubbing the floors on his hands, and knees with a brush and bucket from morning to late at night. Without being allowed to eat, or even go to the bathroom without her permission. Just because he had the audacity to say "No" to her.

Then all those time that bitch used her mentally deprived mind, to alienate, and torment him. Until Pat had enough of her abusing him.

When he accidentally spilled a glass of milk on the scum-bags dress, and she demanded that he lick up every last drop from her dress.

When she became so enraged, that she literally threatened to whip me if I didn't. As he just stood there to terrified to move.

When that did it for Pat! As Pat infuriatingly shouted out. Jumping up from here seat at the table." I've had it …! I had it you bitch! Now you listen you Bitch! Just lay so much as a hand on him, and I'll kill you…!

I have had it with you! Always picking on him! Just treat him unjustly one, more time. Your fat slob! And I'll see you in hell…!"

That was a year and a half ago. Where since them then that bitch never did anything to me again. Mainly because she felt certain that Pat meant every word that she said, and Pat made damn sure that she didn't forget neither before she left.

Where Pat keeps coming back to visit me reminding her that I would be sure to tell her if she dared to abuse me.

* * * *

Art's minds thoughts became startlingly interrupted by a besieging voice calling out his name. As he was in the bathroom taking a shower. Causing him to nervously replied back to the bitch's horrid voice. "I'm in here… I'm in the bathroom I'll be right out…"

"Like hell you will!!" She irately shouted back. Bursting in through the door catching him. As he was wrapping his towel around his waist. Coming out of the shower.

"Hey…!" Art alarmingly blurted out." Seeing her standing inside the open door with her irate hands on her fat hips.

"Hey…! My Ass…!" She argumentatively snapped back." Just who in the hell do you think you are any ways…?! With telling to Wait! Wait my Ass! And another thing…!

What makes you think that you are such a privileged character around here?! Coming and going any damn time you please, and returning at all hours of the night!

I've had it with your defiance! As well as that independent attitude of yours …! You are going to have to be taught a serous lesson! That will teach you obedience, and just who is the boss around here!"

"Oh, Yeah…?!" Art challengingly blurted back at her." By who?! Surely not you. You won't dare to touch me…! If you so much as attempted too...! I'll knock your teeth down your throat, until come out of your damn fat ass!

You are not going to push me around anymore! You old decrypted old hag! Not anymore, or ever again! Shove your damn threats up your ass, or come on let's get it on! Right here and now!"

Art took up a fighting threatening stance, standing up against her once, and for all. Openly threatening to carry out his threat.

"Why you rotten, no good brat...! After all I've done for you! and this is the way you show you gratitude."

"You done...?! You done nothing for me but, terrorize and intimidate me ever since I came here!

I never did forget all those things you did to me. The way you abused, and humiliated me, and literally scared the hell out of me then! But, you don't know you fat decrypt cow! The only thing that frightens me about you is my hatred for you!

That it's all going to come out all at once, and it will overpower myself control. While I'm ringing your grotesque neck! Do us both a favor, and get the hell out of here while you still have the chance!"

"Why, I never...?!"

"That's right you'll never again! And don't you ever forget it!"

"You haven't heard the last of this...!"

"Shut the damn door on your way out, and knock next time...!" Art shouted out at her as she went storming out slamming the door behind her.

Where Art felt as if the weight of the world was suddenly uplifted from off his shoulders. He felt as light as a feather. As he slipped his wet body into his pajama's, and walked out of the bathroom going into the dorm.

Flopping down upon his bed, and slumbered off into a peaceful sleep. Reliving all what happened to him on Pat's visit.

Chapter 8

The next day Art was told to report to the head master's office at 11 o'clock. Art immediately thought that the shit was going to hit the fan, over what he said to Miss Rains.

Where he then went to report to the head master's office, expecting the worse to happen.

When he startlingly discovering that his apprehensions were unwarranted. That the cum-bag hag didn't report the incident to him.

Where instead he was informing Art that he was going to have a special visitor on Wednesday night.

His mice, from back east. Who just moved here, and was making inquiries as to his whereabouts, on his mother's behalf.

He knew instantly that it couldn't had been anyone else but, that waitress Sue. The lady he met at the restaurant.

It was Monday, he had two, days before her visit. During which he couldn't stop pondering over in this mind.

'Why she wanted to come visit him to begin with. It just didn't make any sense what so ever for her to want to visit him, or to put herself through so much, just to come see him?'

Art's curiosity was getting the better of him to a point where he was finding himself actually anxious for her to come visit him.

Wednesday, night finally came. Still without any incident from Miss Rains, where that was putting Art on alert. Anticipating her to come springing out at him all of a sudden. Where not knowing with what that was bothering him the most.

Art foregoes supper. To shower, and dress in his Sunday, visiting clothes. Wanting to look good encase she did show up.

Impatiently standing before the window beside his bed, staring out at the driveway. Getting increasingly more apprehensive... Wondering if she was really going show up?

Feeling all wound up, and hypertensive. Nervously thinking that she very likely changed her mind. Knowing that he was obviously a lot younger than her.

For her to even think about more than becoming just a friend, while uneasily not knowing what she was expecting if she did come visit him.

When a Car pulled into the driveway pulling to a stop in front of the main entrance door. Where sure enough Sue appeared, emerging from the car. Wearing a full dress, looking like a country farm girl going to a square dance.

Where upon instantly Art noticed that she wasn't alone. Another woman emerged from the car. A tall black, and very attractive women. Standing tall and very proud of herself, wearing a white dress buttoned up to her neck.

Art stood staring diligently out the window. Watching them approaching the front door. Following them with his contemplating eyes. Straining his eyes until he lost sight of them, as they disappeared out of his sight beneath his window.

'Oh, come on... Call my name dammit...!' He anxiously paced impatiently back, and forth in front of the window.' Nervously saying to himself.

"Art... Oh Art." Miss Rains called out. Standing at the foot of the staircase.

"That's it, that's me...!" Art ecstatically blurted out. Running out the door of the dorm, hurriedly jogging down the stairs.

Stopping abruptly on the last step, to compose himself. Before preceding to walk into the polar where Sue was waiting to greet him. Standing beside the black women.

Where Art just stood staring bewilderingly at them. Standing side by side, not believing how utterly gorgeous they both were.

No longer thinking apprehensively but, as a young ecstatically healthy young man. With his imagination running ramped. No longer concerning himself about any why's. Only thinking about what his imagination was contemplating going to happen.

" Hello Art I'm Sure your mice from New York." I greeted him speaking out to him. Opening her welcoming arms. Gesturing for him to come give her a big welcoming hug.

Art nervously walked up to her giving her a welcoming hug. Whispering in her ear.

" Sue I can't believe that you are actually here…?"

"I told you that I would come visit you." I whispered back. Watching the fat matron leaving the polar.

"Yes, but I didn't believe that you meant it?"

"Believe it. I'm here aren't I?" I replied back, breaking his hugging embrace. Holding him back at arm's length away from me." Art I would like you to meet my closest and dearest friend Connie."

"It's a pleasure to meet you Connie." Art warmly greeted her walking over to her extending his hand. Welcoming shaking her hand.

As she stood staring at him, giving him an in-depth look over. As if not believing what she was looking at. With such intensity, that I found myself wanting to run away from her. From becoming overwhelmed by terrifying fear.

"Listen you two" I spoke out getting their attention. "I want you two, to stay right here and get to know each other better, I'll be right back."

I spoke out to them as they stood sizing up each other trying to break the ice between the two, of them While I go ask permission to take Art outside, now the two, of you be good." I left leaving them alone

Connie waited for Sue to leave the polar. Where not more than a second lapsed before she became argumentative ,speaking out saying.

" Now you listen you young upstate!…! I don't want you to misunderstand my reason for being here. I'm only here to satisfy my own curiosity, and nothing more." Connie defensively said to him.

"Yes, I can see why Sue has done nothing but, talk about you for the past couple of days. Where from strictly out of my won curiosity. I just had to see for myself.

However you're not fooling me none. Even though I don't know what it is you are trying to pull off here but, I assure you I'm damn sure going to find out!"

She angrily spoke out. Refusing to remove her eyes from examining me herself. knowingly seeing the strong resemblance between him and Tommy.

" Do you've any idea why Sue is here? Where I do and I sure as hell don't like what she is thinking. Simply because it's not possible.

She's a twenty-five, year old highly educated women. Who is seeing something in you, that I must admit is uncanny as hell. In any way one might think including me. Where at the same time, doesn't make any damn sense at all…!

The more and harder I look at you. The only thing that I can make any sense out of any of this is. Is in fact absolutely insane. Where there has to be so logical explanation for what's going on here. Where in the way I'm seeing you? Is nothing more than a look alike, and nothing more."

"Connie is it? I'm in agreement with you. I do think that there's some sort of a mistake happening here. However, there was no saying to no to her.

I might look young but, I'm not stupid. Don't you think that I haven't already said the same thing to myself? By the way who is this someone she is apparently so obsessed about anyway?"

"Don't ask me. That's her thing not mine. At least we are in agreement about this being a huge mistake on her part."

"That's easy for you to say. Where ever since I was informed of her coming here I've been asking myself why? Where I still can't come up with the answer. Where to tell you the truth about her being here. I don't care what her expectations are.

Even though I'm not seeing the same thing she is in me, or even you for that matter. I'm looking at it selfishly by asking myself.

'Is it such a crime to have a friend. One who I might even come to trust, and confide in? I have no life outside of this Godforsaken place until now. Nor in it as well for that matter.

Where I'm no fool either. I know it's never going to last but, there's something about me that attracted me to her. That has also attracted your concern of not being possible. That I'm now very curious to find out what it could be.

You might think it is crazy. Maybe it is, from your point of view. However you are only assuming what my intentions might be but, let's be realistic.

When you said it yourself. I'm only a look alike but, now I'm a curious look alike, as well as a selfish one at that. Look around you. This is where I have spent my life since I was ten.

I look at her, and I. Where I have no idea what is going to be expected of me. When on the other hand. With me only going on fifteen, and being as human as anyone else.

Don't persecute me for being human and having human aspirations I sure as hell not. Where I know knowing even near to as incredible as this is. Is never going to happen to me again, in my lifetime.

Where you know as well as I do, that I could no more never live up to my own expectations of myself. Where let's be realistic about this whole thing. When we both know that it will only be for this very night before it's over.

Look at the two of you, and you tell me. If you were me. That you wouldn't be ecstatically ambitious about making this night last for as long as I can.

Knowing that nothing is ever going to come off from any of it, and it most likely won't last any longer than right now.

You think the worse about my intentions, and I will alive them when neither of you are around to care how I think about my intentions.

Knowing that I'm quite aware of my limitations, and only going on fifteen, Who's the first to admit I have one hell of an incredible imagination, and I'm not about to forget for one very long time. Everything I can dream out about what transpired on this miraculous night.

Where I'm just as confused as you are about who I'm supposed to be. However to every guy here who watched the two of you coming to visit me. I'll become the most envied guy here.

I'll be living their every dream for the rest of the time I'll have to spend here. Gloating about everything I can makeup. Even if neither of you never show up to visit me again."

"Oh, brother..." Sue wasn't over exaggerating about you one bit. You are something else kid..."

"You must listen to me Connie. It wasn't my intention to take advantage of this golden opportunity in any other way, other than to benefit my existence here for as long as I have to make it last.

When the two of you leave. I'm going to be left behind. Having to accept my being here, and what doesn't happen between us. I'm damn sure going to make up.

So you better believe I do want to ravel in ever illustrious moment of her attention towards me. If you feel that I'm placing an imposition on her. You have every right to tell her anything you want.

Whereas I'm sure you are quite aware of. She does have her own mind but, where you as well as her have to speak for yourselves.

I'll not interfere. Where the fact that you both are already here, speaks if yourselves. So if you can talk her into leaving. Far be it for me to keep you here any longer than you want to be here.

"Art why don't we wait until we are all together to sort this out? It's obvious that I'm treading on very traitorous ground here.

Where I myself can see what she has been referring to while concerning you. I'm not going to be voicing my opinion. When I myself am finding it hard to believe what I'm seeing, and hearing here.

Even though I know it isn't possible. Maybe in looks but, where everything else is concern no way, or at least that to wasn't possible."

"Hey, you two come on let's go outside..." I stood before the polar door speaking out." Interrupting the conversation, the two of them were having. "It's all clear to take Art outside so come on."

I lead them out the front door. Looking for a place where we all could go to sit down and talk. Spotting a picnic table, sitting between two trees, across from the parking lot. Leading them to it as they followed behind me.

" Let's sit here." I sat down on the bench saying. As Art nervously left looking back towards the front door of the center.

" Well, come on Art sit down beside me I don't bite." I called out to him as he stood nervously staring all about himself.

As if in a state of total bewilderment finding it hard to believe what was happening. Was really happening, not knowing what that what was.

Skeptically sitting down between Connie, and I on the bench. With me relaxing leaning back on my elbows, reclining back bracing myself up against the picnic table.

"Sue I think it's time that we have a talk." Art uncomfortably spoke up

"Oh, what about?"

"About us."

"What 's there to talk about I like you, and I know you like me, don't you?"

"Yes, but, there's something very wrong here? It just doesn't feel right for me to be sitting here with the two, of you like this.

I know why I wanted you to come but, why have you? Tell me what you want, or what you are expecting from me. So I can understand your being here."

"Sue listen to the boy. You must get this strengthened out between the two, of you. You owe him that much. Come on Sue he's only going on fifteen, can't you see what he's trying to tell you?

He's trying to tell you to break it off girl. Nothing can come from this association... He's gone and this boy isn't him, nor has Tommy come back you inside him."

"No, Connie I'm sorry I'm not going to break it off!" I rebelliously snapped back not willing to rescind my ground where Art was concern.

"I admit I'm finding his bewildering to say the least but, I have given this a lot of thought. Where I want the both of you to know that I'm thinking very clearly about this."

" Sue I don't think he's asking too much of you to tell him. He's talking straight to you, the boy is being honest, sincere and open with you. Just come out, and tell him why you came here, and be done with it."

"Alright Connie I'll tell him but, this isn't the time. He might not understand but, you are right its best that he knows now right from the start. That it's me that's going to ripe the benefits of my coming here.

Where you just have to look at him Connie, to know I'm right about him. He's prefect up to and in the minutest detail. Surely you can see the striking resemblance. Why didn't even mature like him. Look at him. He even carries the same feminine feathers just as he always has. Looking like he still has a lot of growing up to do, to mature into the handsome debonair young man he was going to become.

Art I need you to look at us. I mean really look at us. Not only I but. Connie here as well. We are in our prime of lives.

Who's managed to get where we are by having to deal with the implications, and improprieties of coping with being women in a man's world.

I'm not crazy by any means. I know all too well how all this must be confusing on you. Where in time I'm hoping that it will all become apparently clear.

Art I didn't want to tell you this until I felt the time was right to do, but Connie is right you should know.

Art as crazy as this might sound I have to tell you that you are the sipping image of my nephew. This name was Tommy. He was killed in an automobile accident about 6 months ago.

I love him as if he was my own son. Where his untimely death has made it unbearable for me to cope emotionally. His death has affected me extremely, as well as my career

The second I saw you. You inflamed the dwindling spark that inspired me to want to get back wanting to live and prosper once again.

Art I don't want to escape from the human race I just want to live my life as I want to live it. With you I can once again concentrate on one aspect at a time, and not having to disrupted, or imposed upon by other issues. That are always getting in the way and hindering me.

Art I want you to understand what I'm going to propose to you will not go without amble compensation.

I want you to know I'm in the position to make what I'm going to offer you. Worth your while.

Art what if I was to offer you the means to get yourself out of here. Where all it would take on your part. Is for you to come with me as my deceased nephew Tommy.

That for right now all I want, or ask from you. Is for you to just trust in me. That it \is going to be for all are interest. If you just say yes, and let me handle everything."

" Yes of cores! I would risk everything to get away from here. Yes, I would like nothing more, but, why me? I'm only fourteen, and you don't know anything about me? Is it because I look like this Tommy?"

"Art I felt certain that you would agree once you saw the opportunity I can offer you. As well as ourselves, to give us all newer, and much better lives for ourselves.

I know how strange this must sound to you. It did at first to me when I first thought of it, but it really does make sense.

Art Connie, and I are wasting the best years of our lives struggling getting nowhere in this so called man's world.

Where you alone have it in your means to rise us all above the obstacles that are blocking us from achieving all that we want and desire out of life.

You being where you are being locked up, With the two, of us trying to get over the barriers that keep us battling getting nowhere, and me tragically losing the someone who I loved with all my heart and soul.

Where all it would take is some couching on are part for you to come back alive to keep up with what your parents are going to leave you with. Once they find out you weren't killed in that car accident.

That it was someone else in that car besides you. Who was killed and not you. Where you had amnesia and came out of it and immediately called me.

Where you will have me a practicing psychologist, and even Connie here, who is even a practicing M.D. to substantiate you mental and physical condition.

You see Tommy comes from an extremely rich family. Who I knew personally. Where in fact Tommy was living with me, at the time he was supposedly killed.

Where not even I knew for certain that I could help you recuperate before taking you back home to your parents, to be able to tell them how it was you miraculously survived the accident. When you were tossed out of the car window, and were knocked unconscious. Where in the process you suffered akinesia?

Where it was thanks to Connie here, who found, and cared for you. Until you were able to regain your memory. Where you instantly contacted me, and the both of us then aided you back to health before bring you back home.

We can figure out all the necessary details to prepare you for when you are rejoined with your parents. When them all it will be is a matter of them accepting you and just waiting for the right time to collect. Where hopefully it won't take too long.

Meanwhile you will be free, and Connie and I can jump ahead of everyone else. Where the three, of us will be able to do whatever we want without having to account, or explain to anyone about anything anymore."

"Yes, Pat I am very enthusiastic with the idea." I ecstatically blurted out.

"Yes, I was so hoping that you would say yes. Where with you taking his place, and you taking up his role in life we call all get on with living normal lives again.

Meanwhile I will still my career to think about. Where you can get on living your life away from this horrid place.

Of course you'll have to stay out of trouble, and keep a low profile I'm sure you're intelligent enough to handle yourself properly

Think of it Art. With the arrangement I'm proposing to you, we all can all finally find peace of mind, and the time we want just to devote to ourselves.

It's the opportunity to secure are happiness, and tranquility. Where we can use are youth for other things. Such as applying all the time we need to other ambitions, or just living leisurely. While we will receiving the benefits of each other's company together.

Art this might sound like an opportunity derived from out of desperation. Where in fact it is. Only because you are making it all possible.

Where it's also the perfect resolution whereby you will have the perfect opportunity to reap the benefits from as well. Where you will no longer be forced to live as a nobody like you are known.

The way I see it is. It's only going to take a little time for us to become better acquainted to when we can figure out a way to get you to hell out of this place.

I'm not hard to get along with, or for that matter to live with. Where all you have to concentrate on is your conduct, and staying out of trouble.

Whoever you do realize that there will be rules. That I will be expecting you to obey by at least until you are back home with your parents.?"

"Holy Moses...Sue!" Art ecstatically jumped up and down before

Connie and I. "Can't believe that you are really serious?!

Connie are you comprehending what Sue is saying, and what are your thoughts about this...?!"

"Art I'm not going to lie to you. I really don't know but, I do know this. Sue is making a hell of a lot of sense, and you can gain so much out of it.

With her, or maybe even us taking care of you, and with us promoting ourselves. There's no telling what we could accomplish. Then where with you connecting with Tommy parents. With the three, of us together there's no limits that we can't excel to.

However, that's a great responsibility on your part. Where to tell you the truth I seriously don't know if you can handle staying out of trouble. With you being young and extremely impetuous, not to mention impulsive as well.

When I say us. I say us because we will most likely be living together, and I'm still harboring doubts about. Whether this will work out the way she's thinking it will. In either case you wouldn't be prevented from pursuing your own ambitions. Where theirs is still a lot of if's where your loyalty to us is concerned.

The three, of was could have something wonderful together. However, the fact remains that you are still a teenage boy. That is on the verge of becoming a man. Where the fact still remains that we don't know nothing about you, or you us. Does raise a lot of concerns.

I want to say that I don't feel as strongly towards this arrangement as Sue does but, I also have a lot more to consider than she does.

This is one hell of a situation we are going to be getting ourselves into here. Sue in my opinion, this is never going to work.

It might a beneficial arrangement between the two, of you. Whoever between me and you Art it will most likely not be all that comfortable but, if Tommy and me managed to get along like we use to.

There's always the possibility that things just might work out. So I'm willing to give Snus's idea a chance.

Sue you know why I say that but, I just can't get comfortable with the idea but, I'll not stand in either of your way to find your happiness.

However I feel I've to encourage you Art to think more about this, and the ratifications that will become involved in such an undertaking, and your, as well as our current position."

"Ladies please listen to me. Connie is right. I can't believe that I'm actually saying this. But, here it goes anyway. I wouldn't have the vaguest idea as to know how to relate to either of you. You don't know nothing about me. Where all I've ever felt in my life was misery, sorrow and despair. Where the older I get the more intolerable it becomes for me to handle mentally. Where as you can both see I'm not all that masculine to look at. Where I have never been all that much physically endowed.

So if either of you look to me to come be your hero. You're going to be sadly disappointed basically because I can't fight worth the damn.

Where I'm no stranger to aspirations, and impulsively irresponsible. Where I'm far from not being susceptible to persuasive persuasion. As for being able to handle rejection. You might as well forget that as well Especially when it comes from female persuasion if you know what I mean.

I'm a teenage boy what more can I say. Where any form of philandering isn't permitted especially where boys are concerned. Where if I would get caught I like the others before me will winds up in the reform school.

Where my concerns lie, is that. I've lived with my brother, and two, sisters in one room but, never with fully grown women.

Sue you really do compliment me by coming to visit me but, you did so seeking hope for a way out of your frustrations. Whatever they might be without knowing more about me.

Where in order to do that You should come live in my world, where misery loves company. Where every kid in here don't belong here. Where I'll not shear mine with anyone but, myself. Not because I don't want to. It's because I have learned to trust in no one but myself.

Where neither of you have known idea how desperately I want to escape. Where I now I look upon both of you, and I say to myself.

' Art don't be a fool. You just struck it rich! Only to then see the horrors of it, and that all I could bring upon it is more hardship, and despair ...'

You have no idea how much I want to be wanted but, those I touch with my personal desires from out of my want for it. Will be those who will be the most tormented by it . I honestly think that it's best that you both leave me now.

It's bad enough I have even a harder burden to bare. To have the two, of you on my conscious as well."

"Art." Connie spoke up to me. Raising up to stand before me." No one is placing anymore burdens on you than we are onto ourselves. We both know the consequences of are actions.

Where to be totally honest with you. It's not from out of sympathy that I chose to remain. It's from out of admiration, and your honestly alone with selfishness as well. Believe it, or not.

I'm damn good at what I do. Only because I have to be. Where the burden of having to always be better is extremely trying, as well as nerve-racking on me.

To look at me now, you couldn't see now how the stress of it all isn't showing too much on me now. Where I know personally, if I don't jump at this chance that you are making possible. I'm going to looking like I'm 60 years old in less than a couple more years.

Once when I was but a little girl my mother told me. For one to walk amongst many. One must first walk alone. We all have our own paths in life. One must accept the hardships, anguishes, and suffering of those who will cross that path. To fully understand when to take risks, if one is to revel in their labors to become successful.

To bear the burden of their own decisions from those who have already taken the path they might themselves even embark upon.

Are paths have now crossed. All that was, is no longer. We must now all accept that can, and might be. If we are to move on. Where we alone will create our own paths for ourselves.

Because we can't judge, or be judged from no other but, ourselves, and not by those who has walked are similar paths before us.

Art we Are here now, and we came with a ray of hope. There's no promises in life. All there is from here on is are accomplishments, or failures. Which appears are going to be left up to us. If we decide to venture into this arrangement.

We all have been talking about it but no one is saying, what they really want to say. Denying ourselves of the possibilities because of fear, uncertainty, or personal involvement. That we all have to admit will become inevitable the deeper, and the closer connected we all become.

As irregular as it is, and sound sounds. The concept is genius to say the least but, in saying that. I must also say. It's most likely been tried before.

Where weather it works, or not for us. I guess depends on us, who's actually going to be taking part in the undertaking. Where it hasn't been successful by those before by the three, of us

What do you say Art. Do you want to take a chance for an opportunity at happiness. Even knowing if it might only last but, for a fleeting moment?"

"Yes... My God! Yes." Art anxiously agreed, hugging himself up to them. Being sandwiched in between them.

"Well Sue it looks as though we have ourselves a young man on our hands."

"Yeah, we do Connie... Isn't it wonderful...?"

"This has to be a fantasy come true...!" Art zealously blurted out joyously saying." This is to spectacular of a dream to be really real...! What troubles me is waking up, and finding myself all alone again... I'm not am I...?"

" Art it's not a dream... " Connie assuredly ran her fingers through his hair encouragingly saying. We are real Art. We are as real as you are feeling right now. This is as real as it gets."

"But, what's going to be expected of me? I've nothing to give. I can't expect to take without giving nothing in return.

I'm a nobody. All I've left in my life is my self-esteem, and here I am being blessed by the hand of God himself? What did I do to deserve this miracle...?"

"You just let us worry about that. You just concern yourself with just being yourself. Now come on let's all sit back down. We can't be standing hugging each other all night someone is sure to notice."

Connie stepped back going back to sitting down again. Leading the way for Art and I to follow, but, this time, we all sat back down on the other side of the bench with are backs facing the main building.

"Art let's get one thing clear first, and foremost. You did bring up a very good point. You know nothing at all about us, as women that is. Where you are most diffidently a healthy teenage boy. Who's obviously hasn't been exposed to learning how to deal with certain urges. That you are going to be suddenly be exposed to. Having two, grown women prancing around while not giving much concern to you, and what you might see. Where that goes for us as well as far as you are concern.

There's obviously going to have to be a period of adjustment that we are going to have to go through. That I've no doubt is going to be somewhat strenuous, and very difficult to deal with

The reason I'm bringing this is up, is because I personally what you to be openly honest, and forthright with me about everything.

I don't want either of us assuming anything about what's going on, as far as their feeling are concern physically, emotionally, and mentally. Most important mentally. That is absolutely essential to our success.

They're going to have to be a lot of time that we're going to be sharing together. What we are contemplating is going to take a lot of time. Where that time isn't going to come without a cost to all of us. More so you Art, where you are the one who is going to have to extra careful to not being seen.

"I know Connie. However, I really don't understand what you are attempting to say to me. How as for what we were previously discussing. Let me be the first to say.

Yes, it is extremely important that we don't create any unnecessary tension between us. Where I'm also the first to admit, that I'm besieged with astonishment by the radiance you both possess, and you are assuredly right.

I have been inhibited from exercising my urges as a healthy teenager and I can see where that might be a problem.

However, I see that as more my problem than yours. Where you can be assured I'm not going to hesitate for a second to openly express each and every one of them.

I can hope that the two of you will be able to tolerate my ignorance. Since the age of ten, I've been living segregated from the girls in that place.

Where I haven't been allow to have any close contact with anyone of them. So you have every right to be concerned. Where I too see that as problem area.

However, I'm not all that naive neither. Up until I was forced to come here I slept in the same room with my two, sister and an older brother. However, I don't want to be apprehensive either over my closeness but, also wanting to be blunt as well.

I would like nothing more than to reach out and touch, as well as hold the both of you. Without feeling, or harboring apprehensions about my doing so.

However there again I also don't want either of you in doing so. Thinking that in doing so I would be doing so in an offensive mature. In the way of trying to impose any demeaning upon either of you as a person.

I do have morals, principles, and deeply embedded convictions that I will impose upon myself. As not to infringe upon either of you. That might provoke some form of hostel reaction or resentment towards me. I want this to work out for all of us. Not turning ourselves against each other.

Believe me. I know what I'm saying doesn't sound anything like a normal healthy teenage guy but, my sincerity is prompted by desperation to get the hell out of this hell hole, and never come back.

You can believe me when I say that until I reach the age of eighteen where I can manage on my own. I'll do nothing to jeopardize my position to shorten, or ruin are association together.

As for after I'm eighteen, I will promise nothing, nor will I commit myself to any agreement that I was bond to previously by either of you..

The both of you might have been exposed to a great many ordeals. The last thing I want to do is add to any of those bad experiences. By becoming to presumptuous, or overbearing, nor obnoxious.

In the years I've been here I really did better myself. I read a lot to where I also do know the difference between the sexes. Due to having to grow up with two older sister.

I know my feelings, and yes. I can even go as far as say that I've even known a few girls intimately while being here.

Now do I need I have to say more than I already have. Where I might admit I might not have been all that successful with them. It doesn't me that I haven't leant a lot from them.

Now if you don't mind with that being the case. What chance do you think I would have with two, grown women such as yourself?

No thank you. If you don't mind. I'll stick with girls my own age. With the request for a lot of couching in my favor."

"Art all we want you to do. Is to look upon us with the respect, and admiration, that you would expect others to look upon you, and as you would look upon yourself as for the way you want to be treated, and respected.

If you dare to think that you are just going to use, or take advantage of us. You better think again.

It's like Connie said before. We are just going to have to get use to each other's likes, and

dislikes. By listening, and learning from each other where eventually it will all come together."

"Sue please lighten up on him. I don't think we have to say anymore for right now. I'm the first to admit that this is extremely unorthodox position we are all placing ourselves in.

Especially with so many obstacles against us already

I'm not about to go lying to any of you. I was and still am harboring reservation about all this, and I'm sure Art is having a great many aspirations on his own about us as well.

However after hearing all that's been said, I find several elevating factors that are minimizing a lot of my concerns. One, being the fact of his obvious intelligence, and another, us being able to relate comprehensively between each other. Now that I'm finding incredibly amazing to say the least

I've no doubt that he is thinking of himself as the most luckiest person in this world right now but, under all the enthusiasm, and prestigiousness. He's harboring a great deal of doubt, not only about himself but, us as well. Where the way I see it. He's already ahead of us attempting to address the level of importance. Above that of being a fourteen-year owl teenage boy where the opposite sex is concerned.

Sue you came up with this idea, where their again I'll be damned if I know how to implement it. Without placing everyone in a precarious position of extreme doubt, or apprehension.

I really think that it's time for us to go back to are perceptive homes, and give this idea time to sink in.

If we don't leave right now. We might start getting involved in something that none of us are prepared to deal with right now. So let's just take it easy shall we, and not let presumptuous expectation ruin everything before we even get started."

"You know I'm in agreement with that idea." I spoke up agreeing with Connie." Let's all think about this for the time being. Besides its getting late, we best be getting Art here back inside."

" Art I hope you're not too disappointed over us cutting are visit so short but, I honestly believe it's the best thing for all of us. Especially now that everything is out in the open.

The last thing I want you to start thinking is that we easily compromised are position where you are concerned. Over thinking we are anxious to enter a life style of fortitude with you. I can assure you we are far above that level. Where Sue here is right, we all have to consider every obstacle we all are going to have to face."

Connie rose from the bench saying to stand beside him.

"I understand." Art forlornly rose up." You won't forget about me now will you?"

"No, Art I answered him." We are not about to forget about you but, we have to leave sometime. Besides we have things to do if we are going to pull this off. However, you have to respect are position over yours right now.

Seeing how we are the ones who are capable of moving about. Where you are going to have to compromise your position. As just going to have to believe in us."

We walked Art up to the car, then let him walk by himself up to the main building, as we sat and watched him enter the front door.

"Well he's inside Connie, we best be going as well." I started the car, driving it out the main gate.

"Sue I hope you took into consideration the repercussions of our involvement with him in the eyes of the law. We could be getting ourselves into some very serious trouble here."

"Forget the law. What does the law know about human nature, or the fact that we knew beforehand what we will be allowing ourselves to get ourselves into.

He's as much like Tommy, As I knew him, he would jump on the offer. As the one we are offering him. If I wasn't sure about him I never would have brought you here to meet him."

"Sue you can't go on thinking like that about him. I know what you are saying. You forget I knew Tommy as well. As much as I would love it to be him. We both know it can't be where we both are going to have to accept the fact that he isn't.

We both read his case history, as to why he's in there. It still is beyond me how you got hold of his last name.

What you're contemplating is far more than unorthodox. Its unnatural, and uncanny as hell Where I grant you, we have to be realistic about all this. As hard as it is for us to accept we are going to have to.

Sue we are two, grown women. Involved in professional careers. Not teenage girls Where as much as we both might want him to be Tommy he isn't.

With you being a psychologist you yourself have to know just how irrational it is to be thinking otherwise."

"Connie all I did was ask, and I received. From there on it, was simple to obtain his records. Being an interning psychologist does has its advantages. I know in my heart and mind that he's dead but, spiritually you yourself have to admit that anything is possible. Then again let's not forget about fate, and the fact that we both took to each other like ducks due to water

Then there's the two, of you and the way you hit it off. You always wanted him to be smarter than you. Now he is. He sure appeared that he was from what I was hearing him putting you in your place.

Now you had to admit that he was way ahead of you. Trying to find fault in his motivation simply by agreeing with what you said."

"Speaking of advantages. I hope you did a great deal of thinking about a fourteen-year-old boy glandular infatuation, and along with the fact about him wanting to get physical?"

"Why of course I have. I don't know about you but as for me. I'll did with it. After all its a natural think for a fourteen year old boy , now isn't?

I'm not about to give up an opportunity to bestow upon him the advantages of his lifetime where females are concern.

I want him totally independent just like Tommy was. Where as far as

I'm concern the quicker the better. I've no doubt in my mind that Art is as ignorant as a new born baby when girls are concern. The last thing I want is not being able to keep his mind on getting reestablished with his parents, and off other things and blowing everything for all of us.

At his age that's the very thing t\hat is going to make him very venerable. Whereby relieving his obsession towards sex, will establish a long lasting relationship with me.

Hell, girl it's not as if I'm not women enough to handle him. Where I never known what it was like to be a millionaire

Connie you're not regretting me taking you to see him are you?"

" No, he's an astonishing to say the very least but, I'm also harboring aspirations over certain facets of this arrangement. I know you make it all sound so reasonably simple but, two, grown women, and one, fourteen old boys just doesn't add up."

" It's crazy I know but, it's not anymore crazier than what's been taking place in our lives thus far. Whereas if you look at it rationally like I've. It's a perfect solution for us.

It hit me the second I saw him. Where even if it doesn't work out, what have we lost, compared what could be gained.

The way I see it, it's not going to hurt him in the least by catering to him, and it's not if I am going to be telling anyone about it, so who the hell is going to know?

You need to stop frustrating yourself over his infatuation for us, it's only natural. We are two, gorgeous babes, if you don't mind me saying so, and he knows it.

You did see the way he was ogling us…? We need to encourage him to continue to do so to ha\stem the time he's going to pursue his sexual attractions for us. The sooner it's satisfied the quicker it will fade.

Where we could apply his energies where they are needed to be applied. That would benefit us. After all that is going to be what it is all about now isn't it, us?

Once he's accepted back into the family the hard part is going to be over for us getting him back into his family. The harder part is going to keep him loyal, and dedicated to us so that nothing changes his mind about having a change of heart towards us."

"I understand where you are coming from but, what if it doesn't work out?"

" It's going to work out. All we need is a chance to make it work. I refuse for it not to work, where we are in a perfect position for it to work.

As far as anyone is concern I'm his mice. Besides what kids in his right mind would say anything about the best thing that ever happened to him in his lifetime.

Really Connie if you don't want to get that involved with him, then don't. I'll do it for the both of us. I'm not going to stop at anything to get my hands on my share of his family's fortune. Nor am I'm going to feel the least bit infringed upon."

"What about that sister of his, and the rest of his family?"

"We'll handle his sister. First, then worry about the others, and anything else if and when it ever comes time for us to have to deal with it.

Where the hard part of this whole think is. Keeping it from becoming known where he's been, and who he really is from being discovered in order to pull this off.

Somehow I'm going to have to get a hold of his parents records, and all the information I can get my hands on concerning everyone in his family. Are primary concern is keeping his previous, and present life a total secret. So that we can manufacture this new one. From the time of that accident, up until the time we take him to be reintroduced to his parents.

We know that his sister Christ was adopted. That she's never even tried to contact him. As for his older brother. We don't need to concern ourselves about him. He's a queer as a three-dollar bill.

It's his sister Pat who is the only one, it seems that we need to concern ourselves about, and I know where to find her, she's living on welfare."

"Sue you seem to have it so all together but, aren't you overlooking something. I'm black?"

"Are you...? He didn't seem to notice, and if he did he didn't seen all the self-conscious about it, it's obvious he hasn't noticed, like me.

You also heard the way he thinks and feels. He thinks of you as he does himself. You just have to give yourself time to get over feeling apprehensive where he is concern"

"That's what I mean? He's too unbelievable to be for real. I never met anyone like him before. I know where I think his head is at but, yet I don't, and it's the uncertainty that is driving me crazy...

Where there's another thing. It's he's to intelligent to be as gullible, and naive as he's putting himself on to be. He sounds to me like some sort genius manipulating us. To do for him, hiding his own agenda from us."

"So you are feeling it to are you? I felt it myself, the second I first introduced myself to him but, I also felt that there's something very special about him.

Connie even putting aside, that there's no doubt in my mind that he is in fact Tommy himself theirs that certain quality that he projects, that emulates him in so many ways to be Tommy."

"I know what you mean even though I didn't know him as well as you did. If I were to meet up with him by myself. I to would aware that he was Tommy himself.

Susy baring everything we have discus between us. I need to ask. "Why me?"

"Connie you are just like me. We are practically sisters; we are so much alike in so many ways.

I knew that once you saw, and talked to him. You would become to feel the same way I am about him. You are just uncertain about everything else because this is all coming on you so fast. Where I can't blame you because you never went after anything to the likes I'm using him to get at.

That you're denying the fear you are feeling over having to risk placing your life in the hands of a fourteen-year-old boy.

I knew the second I thought of it myself. Where it terrified the hell out of me. Going to prison is something I'm looking forwards to. Where I'm going to do everything in my power to avoid doing.

" Sues I don't honestly know if I am feeling the same way. For reasons that I'm thinking rational about all this, but, I'm diffidently feeling something, that's for damn sure.

You know Sue I admit I felt myself wanting him to reach out to him. I haven't felt that way in such a long time towards anyone.

His very closeness was making me feel uncomfortably desirous towards him. I truly wanted to hug the life out of him. That's how affectionate I was beginning to feel towards him."

" You're not alone there, why do you think I cut are visit short? Well, it didn't happen, so let's just drop it." I frustratingly said driving towards the city.

Chapter 9

The next several days that followed Art just mindlessly mopped about totally depressed. Isolating himself form the rest of the kids.

Harboring the expectation of wanting to run but, not being able to. Not knowing for certain if Sue and Connie were going to come back.

Where it was due to hearing that they were going to come visit me. Was the main reason behind him hindering himself from running away from the orphanage. Just a few days before he was going to put his plan into action.

Which was running away and going to live with my sister Pat. Where I would change my name, and go back to school to finish getting my high school diploma, and joining the military when I was seventeen,. Where from there he could make his own life from himself

Where when Sunday came, and went, without anyone coming to visit him. He felt certain that he was all but, forgotten.

Where forlornly he sat on his bed contemplating over in his mind, whether to follow through with his plan of action, of running away once and for all.

It was while he was sitting on his bed formulating, how he was going to go about making a life for himself speaking out. 'What the hell.' Sorrowfully said to himself.

' What do I've to loss by trying? The worst that could happen to me would being sent off to some boy's school. It sure couldn't be any worse than the hell I'm living in now.' Where he was annoyingly disturbed by hearing Miss Rains voice calling out for him saying.

" Art will you come down here? There's someone here to see you."

'Someone to see me…?!' He excitedly said to himself.' Running out of the dorm down the stairs stumbling. Rolling down half of them to the bottom.

Where everything went totally black before his eyes, and he dizzily spun around in the emptiness of total darkness.

Finding himself lying on the sofa, in the polar. Having his forehead caressed by the smoothing hands of two diving angles. As his eyes vision cleared, looking up onto the faces of Sue and Connie.

Where he instantly reached out with his eyes watering over from tears of joy grabbing them both around their necks. Pulling their beautiful faces down towards him. With his flooding eyes couldn't hold back the tears of his zealousness, whispered into their ears.

"I thought that you forgotten all about me..."

"Art." I spoke out to him forcing him to release us. Rising up my head to look down upon him, with Connie doing likewise. As she rose to stand behind him lying on the cushions of the sofa. While I remained kneeling down beside the sofa tending to his forehead.

"Art it's only been a few days." I whispered back to him. Uncomfortably looking around to see if anyone was close enough to hear what I was saying.

" We told you that we had a lot of things to do. Surely you can't be all the insecure about yourself, or us for that matter. To be so dependent on us coming back to see you?"

"But I am Sue. I can't help being so apprehensive after the other night. Where I had time to think. Thinking of all sorts of reasons why you could have had a change of mind about everything.

Sue it's not been easy for me. I had only my sister Pat caring for me. Especially where I have everything against me thinking that either of you would want to come back. When you really know nothing about me. How could I expect you to care about me?

Where I so desperately want a chance to live my life... A life that I've never had the opportunity to live. I still can't bring myself to believe that just a wonderful could be happening to me."

He forlornly spoke out attempting to explain his skepticism concerning us showing up.

" Art nothing's changed. We made are decision. You've to stop doubting yourself. and us. You are tormenting yourself unnecessary, we are here now, aren't we?"

"Now that, that is settled." Connie uneasily spoke out saying." Just what in the dam hell do you think you were doing?! Do you realize that you could have killed yourself?

You are old enough to know to pick up those big lummox feet of yours. We don't want to come visit you while you are lying in traction so, knock it off!"

" Alright let's all just calm down." I spoke up breaking up are reunion. "Connie go close the door, so that we can talk in private. As for your young man come on get up."

I helped pulling him up into a sitting position on the sofa, s Connie came back after closing the double doors of the polar.

" Now just sit still and let Connie here check you over, she's an interning doctor."

"She's a doctor…?!" Art ignorantly blurted out.

"Yes, so don't be giving me a hard time about it." She snapped back.

"I'm a doctor as well Art." I spoke up telling him." Connie is into medicine, where I'm into psychology. We wanted to tell you the other night but, you didn't give us a chance to."

"But how can that be… You are both so young…?"

" Art women need more than their looks to go along with their youth to get ahead in this man's world." Connie preceded to check him over saying." We also have intelligence that's somewhat higher than the average persons. Sue has a IQ, of 165. Whereas for myself I don't mean to brag but, it's slightly higher about 175."

"Why that's utterly amazing!" Art dumbfounding replied." The last time they tested me mine was 145. Like I said I do read a lot, where I've what is known is a photographic memory.

I've already ready all the book you see in here.

They tell me a lot but, really nothing about myself, and they only tell how things were, and how they are supposed to be, but they say nothing about how things really are.

Stories is all they really are. They teach everything but, yet nothing, and yet they actually govern the lives of us all."

"Damn Sue..." Connie nervously blurted out." You said that he was special but, not this special, and he's only going to be fifteen, where his mental attributes are already off the charts.

"I really don't want to get into a philosophical discussion with any of you over are intelligence but, when I've the time. You better believe I am, where you are concern Art. However as for right now I've more important things to discus with you

Art since Wednesday evening Connie, and I have been very busy making inquiries, and plans. Art we went to talk with your sister Pat. We told her about us coming to visit with you.

She was surprised to say the least to see us. Then we all sat down to have ourselves a lengthy conversation. After which we arrived at a mutual compromise."

"You needn't say any more Sue. I knew all along that it was too good to be true. Where I want to thank the both of you for a marvelous dream." Art rose from the sofa saying.

"Knock it off Art, and sit back down!" Connie authoritatively demanded." And just listen to what Sue has to say. Now sit dammit! And listen up boy!"

Connie aggressively stood up blocking him from heading towards the closed doors. Holding her hands on her hips so he couldn't get past her.

Art sat back down on the sofa beside Sue. Looking up at Connie standing before him.

" Alright I'm listening..."

" Your listening but, you're not hearing a word anyone is saying. Where you are already assuming the worse." I reprimanded him speaking sternly directly at him.

"What I'm trying to tell you is that Pat said that she would be willing to go along with whatever you decide.

That as long as she knows where you're, and that you are alright. Where of course, could see you from time to time. She would go along with your decision.

She however did stress. That we were all out of our minds, and that it would never last. That when it seamers down.

We are to contact her immediately so that she could come, and get you. Of course we didn't tell her what we were really all up to.

We are going to leave that part up to you. When the time comes that it's safe for you to do so. Meanwhile you are going to be stuck with us.

She's fully aware of her position where you're concerned, and wants you to at least have your chance at living the life you want. Regardless how it might turn out in the long run."

"Pat said all that? That doesn't sound like Pat at all. Why would she concede. Even knowing that's the only thing I can think about, is being free?"

"Art you're so damn apprehensive about everything, and everyone. You are afraid to let yourself trust, or believe in anybody." I reprimanded speaking out at him with an agitated tone too my voice.

" Can't you just accept the fact that you are not alone, and we all care about you? Your sister can.

I admit that things are moving kind of fast but, when it all settles down and it will. We will have to look towards to are future together. Are coming together isn't temporary by any means. If you are thinking that, you best get that right out of your head right now.

You have to be made to realize you're not the only one in this world that's been forced to grow up in their own living hell. Hell, in one way or another everyone else had to survive in their own hell. So don't think that you are an exception, you're not.

However, you are right now. You are the one being given the opportunity to make things better for yourself, to put it bluntly.

You're going to have to accept us, for as long as it lasts, or not at all, and accept the alternatives. That we determined for you right now. Without question.

Life holds no promises; you get out of it what you put into it. If you don't want to try to make a new life for yourself. I'm just wasting my breath, as well as my time trying to make it happen. Where I'll be damned! If I'm going to offer without receiving in return.

You said you don't have anyone, to have even be a friend with. Where one has to commit themselves to want to have a friendship with. Maybe that's why you don't have any? You are afraid if you did, you would only get hurt in the end.

Well that's not how real life works. You have to stick your neck out if you want to get all that you want to get out of life. Nothing's going to be handed to you on a silver platter.

Connie, and I aren't going to be the only ones trying to make this work. Always having to account to you, with you harboring doubts about what we do, acting in your behalf.

You are going to have to earn the rewards, and the pleasures that can be derived by your achievements, and learn from your failures from sticking your neck out. So you can do so more wisely the next time, and believe me. There will always be a next time.

So what if it doesn't last? You're not the only one taking a chance here, and I'm not going to be cuddling you.

Its time you stop just thinking about yourself, and stop whining about how miserable your life was, and start giving some consideration to Connie, and I, and what we're attempting to achieve for everyone behalf without question."

"Slow down Sue."

"No, Connie once, and for all. He's either going to come out of his private world of solitude, or regress deeper into it. It's time for him to emerge out into the human race like all the rest of us."

"Sue he's only going on fifteen."

"That's what I mean, and only he is going to hack it, or not. He can no longer hide in his self-pity. The world is too big of a place, and it's moving at an all too rapid of a pace.

If he wants so desperately to go out into what's waiting for him in this world. He has to come out excepting it for what it is, or be swallowed up by the hordes that are fighting to survive in it.

He's hiding in books, and blaming his life for not venturing out into it. Feeling sorry for himself holding himself back. Using his age, and the situation he's in to welter in.

Like it, or not. He's going to have to make his own way, and if he hasn't the gumption to do that. We can't be wasting our time with a loser. Not when our own lives are at stake right along with his.

I'm saying all this for his own good. This insecurity of his, is only holding him back, and driving him down.

We didn't get where we are at by stewing over the setbacks life has thrown at us, and I'm not going to tolerate constantly hearing about any of it.

If he's coming with us he's going to use that intelligence, he has to better himself. Learning out of book is one thing. It's learning how to apply it when and where it counts, is all that's matters.

"I'll do it." Art replied." I told you I would. You're not giving me the chance. That you yourselves are expressing about your own apprehensions towards me.

I haven't said anything contradicting my feelings towards any of this. I might be confused but, I'm not one for cutting off my nose to spite my face. All I said is that I didn't understand why my sister was going along with the two, of you.

As for my insecurity. Your right in everything you said, and I know if this is to work for us. It's going to take all of us to want it too. You needn't concern yourselves about me. It's the last thing I want is to be a ball, and chain to either of you. I'll hold up my end> It's just a bit hard right now comprehending the lever of my responsibility. It is going to be a bit challenging but, nothing I can't handle.

I'll carry my own weight once I get my footing as to what I'm dealing with. I need to know how to act, and how to fit in to this Tommy's life style.

The two, of you might of had some hard times but, I spent four years of my life isolated in a controlled environment having very little contact with the world around me. That I'm going to have to become very familiar with very fast. I'm not looking forwards to hanging out here very much longer that's for damn sure!"

*   *   *

While Art was defending himself against his feeling about his insecurity. That I mainly incited in order to determine. Just how strongly his aggressive natural was.

To determine just how much, I would have to donate of my time. and efforts, to prepare him for blending into the environment of the world outside the orphanage he was forced to live in.

I was also contemplating why his sister Pat didn't contest to much about why I was taking such an interest in him. Trying to get at some answers I wasn't getting from his sister.

Knowing that I couldn't tell him, that his own sister was whoring herself out, and that we agreed to pay her for her silence, and collaboration to go along with me.

Avoiding most of all of telling him. That when money entered into the picture her loyalty towards Art drastically changed.

*   *   *

"Art your sister is are concern now. Whether you realize it, or not, you're not a kid anymore. You have just surpassed your age, and grown ten, years. You now have a responsibility to us as well, as yourself. Where the older you get the more we will be expecting from you where we are not about to ease up on you.

We will assuredly help you to adjust to the changes you are going to have to make. Where I don't think you will have very much of a problem doing so with your lever of intelligence.

Look at us Art and ask yourself what do you want to be a man, or a boy? You and only you alone can excel yourself to the heights you want to soar to. However always remember that life, nor the world is going to stop to revolve around you solely. There's no getting off, nor running away, or feeling sorry for yourself. Regardless what life might throw at you.

Where in our case the three of us are going to be willing to risk it all in order to rise above the rat race where we can set ourselves aside from those who are trying to get ahead, and staying there.

I'm telling you what I am to forewarn you of what lies ahead. Not to intimidate you, but to prepare you for it not to be easy by any means.

"Sue I don't need you, or anyone telling me about my life. There's nothing I don't personally know about it already.

While everyone was thinking that I was (wailing) in self-pity. I was advancing my comprehension to overcome my insecurities.

As for my expectations they are limitless, as well as my perseverance and determination to do anything, and everything necessary I have too, to rise above any anyone who might stand in my way to achieve what I want for myself.

As for my ideals, and conviction they far exceed my appalling status. That I've to be constrain in that might bind, or becomes an obstacle that stands in my way . Welling to apply any and all means necessary to remove it when I have to.

You haven't realized it what sort of person I can really be when I have to be. My localities, and concerns are only to those who serve my purpose, and who receives my devotion, dedication to risk everything for.

Your analyst of my retardation is hypothetical at best. Your contention is to tell me, that which you yourselves don't know the outcome to, and you yourself are venting your concerns over. Whether I'll be able to handle myself under stressful situation, without losing control of me constrains, and resort to violence.

I like mentally challenging mind games when they present a challenge, and the way I see it.

You're as frail as I am.

I never once denounced you, it's you that denouncing me. Thinking that I'm incapable of seeing beyond my immaturity, and my infatuations towards the two, of you

Pat should have told you about me. I don't want to be above either of you but, neither of you are leaving me much of a choice but, to become concerned about the both of you.

I will if need be. Do all within my means to survive. Pat knowingly knows of my fortitude as well as my being intellectual advanced. However, when it comes to dealing emotionally. I'm unstable.

My life isn't based or concentrated about wanting things...Material possessions never last, and it ties one down.

I don't want your sympathy nor your patronization. I know what I am and where I've been along with knowing what I might have to do to get what I want from out of my life.

I don't need to be taken down memory lane. Living in the past is a hindrance where I no longer want to have existed in but, to advance above where I only have a need for several things.

That is your trust, and acceptance of me as for who and what I am. For as long as are relationship might last.

I don't want to be controlled, or protected. Where the last thing I want is to be is a crouch on anyone, is that asking so much?

The two, of you are only seeing the teenager. You've yet to see the person lurking within waiting inside me. I don't need a chance. What I need is the opportunity to excel using my potential to my fullest advantage.

Along with both of you to just stop underestimating me, and let me be dependent on myself. I just might shock the hell out of the both of you.

" Alright let's just drop the subject." I spoke out to him." We all understand that we are not impervious to are imperfection, and we all have are fragilities. Along with being all susceptible to are past. Not to mention being all that prepared for the uncertainties that lies ahead of us. Along with the fact that it's going to take time to bring us all together. However, nothing can start without having a beginning at some point.

Where your right Art, we all have to start trusting in each other. So that we can move forwards, where we can only do that by opening ourselves up to each other. Instead of being evasive, and trying to feel each other out if there is anything that we might have in common besides the obvious with each other.

It's obvious that there is a lot we aren't doing properly, and by doing so, we are overlooking a lot about each other. Because we're harboring hidden agendas ourselves, and over thinking the others intentions.

However, we do all have one thing in common. We are all in this together. Where I might remind both of you. No one is going to make it alone. If we all don't make it, no one does.

Now that we have that out of the way once, and for all. I hope we can now concentrate on getting you out of here. Where it's going to be tonight. Where afterwards we can work out the final details later. Especially the legal details.

Now, I did some investigating. Regarding going legal. Where that's going to take too damn long, and cost a fortune. Where I for one know that isn't going to work for us under the circumstances that we are going to be working under.

Where the overall better approach is getting you out of here without anyone being the wiser as to who's who. The less known about you Art the better it will be for all of us. The last thing we need is notoriety about you running away from here.

Where it's best to have you as just one of the kids who run away from here. Where it dies in a day, or so.

We don't want anyone making a big deal about you taking off. The less we have associating with you being here the better it is going to be for all of us.

Don't forget we have a lot of time to account for while you have been gone, and it's going to take time to bring you up to date on what's been going on in your life. When we walk you back home to your parents.

Where once we have you out of here we will be in a much better position to deal with the situations as they come up. One, at a time, where we can maintain control of everything while getting you back to living your new life, and Are's as well."

"Sue you can't be serious?! Tonight...?! But how...? They lock everything up at night, and there's bars on the windows and let's not forget that damn iron gate? Art uncomfortably blurted out saying. Nervously looking all around the den we were in. Mentally questioning her decision.

"We know all that Art. That's why you are going to go out that window over there." I pointed towards the double pained window to the left of the fireplace.

" Do you think that you can crawl through that bottom pane of the window?"

"Sure, easy. "

" Yes, we know, and there's bushes right below it, where no one would ever see you once outside. However, there's all that distance between that window, and the brick wall. Then there's that iron gate that they keep locked, so you are going to go for the brick wall, and that tree. Where you are going to climb as high as you can go, that would be almost to the top of it. Where you are going to have to leap up to the top, and jump down. Too where we will be waiting down below. Then form there on you let us worry about the rest.

Now listen up. All you have to do is to wait for everyone to go to sleep. Them come down here, and climb out that window. Connie go loosen the pane of glass."

"Wait a minute Connie." Art stopped her from going to the window.

" What about miss Rains she might see me? She practically lives in that damn office of hers, and that's right across the hall. Facing the double door, we have closed?"

"So she sees you? Just lock the doors, that should give you enough time to crawl through. Then run like hell towards the that damn tree, where Connie and I will be waiting on the other side to pick you up, and your gone.

We have this place where we can hide you out for as long as need be. Once in the city no one will ever be able to find you.

Where we will be able to go on with our lives as moral, until we can relocated, and move elsewhere. Where in time you will be forgotten. During which we will use to prepare you to meet your parents.

However just in case something might happen and you can't make it to the tree, Head for the gate. Where Connie and I will take care to have it unlocked for you. But, avoid heading towards it, if at all possible."

"Sue what if I don't make it?"

"You have too Art. We wouldn't be able to come in to help you. We can't afford to be seen.

As it is we're going to be questioned about your disappearance. You are going to be a typical runaway. In a city filled with thousands of other runaways.

The police probably won't even bother with wasting their time looking for you. They will just wait until you get yourself caught. Where that's not going to happen because you will be with us.

However, we are going to have to come back here, and act as if we don't know anything about you running away. In order to be eliminated from being involved.

That's why we can't afford to be seen helping you. You have to make it. Where I know you will if you do what I'm telling you.

Once you are outside and over the wall. Just encase if you don't spot us. Don't panic, just keep running. We will catch up to you.

We will be driving the same car we came here in. The red convertible. You won't be able to miss it.

Art it's going to be tonight at 9 o'clock, You go, or stay is up to you. Just so there's no mistakes we best make it ten o'clock. Just to be on the safe side. Now go on Connie, go do your things on that window."

"I'll be there Sue you can count on that." Art watched Connie walking over towards the window kneeling before it on her knees pulling back the curtain.

"I know you will Art. Now listen to me, this is very important. Once we have you hidden, we won't be able to stay with you.

I don't want any police involvement therefore you are going to have to stay inside. I don't want you to do nothing to draw attention to you being where we put you."

"Got it Sue." Connie rose up onto her feet saying. Walking back towards the sofa. "Art all you've to do is tap on the window pane, and it will just pop out."

"Alright so it's a go. At 9:30PM I want you to be standing at your window, where I can see you when I drive by the front gate.

I'll flash my headlights three, times to let you know we are out there. You will have to judge your own time, that it takes for you to make it downstairs.

However give yourself a few minute, just in case we might get caught up in, or get stuck in traffic. To get in position where we will be waiting for you by the tree.

Art you do realize that once you're outside there will be no turning back. That there will be no second tries for you to pull this off. It's going to be all up to you, and you alone to make it over that wall. I want you to understand that?

There's one more thing. Don't bother taking anything with you. We will have everything already taken care of. Just bring yourself.

Art this shouldn't be hard. Just take it slow, and easy. The hard part is going to convince the police that we weren't involved.

We lied about our names to get in here to see you. We can't afford the police to investigate us. We have been professions to think about. All are comings, and goings from here, must stop right here. From having any connection with you.

That's why we are going to have to come back one more time. Hopefully without having to be questioned by the police. If everything goes as planned you are going to be just another runaway like I said."

"Sue what could happen to you two if you get caught?"

"Don't ask but, if we are. Just remember we will be thinking of you."

"Sue wouldn't it be best if we would wait until your next visit. You could say that I just ran off on you when we were outside."

"We thought about that. This way is uncomplicated. That other way there would be far too many complications, and the police would suspect us right off. It has to appear that you are doing this on your own."

"Sue I don't want anything to happen to either of you. I want you to promise me, that both of you will stay away until I'm out, and on the other side of the brick wall.

No matter what happens don't come in after me for any reason. Just get the hell away from me, if things go wrong. I'll not place either of you in any sort of danger because of me."

"Alright Art we hear you." I compromised replying back." Then it's a go win, lose, or draw it's coming down tonight.

Connie its getting late we have a few more things to do." I rose from the sofa saying walking towards the polar doors opening it." Come on Connie let's move it."

"Yeah, sure I'm coming." Connie reluctantly replied, walking towards her as she stood before the now open polar door. Then following her out into the hall.

" We'll have a nice visit did you?" Miss Rains came walking out of her office asking. Stopping them in the hallway.

"Yes, thank you." I answered her." And thanks again for the late visit. I really do appreciate it. I promise not to be so late next time.

It's a pity though that my visiting him is going to end shortly. I'm going to have to leave soon, so at best I'll only be able to visit him a couple more times."

I apologetically apologized about not being able to continue visiting Art on a regular basis. While walking towards the front door beside her. Leading Connie towards and out the door. Then towards the car parked out in front.

'Well Art this is it... This is what you wanted, and now you got it.' He sat upon the sofa saying to himself.

Pondering over in his mind his strategy as how he was going to get from the dorm down into the polar. Looking at the clock on the mantel over the fireplace reading 7:30 in the PM.

'Hey...! I know. I just won't leave the polar I'll hide... No, that's no good. That bitch will only come looking for me. If I'm not in bed during bed check.

I've to make her think that I'm upstairs sleeping... Damn it! Why can't it be ten, 0 o'clock...?! Come on clock move it! Dammit!'

He frustratingly watching the hands on the clock just sitting still entrapping him in time as if it was standing still.

Hey...! I got it...! Damn... It's so simple... I'll just make myself visible but, yet invisible... Now why haven't I ever thought about it before now.'

He rose his reassuring head up from out of his hands. To see Miss Rains standing inside the open doorway of the polar staring directly at him.

"My goodness that must have been so visit...? Care to tell me about it." She spoke out saying walking towards the leather easy chair sitting herself down in it. Across from him sitting on the sofa.

"No, I rather keep it to myself if you don't mind."

"Have it your way but, come tomorrow you must thank the head master for your special visit. Where if something might happen that you won't be able to. I'll do it for you." She evasively commented.

" What is that supposed to mean?" Art skeptically asked. Sensing a tone of sarcasm behind her remark.

"Oh, I don't know... Tomorrow is a new day, and who knows what are tomorrow's will bring? You might be in-deposed, or not even here at all..."

"You are trying to tell me something. Stop being so evasive about what's on your mind, and just come out with it!" Art uncomfortably replied.

"Well now that you brought it up. I was rather carious about a few things. Like when I was making my rounds.

I thought that I would stop in to see how your visit was progressing. When I found the door closed.

Now I wonder, why that was? If no one had nothing to hide but, in any case. Try not to let it happen again. Just leave it open from now on when you are having a visitor.

Art I couldn't help noticing that you've become distantly lately. Is there something troubling you?

I'm sorry if it appears that I'm meddling but, you seem to be always so preoccupied with yourself and, so withdrawn.

Not to mention oblivious to what's going on around you half the time. Where the other half, you don't even seem to see, or hear the person that's talking to you.

It's as if you have something locked up deep inside you, and you can't find the key to let it out.

Your inattentiveness is beginning to arouse my concern.

It's not moral, or healthy for you to continue on like this so I've been thinking. Maybe all you need is someone to talk to? I do what to help you."

"You help me?! Don't make me laugh... Why I wouldn't trust you for the time of day. Let alone what's going on inside my mind. I'm not that desperate yet!"

"I'm only trying to be helpful. You don't have to be smart-alecky. I know what you think of me but, I'm not as terrible as you are making me out to be.

Whether you realize it, or not I've a great deal of respect for you. You are an extremely bright young boy, who devotes a lot of time, and effort to disguise it. I'm only looking out for you."

"Sure you are." He argumentatively replied. Stopping himself before it took possession of his hatred for her.

Knowing that it would be the last time he would have to look upon her grotesque face. "I'm sorry I don't mean to be advantageous, I just have a lot on my mind right now."

"Yes, I'm sure you do. It also appears that its more than you can handle. Art you can't deal with it alone. You are going to have to unburden yourself onto someone.

Someone that can help you unburden yourself, with those dilemmas that are going to add even more of a burden on you.

Like I said, I don't mean to meddle in your life but, here you are going on fifteen, and I haven't seen you with any of the young girls around here. I'm sure that you must have taken a liking to at least a couple of them?"

"Sure I've but, my feeling our my own."

"That they are but, would you mind telling me why you haven't even attempted to become even friendly with them?

It's not moral for you not to want to become close with at least one of them. Surely you must want them to flatter you. With their affections, or maybe with a simple kiss?

Art if you haven't already selected your roll in life. Such as your brother has. How is it that you have lost your desire for the affections that could anointed the growing boy that you're?

You're at the prime of your youth. Don't you desire the affections of a girl...? You have no idea of what you are missing out on. Where for the life of me I don't know why?"

"What are you up to?" Art rebelliously reprimanded her." That's what I want to know! You sitting there talking to me.

Like this doesn't come without you having ulterior motives in mind. Besides just what business is if of yours what I do with my life, or how I choice to live it?

What do you take me for some stupid gullible fool?! Knowing the way things are between us. You would like nothing better than to catch me with just one of the girls around here.

So you can pack me off to some reform school for being uncontrollable. Like you did all those others you caught kissing you precious girls here."

I didn't do that; the head master did that. I warned them but, would they stop? No, they did it to themselves. I had nothing to do with it. I'm not the only one on staff here but, I'm held responsible. You have me all wrong.

Art I'm not trying to entrap you. All I'm attempting to do is understand you. It's obvious that something is troubling you? You do have all the systems of a boy in need of affection."

"Just where is this conversation leading us... Why don't you just come right out, and tell me what you have been trying to say? I'm tired, and it's getting late. I do want to get some sleep sometime tonight."

"Oh, are you going to sleep tonight...? I thought..." She stopped abruptly catching herself from saying something. That she didn't want Art to hear.

"You thought what?!" Art defiantly replied, as his mind panicked. Feeling an icy chill running up his spine.' Oh, my God...! Does she know...?!'

"Nothing Art. It's not that important that it can't wait. All I'm trying to say is that the way you are going about it. Isn't going to work, and that your burdens. Can't be released by the way you are going about it."

"What are you talking about?" He defensively retaliated. Being caught up in an abundance of gibberish. Jeopardizing his plight to escape.

"Relax, Art I can't see what you're getting so defensive about. All I'm saying is that you are not finding any satisfaction. Where I'm going to see to it that you do the right thing. Especially where I'm in the position where I can surely help you were all you've to do is to entrust yourself into my hands."

She said rising up from the chair she was sitting in, walking towards the open polar doors.

Stopping to turn too look directly back at him.

" Trust in me Art I know all too well that your way isn't going to work. By the way it was

rumored that someone was going to attempt to run away tonight.

I called the police. I've no idea who it is but, if someone is wanting to aid anyone plight to run away. They too will get caught, and arrested for aiding and abiding. If I were you and if you know anything about it. I wouldn't be getting yourself involved. Now that will most diffidently get you a trip to the reform school.

You know what gets me. Is the night they picked. I mean there's only a few of the staff here. While all the others have gone to the baseball game. Now you wait here I'll be right back." She walked out of the polar saying.

'What's that bitch up to…?!' Art nervously asked himself.' There's no way she could possibly know is there…?! Damn her…!

If she thinks that she's going to intimidate me! She has another guess coming.' Art disturbingly looked towards the open polar doors. Frantically attempting to contemplate what she was up to

"Hello again Art." She said appearing moments later standing before it." I didn't make you wait too long now did I?"

"Just what are you trying to pull?" Art demandingly replied. Rising up preparing himself for the unexpected.

"Now you just sit yourself right back down and be patient. Once you see that I'm only trying to help you learn to trust me. You will understand, now kindly sit back down."

Art sat back down again. Not during to take his eyes off her. As she stood just outside the polar doorway.

" Art all I want you to do, is to meet a new arrival. She's been here for only a short time, she's an oriental girl he name is Swag.

I just know that the two, of you are going to be quite taken with each other. And she's so very lonely. Where she herself is also having such a hard time adjusting just like yourself but, if you rather not take advantage of the golden opportunity I'm offering you.

You will leave me no other choice but, to go to the Head Master, and inform him about what you're planning to do this very night."

"What are you talking about?!" Art panicky shouted back at her." I've no plans on doing anything tonight but, go to bed."

"Oh, yes you do. You're going to attempt to take off from here tonight. With you Mice, and that friend of hers."

"You're crazy!" Art denied. Shouted back at her. Struggling to control his aspirations over her knowing." Where did you ever get a crazy idea like that?"

"Right from this very door. I overheard the three, of you planning the whole thing. Not all but, enough to inform the police about an appending escape.

They are going to be watching this place tonight. Looking for anything strange going on. They will nail you. The second you hit the street, and those two as well.

The only reason they are not here now. Is because I told them that I didn't know who it was going to attempt to run away.

You might as well set your mind to it. You are not going anywhere. If you don't believe me just try to, and see how far you will get. Go ahead and throw your life away. Throw away all that you can have here.

Art you could have it made here. You could have everything that a boy could ever dream of, if you will just believe, and trust yourself in me.

As for your mice, and her friend. I'm going to make sure that you'll never see them again. From here on out. It's going to be you, Swag and me. Do I make myself clear?

If they are out there, and you attempt anything stupid. They will go to jail. In any case you will never going to see either one, of them ever again."

"Just what are you expecting to get out of all this?" Art argumentatively asked. Realizing the parlous position, he as well as Connie and Sue have been placed in. Hoping to open up a form of negotiation.

"Nothing but, yet everything. You are going to be my key out of this purgatory...! and all you have to do. Is what coming naturally, and we will all rip the benefits of your attentiveness.

I know that you hate, loath and despise me. At least now you do but, in time you will come to appreciate what I'm doing for you now.

What more could you ever want for? You will be taken care of, and at the same time. By being

Embellished within the comforting arms of a woman lavishing you with her body, and attentively affections.

Just imagine of it Art. You basking in the realm of a women femininity, while ingratiating yourself. Feeling the inner warmth of her compassion."

"Your sick! You have a warped deranged mind...! You are a mental degenerate with no conception of any morals! Who's infringing your conviction upon others. While you are lost up in your delusions that brought you to tolerate your own insanity.

You are using that girl, and me. To rise above your own inequalities that were conceived from your own miserable life."

"That might be Art but, I've you where I want you. Look who's calling me sick when you as well as your whole family are nothing more than perverted!

I hope for your sake that you don't force me to elaborate on the improprieties of my demented mind I've had far more time to devote to it than you have.

I know what my madness will bring. Mad, sick you say. Yes, I'm all those and more but, I have you by your ass! And you sister Pat as well. I have picture of the two, of you together being a lot more than just brother and sister.

Now I'm going to fetch her for you. I warn you not to try anything foolish. I don't want to lose her. Where you can't afford to either the way I see it. Where you also have two, others to think about. Where I only have myself.

I must admit I've longed planned for this moment but, I never expected it to turn out like this.

As long as you keep doing your manly thing under my control of course.

I could care less how you feel about me but, remember this. You can be replaced, you're not the only boy in this institution but, I've you until you are eighteen.

Try something stupid, and I'll have your ass in a reformatory most like turning yourself into a bitch lust like your brother. Do I make myself clear?

As for your two, bitches. Do them the favor I'm offering to do for you. Let them waste their time waiting, so that they can go on their way, and accept the fact that you will never see them again. I'm going to make sure of that. If they ever show their faces around here ever again."

"I still don't understand why?"

"Intelligence doesn't come cheap but, put together two, intellectual mind, and you figure out what could come out of it.

Where meanwhile until the obvious happens I'll be able to profit from the interaction taking place, and selling it to the highest bidder. Besides having the evidence that I'll need. If either of. you two, decide to betray me.

Don't blame me for the idea. Blame your sister Pat. She's the one who gave me the idea from having to watch the two, of you. Thinking that you were getting away with something sneaking behind the laundry.

The two, of you are going to be my retirement. With the monies I'll make from the two, of you following your primal instincts. For the next three, years. Is going to allow me to retire in luxury. Where I'm still going to be young enough to enjoy lavishing myself in all the benefits that money can provide me.

I'm sick, and tired of having to put up with retarded brats. I've waited for this opportunity to present itself. Where now that it has I'm going to take it.

As long as I get what I want out of it. I could care less what you do with your damn life but, until I do. You're not going anywhere.

At first after reading your diagnoses reports. I attempted to get you to get caught with your sister but, that failed because I thought better of it.

When I did that really upset me. When I thought how I could have made been making a fortune. Breeding you with the other girls here but, I know your sister would never let me get away with that, so I had no choice but, to wait.

When until a fellow weeks ago I heard about this very special girl who would be more than happy to collaborate with me. Where you came popping into my mind as you being perfect to suffice for my idea, and here we are. Where I got you by your very balls that I'm going to be using the hell out of. I'll be damned if I'm going to wait any longer.

Whereas after overhearing what I did. It makes you the prefect partner for me to affords my early retirement. After which I could care less what happens to you. Noting personal you understand. Where I know you have nothing to lose by this arrangement, and everything to again. If she wouldn't have shown up when she did I wouldn't mind in the least, you running off. Hell I was hoping that you would have done it long before this.

Now I want you to relax, and appreciate what I'm doing for you. I'll see to it that you're not disturbed. Just don't disappoint me now.

This mare is high breeding material, and she's been all primed, and prepared for you. That's how prefect she is for you. You know I was even seriously considering taking you on as a partner. Until you blow it. With that mice of yours." She obnoxiously commented.

"Now wait here I won't be long." She said walking away from the doorway.

Chapter 10

Art sat knowing that his plight was hopeless. Panicky looking at the clock on the mantle reading 9 PM. Knowing that he had to get out to warn Sue and Connie but, his mind was a total blank.

Deeper and deeper he frantically intensified his minds ability to think. Probing through its emptiness. Until his head was pounding, and his eyes felt like they were going to pop from the pressure! That he was placing upon his blank mind. Until his mind was in a constant state of turmoil that he didn't even know his own name.

When from out of shear desperation. His mind snapped upon an impulsive act of utter desperation idea.

Sue Wong 'Thinking to himself that it was a slim chance but, the only one he seem to have.

Thinking that just maybe she would help me? She has too...! I've to get her alone so that I could talk to her, and make her understand. Just how much I need her help.

I've to try...! If she doesn't. I'll do whatever I've to do to get out of here. To at least warn them that it's a trap!'

"Art." Miss Rains stood outside the polar doors. Holding her hands on Sue Wong shoulders, while standing behind her. Presenting her before Art. Having him turn his eyes attention towards her.

" Art this is Sue Wong."

Looking at Sue Wong wasn't hard at all. She was a true wonder to look upon. Where she was nothing less than stunning to my eyes.

Appearing so serene with a reddish blush upon her cheeks. Looking at me with a shy expression upon her face, as she bowled her head to me.

Making me feel above her. Making it very difficult for me not to accept her from the way she was making herself appear. Causing me to ask myself.

'Why would she humble herself so quickly before him? Even if it meant respect in her culture. He failed to find any respect in her as a person, by not standing proud with her head held high as if saying.'

"Here I am, I'm Sue Wong the person, and damn will proud of it. Allowing myself to be displayed for your approval." Instantly telling him that there was something seriously wrong with her."

"Art isn't she absolutely gorgeous? Well come on you two, this is no time to become shy someone say something."

Art looked straight into her eyes, as she rose her face up. Startlingly discovering that her appearance took on a drastic change! The instant his eyes made contact with hers.

When that of an aura of ungodliness projected from them. As her leering eyes caused a cold chill to run straight up his spine. Sending billions of goose pimples scurrying throughout his entire body. As her facial expression, took on an entirely new, and grotesque appearance. One of a viscous contemplating person.

'Holy shit...!' Art gasped out to himself. Feeling as if he was at deaths door. Thinking that he was looking into the devilish eyes of one of Satan's she devils.

When her reddish blushful shyness literally dissipated and her exalting eyes widened. Her eyes felt as if they were cutting right through him. Scaring the holy hell right out of him.

Too such an extent, that he actually began to tremble from their coldness. Feeling them piercing right into his very soul.

Her transition from the meek humbling girl. Into a satanical thing! Was not to be believed. It was nothing less than horrifically frightening.

"Come on girl." Miss Rains lead her into the polar saying. Sitting her down beside Art sitting back down on the sofa.

"You just sit right down here, and get better acquainted." She said going to sit down in the easy chair beside the sofa.

"He must be afraid of me Miss Rains." She spoke up saying.

"He's just a bit shy. Come on Art say something nice to the young lady."

"What's there to say?" He sarcastically replied. As he sat freezing right down to his bones from the touch of her knee against his. Not daring to look into her cold devilish eyes.

"Boys always find something to say to me." She broke the ice between them saying.

"Yeah, I just bet they do but, like what?"

"Like how old are you? Stuff like that."

"Alright just how old are you?"

"I'm sixteen."

"Well I'm only fourteen, that makes you older than me."

" Young boys like it when they have an older girlfriend."

" But you're not my girlfriend. I don't even know anything about you, other than your name."

"But wouldn't you like me to be your girlfriend? Being older means that I've that much more to offer you in so many ways."

"Like what?" Art turned his eyes attention onto hers. Meeting them as if challengingly combating her devilishness, putting her on the defensive.

"Well for one thing wisdom."

"Wisdom is recognized by the company it keeps. It takes years to come by, as well as to learn how to use it intelligently. To which you have far too few of being that. ? Seeing how you are only sixteen."

"I'm impressed Art. Your criticism must be respected, as well as admired. You are right I'm far too young. I must thank you for showing me the errors of my ways.

Please be so kind as to show me what-else you have hidden under that hard shell. That you are trying so desperately hide under.

Just what is it that you are afraid of. That you fine sanctuary in impertinence, and criticism. That's harden about you like a protective shell?"

"The way I see it. You're not in any position to be cynical. If I have to guess your life has been filled with turmoil, and frustration, along with overbearing men. Who don't have enough brains to know when they're not wanted."

"What did I ever do to you? I didn't agree to meet you. Just so you could insult me! If I irritate you that much maybe, I better leave?"

" Sue Wong you're not going anywhere." Miss Rains authoritatively spoke out." Art apologized to her right now for your rudeness! If you don't, you will leave me very little choice, but, to have to deal with your insolence more harshly." She threateningly implied, what she was speaking about earlier. Placing him back under her control again. As he glanced over at the clock sitting on the mantle.

"I'm sorry Sue Wong. I really didn't mean to insult you. It's just that I'm very tired, and upset right now about something."

"That's alright Art. I know how it feels to lose something that means something special to you. But, you'll find as I have that time heals all wounds."

"Do you know why she brought the two of us together like this, and what she's expecting us to do?"

"Sure I do. In fact, I was inspired by the idea. I know very well what she's expecting. I was quite taken with you from the very first moment I seen you. To the point where I even willingly accepted the opportunity to meet you.

I think that it's time that I tell you my reasons for being allowed to be placed in this position we are now finding ourselves in. Where even why Miss Rains here has taken it upon herself to bring me here.

You see my mother doesn't want me near her, and because of her. I was placed here from being assigned from out of a sanitarium.

That I was at for murdering my father. While suffering a nervous breakdown over his death. Where you must believe me when I say. I didn't kill my father, my mother did.

She framed me by making it appear as if I did it. Because she was jealous, and hated me since I was five, years old.

Both my parents were aristocrats but, my mother was an American. Where she just couldn't handle being undermined, or couldn't stand being diplomatically ignored, or placated.

Where my father wasn't. Where it got to the point where she just couldn't accept it anymore. So she killed him. Knowing that she knew that I knew that she did it. Where killing him was her way to get rid of me. All at the same time, or should I say shortly later.

Though my father was highly intelligent, he also suffered from admiral admiralties. One of which, was that he was a pedophile since the age of fifteen.

I was incestuous with him from the age of seven, up until the age of twelve. When my mother killed him.

She murdered him with a meat cleaver, while he was sleeping. By the time she finished chopping him up into chunks of meat, them while attempting to grind him up in the meat grinder. When I came into the kitchen to get a glass of water, and caught her.

It wasn't until about three, years later. That my mind unlocked itself, and I found myself laying in a bright white room. Where I previously spent another year of my life. Being mentally treated for whatever they said what was wrong with me.

Believing that it was me who murdered him. When my mother already confessed to murdering him, just before she died during being confined due to the nervous breakdown I suffered.

Well to make a long story short. During the past year that I've spent in the isolated building. Blocked off from the rest of this orphanage center undergoing evaluation

Miss Rains, and I became extremely close friends. In fact, she's been like a mother to me. We became that close.

That look you obviously seen on my face was intentional. It comes in very handy to keep the boys, and others the fuck away from me.

However, the fact remains that I have been having sex since I was five, and I came to really loved the intimacy, and the sensation I derived from taking part in different aspects of it.

I found it not only stimulating but, even more accelerating as well. My father taught me a great many various as well as vanities that I became addicted to as well.

I didn't mind so much when I was being sedated for my nervous back down but, I'm been far over that for some time now.

Even though I wasn't participating in it with anyone but, my father. He's no longer alive, and I'm finding it extremely nerve-racking having to be denied.

Where I just don't like having to participate in it just anybody. Where I most assuredly do miss indulging myself with the raptures of succumbing to it.

Then when I found out about you, from your sister Pat. That's right Pat. You were all she seemed to want to talk about, and when she started talking there was no shouting her up.

I don't know how it was she came to be placed in the same room as I.

However over those times that she was admitted and placed in my room. She told me about her being admitted for behavior evaluation towards the head matron. Who turned out to be none other than Miss Rains here.

Where after hearing all about you from her as well. I didn't hesitate to propositioned my best friend here/ In a way that would in her best interests for her to get us together.

I'm sorry but, I was the one who told her where you and your sister would go hide. Along with what she herself told me what the two, of you would do together.

I couldn't help myself I was so damn jealous of her. Now if you would have invited me, things might have been different, but you didn't.

Where in exchange for what I told Miss Rains here. We both hit on a golden opportunity to establish a common link. Where we both jumped at the chance, seeing how we both had the same thing in common with each other."

"You see Art I told you that the two of you had a great deal in common." Miss Rains rose from the easy chair saying.

" Now I think its best that I leave the two, of you alone but, don't become too involved before I get back now. The two, of you have to behave yourselves for a little while longer."

She walked out of the polar speaking out loud. "for Art's ears only." Don't be stupid. "

'Thank God, she's gone...' Art nervously said to himself.' Now's my chance to talk to Sue Wong.' He looked towards the clock on the mantle reading 9:35.' Oh, Shit...!' He panicky said to himself.' I've to get to that window...!

No... Maybe if I don' show myself at the window they might go away...?! Dammit...! That's no good...!'

He nervously said to himself. Knowing that they wouldn't, and he couldn't let them sit out there waiting for him, with the cops patrolling the area. Where they were bond to be stopped, and questioned. Maybe even arrested and taken to jail. '

He couldn't let anything like that happen to them. He just had to warn them some now...! I've to get out of here now...!'

He panicky looked around the polar catching Miss Rains peering in at him as she preceded to pass the polar doors. Realizing that his time was running out. That he had to take the ultimate risk to ask Sue Wong to help him.

"Sue Wong." He turned his eyes attention on hers, looking into her cold devilish eyes.

"Yes, Art what is it?"

"Sue Wong you are the only person that I can turn to. I need your help desperately... My friends need your help! If you don't help me, I as well as them will be in a lot of trouble.

I don't have much time to explain but, you must help me get out of here.

For only a few minutes. I promise you that I'll come right back, and we can do whatever you want to do."

"I can't do that. I'll get into trouble, and I have more than my share of that as it is. Just forget it Art there's nothing that can be more important than us right now."

"No, I can't...! I need you to help me! If you don't. You too will lose out. I'll be taken away from here ...! All I'm asking for, is just a few minutes. I'm desperate...!! If you don't help me, I'll do it without your help!"

"Like hell you will! You're not going anywhere...!" Sue Wong threateningly yelled back at him." You are going to have to get past me first! I'm not about to let you go anywhere! Try it and I'll scream for Miss Rains..."

"Damn it...! Shut up...!" Art paradoxically whispered out at her." Do you want her to hear you...?!"

Where without stopping to think about it. He clenched his hand into a fist, and sent it crashing into the side of her face. With all his strength behind it.

Hitting her with such an impact, that her eyes shot upwards in her sockets, and her mouth fall limply open.

As her facial skin rippled beneath the knuckles of his crashing fist, and her lifeless body was propelled sideways onto the arm of the sofa. Where her head just dangled over it. With blood flowing from out of her mouth, with her lips turning blue.

"You fucken Bitch...!" He irately shouted out at her. Jerking himself up from the sofa.

Paradoxically saying to himself

'I've to get out of here...!' As he panicky ran towards the window where Connie cut out the glass.

Where, just as he was about to kick out the plane glass. Miss Rains came walking into the polar speaking out nonchalantly.

"Is everything going alright kids...?!"

To shockingly come to an alarming abrupt stopped. Seeing Sue Wong's head draping over the arm of the sofa. With blood flowing out of her mouth. Into a poodle on the hardwood floor. Then seeing Art standing horrified. Before one of the windows.

"My God...!" She panicky shouted out." What's been happening here...! Why you little ungrateful Bastard...! What have you done...?! You are going to the reform school for this...! Get your ass away from that window!"

"Go to hell!" Art challengingly shouted back at her." I'm getting the hell out of here right now! and you are not going to stop me!"

"I'll show you ...! She irately shouted out. Charging straight towards him. With her hands extended out in front of her. Going for his throat. Screaming at the top of her lungs." I'll get you...!"

Art waited until she was almost on top of him. Then as she made her final lunge towards his throat.

He dropped sideways down onto the floor onto his hands and knees in front of her. Where her speed was too fast for her to stop.

One of her momentous feet, came crashing into the side of his chest. Causing her to stumble forwards. Sending her hurtling head first right through the eight, pane window.

Art couldn't stop to linger. He was certain that someone heard all the screaming, and her crashing through the glass of the window.

When he frantically attempted to get up onto his feet. When he became so besieged with such excruciating pain that the horrific pain sent crashing back down onto the floor.

Besieged by a sharp stabbing pain at the side of his chest. Where her foot slammed into his side.

That caused his breathing to became short, and gasp. Where every time he attempted to move. His whole chest felt as if it was being ripped wide open.

Knowing that he just couldn't lie on the floor. That he had to get out to warn Sue and Connie. He grabbed the side of his chest, and squeezed as hard as he could. Using his arms to constrict his chest, trying to hold it together.

Sucking in a deep breath he grudgingly pulled his knees up to his chest. Summoning all his strength, he pulled himself up onto his knees.

Gasping, and puffing for air to fill his lungs. To push himself up using all his strength to his upper thighs and knee muscles. Raising himself up onto his feet.

Half hunched over besieged with insurmountable pain. He grudgingly dragged himself towards the shattered window seal.

Stopping to look out to see Miss Rains spread out. Lying face down in the bushed below. Not moving.

"You fucken rotten Bitch! I hope you killed yourself. You hurt me... I hope you rot in hell...!"

He resentfully spoke out climbing up onto the window seal. Once again squeezing his arms **constricting around, and against his chest as he sucked in a deep breath.

Then let himself fall forwards out the window down onto Miss Rains back. Stumbling rolling off her back onto the ground. Into the bushes beside her.

Screaming out from the excruciating pain that came from within his chest, as he impacted against the ground.

The pain was so unbearable that he just laid upon the ground in a paralyzed rigid state. Hoping that death would befall him, thinking to himself.

'That it was all over, and he was going to die an agonizingly painful death. As he laid staring up at Miss Rains lifeless face, bleeding profusely, from multiple paces of glass deeply embedded in her face, neck, and chest. Making her look even more grotesque to look at.

'Give it up Art you can't make it...' He spoke out to himself. Feeling his chest flattening out against the ground.' You're as good as dead already just lie here and let it happen... It's over, you're not going anywhere but, straight to hell for what you did... No...!'

Art cried out to himself...! 'I can't... Not yet! I have to warn Sue and Connie... I must... I just can't die now...! I won't let myself die...!'

He struggled forcing his body to move beyond its endurance limits. Pushing it beyond the unbearable pain moving was inflicting upon him. Forcing himself up into his feet again. Not caring about the pain, or himself.

His stomach came gushing up out of his mouth. Causing him vomit profusely. While clutching his arms tighter constricting harder about his chest. He grudgingly dragged himself towards the iron gate. Knowing that he could never climb the tree. Seeing the iron gate wide open. Not daring to stop, not caring to stop to look, if anyone was chasing him.

He made his death defying attempt to reach the iron gate. Taking step by grudging dragging step. He stepped that much deeper into the infernal of damnation. Passing the bench where they once sat.

Before his legs went out from under him. Causing him to fall backwards down upon his back onto the ground. Hopelessly gasping for air, knowing that it was the last step he would ever take.

Where the besieging pain sudden was no more.

As he laid upon the ground looking up into the stars. Watching them disappearing one by one as his mind began to drift into the darkness of nothingness.

"I'm sorry..." Art sorrowfully cried out, as he laid being consumed by his body dying moments. No longer caring or feeling the will to resist what he felt was awaiting him.

Feeling his mind for the first time in his life becoming at peace with itself. As he drifted deeper and deeper into the serene solitude of nothingness.

Only to have his tranquility becoming disturbed hearing the sounds of screeching breaks. Sending an electrifying shock straight up into his brain. Awakening it from out of its solitude of bliss, amidst a screaming terrifying voice panicky shouting out.

"It's Art...! It's Art!" Connie hysterically creamed out.

Then the sounds of clicking heels running towards him echoed in his ears. Then noticing as his eyes slowly closed again. Trying to recapture the solitude of his minds approaching death.

Four, hands came upon him. Catching his mind as if pulling it back to the grin reality of the suffering he had to endure.

Frantically searching, squeezing, and feeling about him. Too startlingly come to an alarming stop upon his chest. Causing him to reopen his eyes by besieging pain.

" It's his chest...!" Connie paradoxically shouted out." He's all fucked up...! We have to get him the hell out of here now...!"

"No...!" Art rasping cried out with a gasp tone to his voice." It's a trap... They know, get away from me...Get out of here ... you promised ... The police..."

"What in the hell is that...?!" I alarmingly shouted out. Hearing a horrifying scream coming from out of nowhere. Fearfully turning my head in the direction of it.

Jerking up onto my feet from my kneeling position beside Art lying on the ground.

With Connie rising to join me. Stepping out before Art's head in defense of him. As Sue Wong came charging straight towards them. Holding a meat cleaver clutched in her hand, waving it about above her head screaming like a howling banshee...

As Sue and Connie stood their ground, looking into each other's eyes. Watching her coming as Sue Wong slashed out at Sue. As they went out to comfort the engraved bitch.

Connie with a executed swift kick sent her foot into Sue Wong's chest. Dropping her down onto her knees.

Sue spun around, catching her in the back of her head with the back of her High Heeled foot. As Connie repelled her to fall forwards. As Sue sent her foot into her forehead, sending her back onto the ground between them. Where Connie caught her in her the lower stomach as she brought down her knee behind the full weight of her body down upon her stomach.

Causing Sue Wong to convulsively tremble in shock, bouncing and swarming upon the ground. As they both disconcertingly walked away from her back towards Art.

" Let's get him the hell out of here, before we run into more crazies... Come on Sue help me with him..."

"No... Please leave me... It's a trap..."

"No, way! You are getting out of here...! We are not leaving here without you ..." Now come on Sue grab his legs."

"Connie he's past out ..."

" Good, that way he won't feel any more pain. Let's just get him to the car, and get the hell out of here."

We carried his limp lifeless body to the car, and laid him stretched out on the backseat. I jumped in behind the wheel as Connie climbed into the backseat placing his head upon her lap. Covering him up with a blanket. As I Sue speed out of the driveway in reverse. Through the iron gate, and drove off down the road away from the center.

"Sue doesn't it strike you as rather peculiar that on one came out to investigate with all that screaming going on, and where are those cops?"

"You are right Connie. It's obvious that someone must have heard. As for the cops I don't think that they were informed but, must assuredly are now.

Connie I seen that old crow-bait matron lying face down in the bushes below the window Art was supposed to come out of.

Then there's that screaming banshee. Why was she trying to kill Art? Then there's Art being badly hurt...?" I pulled the car over to the curve saying.

"What are you doing Sue? Let's just keep going."

" We can't Connie we have to find out if we were seen. We could have killed that crazy bitch! We have no choice but, to find out what if anything the police could have against us. Beside we can't move Art around in an open car in the condition he's in.

One, of us is going to have to do some walking." She said raising up the top of the convertible. To conceal Art laying stretched out on the back seat

"Walking? To where?" Connie skeptically ask.

"Connie there's no telling who could have seen this car. It's a straight link to us dammit! We're going to have to switch cars. One of us is going to have to make it to the apartment, and get Jim's cab.

That cab will be being ticket out of here. Where this car is going to become disabled out of sight."

"Now I understand. I'll go Sue, I need the exercise to cool myself down."

"Alright." I answered her. I got back into the car and drove it as far as I could get it away from the adoption center, and as close to are apartment as I wanted to get.

Not wanting it to be spotted. Where it would still be within walking distance to the apartment.

Where I parked in a neighborhood parking lot. At the far back end of it. So that it would be out of sight from anyone who might be looking for it. Like the cops.

" Now when you get back just pull up beside me, and open the trunk. We'll transfer him over into it.

I'll climbed in with Art where I can keep a close eye on him. Now you best be going I'll handle things here until you get back."

I said climbing out of the car, going to open the hood. Taking off my high heel, poking holes in the radiator. To make it look convincingly disabled.

As Connie climbed out of the back and walked away from the car. Heading for the apartment to get the other car.

I closed the hood partially, and climbed back into the backseat of the car to carefully examine Art's chest. Where I couldn't help but, to notice that someone really fucked him up good.

Although I wasn't any doctor. The nearest I could determine was that at least three, of his ribs were broken. However, his chest didn't feel mushy, or if there were any bone fragments or splinters sticking in any nerves, or vital arteries, or exposed out of his chest.

Knowing all I could do was hope that there wasn't anything else more serious, until Connie could examine him more thoroughly.

I had to do something to hold his chest confined.' But what?' I ask myself. ' I know...' Coming upon an enlightening idea.

' Our bras. The elastic just might work?' I carefully got out, and went to the trunk to riffled through our suitcases, that we happened to have brought with us. Finding three, in Connie's suitcase, plus two, others in mind.

Grabbing them up plus extras just in case, I climbed into the back seat slouching down between the seats. Then preceded to strap them about Art's chest.

Stuffing them with articles of clothing to compress the tension against his chest, to help his breathing. Until his breathing eventually became slow and somewhat strong and his chest appeared expand morally. As he appeared to sleep calmly.

Going to sit up under his head after placing it upon my lap. Compassionately rubbed his head speaking out to him saying.

"Hold on Art, just a little while longer.

* * * *

"Hey you...!" A young cop shouted out at Connie as she approached a roadblock not too far from the parking lot where Sue, parked their car.

" Just hold it right their lady." As he approached

As Connie stopped the cab, pulling it to a stop over at the curve.

" Yes, what is it office?" She asked as he looked through the windows of the cab checking it out the activity going on up ahead of her.

"Connie is that you...?" Police detective Carl Miller called out, walking towards the cab she was driving.

" Why it is you...?" He curiously said standing beside the window." What are you doing around here?"

"Hi, Carl." Connie answered him greeting him. Smiling her pearly white teeth at him." Fancy meeting you here of all places so what's happening?"

"One of the boys ran away tonight from the adoption center. That's about all I can tell you right now."

"Come on Carl all this commotion for one runaway kid, now that I find hard to believe."

"Believe it, and he's not going to get far. He's still around here someplace, it's only a matter of time before we nail him.

This one is by no means your ordinary kid. This one is a homicidal case from the way I heard it over the radio.

When this one left. He left one, person dead, and some young girl in a coma. With her head, and chest crushed in. It doesn't look as if she's going to come out of it either. You didn't answer me what are you doing here?"

"I'm helping out a friend. Well, it's really not my friend as much as it is Sue's. Thanks to you putting him in jail for 30 days, and me on longer hours. Keeping his business going along with Sue.

I was just answering a call in the neighborhood so can I be on my way now? Time is money you know, and I'm a working girl. However, seeing how I'm here. Maybe I could be of some help?"

"No, we have it under control, besides no one could help that head matron. She was found dead with large slivers of glass shoved into her eyes. Face, and throat besides her chest. Where some of the glass went straight into her brain.

As for the oriental girl. No one knows for certain about her condition. She's already on her way to the hospital."

"Carl how do you know that the kid was the one, that did it?"

"We don't for sure but, it obvious that he had to had been involved somehow. All the evidence points directly to him, and when we find him. I'm sure he'll confess to it.

The way we figure it is. That he's most likely holding up around here someplace. That's we're concentrating are search around here.

He has to be on foot, and most likely hurt himself. Pretty badly by the looks of the tail he was leaving. Judging from the amount of blood that was on the meat cleaver that was found beside the oriental girl. We found lying on the ground."

"Hey Carl." Terry his black partner called to him, coming out from the front of the parked squad car that was parked across the street from them.

"Yeah, what is it Terry." He yelled back.

"The lieutenant wants you to report to him right now. That oriental chick just Donated on the way to the hospital."

"Damn...Shit... Alright Terry I'll be right there. Sorry Connie to leave you like this but, duty calls." He said walking away from the cab.

"Hey..." Connie shouted out at him stopping him." What about me I can't spend the whole night here."

"Yeah, alright I hear you. She's alright Pete. Carl spoke out to the officer standing in front of the cab." Pass her through."

"Alright lady move it." The office called out to her saying, waving her past him as she drove by him.

Driving down the street until she spotted the parking lot Sue's was parked in. Pulling up beside her parked car. Finding her sitting in the back seat.

"Come on Sue let's get him out of here…" She anxiously spoke out climbing out of the cab, unlocking the trunk. Jerking it open as I throw boxes of stuff into the back seat of the cab.

"Sue there's cops all over the damn place. I had one, hell of a time getting here. They have road blocks up all over, they even searched the cab. We are Goddamn lucky that they haven't caught you with him, now is he doing?"

"He's holding his own so far." I approached the trunk saying, dumping out the suitcases full of our clothes into the trunk making up a bed for Art to lie upon.

We hurriedly moved Art into the trunk. Where I climbed in to lie down beside him, loosening his belt and unzipping his pants. Not wanting any added pressure on him as I climbed in rolling him over on top of me." Alright Connie lets go I've him."

Connie closed the trunk, and got back in behind the steering wheel, and drove off back down the road.

Art began to stir. That cause him to wake up grabbing for his chest. Startlingly becoming pain stricken again.

" No, Art don't move…" I called out to him using my body to adsorb the bumps of the road. As I laid holding his chest compressed against mind. Holding him in my arms, while the rest of him was being bounced about upon me. As I had to use my knees bent up towards the roof of the trunk to keep him stretched out as much as possible.

"We have you Art but, you mustn't make a sound." I whispered into his ear." Connie, and I are with you. We are trying to get you away. To where we going to originally take you.

You are hurt very bad. I know that you must be in a lot of pain but, you mustn't make a sound. There's cops all around here. We are in the trunk of a cab, Connie's driving it. Just hold on until we get you away from here."

"You should have just left me like you promised me that you would. I'm not worth you risking your lives over..." He struggled to speak out.

" Hush, Art it's too late now anyway. You are here with us now, and that's all that matters."

* * * *

"Holy shit...!" Connie panicky blurted out. Seeing a flashing light racing up behind her turning on its siren, pulling her over.

Pete climbed out of the squad, and approached the cab." Greeting Connie congenially saying. "Hi, again sweet sugar."

"What is it now Pete?" Connie nervously asked but, hiding it from Pete making it sound as if she was aggravated by his stopping her.

"It just drawn on me that call you came here on. That it just might be that kid. I just thought I would come along with you to have a look see. Just to make sure. If that's alright with you? By the way, where did you get all those boxes full of stuff from you didn't have them when your cab was checked out earlier?"

"I found them just a few blocks back and stopped to pick them up. Can I help it if I'm such a scavenger? Besides I know a great many people that could us what's in those boxes."

"Now that's strange I must say. So what about your passenger?"

"What passenger? As you can see I don't have any. It's my guess that whoever it was that called, got impatient and left but, now that I think about. It was very close to where I was supposed to pick him up that I found all these boxes of stuff.

Pete I've also been doing some thinking about what Carl was telling me. He said that he didn't know if the kid did any killing. If that's the case isn't all this police activity a bit much...?"

"If anyone ask you. You didn't hear it from me, but we found another one."

"Another one what?"

"Another body down in the cellar. Her throat was cut from ear to ear..."

"Oh, my God... No...! But didn't I hear Carl right when he said that a meat clever was found outside in some Orientals girls hand?"

"I don't know about that but, it wasn't a meat clever that killed the one, in the cellar, it was a knife but, who knows. He could have put it there after he beat the hell out of her outside while he was killing her in the process."

"Pete what you're saying doesn't make sense. If he's as badly hurt as Carl says he might be. How could he have fought off so many, and still gotten away without leaving a trail?

Just maybe it wasn't him? For all anyone knows it could have been that matron, or the girl herself, and he's just running scare after getting hurt by accident. By trying to break up what was going on.

The police could have it all wrong, and he could be the innocent victim, not the one, that's the guilty party.

Pete it just doesn't add up I'm no detective, but by just putting the facts together it couldn't possibly add up to be him.

What it sounds like to me is a conglomeration of events that led up to his disappearance, and he's just running scare because he doesn't know what-else to do."

" Connie I don't want to see that kid hurt any more than you do but, if he was an innocent victim why doesn't he come forward, and tell us what he saw?"

"Jesus Christ, Pete the boys hurt, and must likely in shock, and most likely frightened to death. You would run too if you were placed into the same position he's only a kid... Right?

What if I'm right and some of your men come upon him laying hurt someplace? He's going to run. You know that as well as I do.

The police could be killing an innocent frightened kid. My question is why wasn't anyone else there to bear witness to what happen?"

" You know I could lose my job by discussing anything with you. If it wasn't for the fact that I know you personally from the hospital you are practicing at. I wouldn't be telling you anything at all.

But, if you must know. Mostly everyone to taken to a baseball game, then went out for a late diner afterwards. The only one that knows about what really happened is that kid."

"Then you don't know what really happened do you? But, yet you're still hurting that poor kid down like a mad dog.

How do you know there was even a boy, and who in the hell called the police…? Come on Pete something isn't right here. Unless that is there's something you're not telling me? I'm no cop but, even I can figure out that something isn't right about all that happen and who's doing all the reasoning about the case. After all I'm just an interning doctor. What could I possibly know."

"Connie I said to much as it is. You best be on your way now."

" Yeah, sure I will Pete I don't want to be around here to bear witness to the police hurting down a poor frightened kid."

Connie angrily pulled away from the curve. Leaving him standing in the road with the thoughts that she left him with lingering in his mind.

* * * *

Connie drove hypersensitivity nervous about Art laying in the trunk with his body was being tossed and jostled about upon Sue adsorbing only some of the shock.

I held onto Art as best as she could be noticing that Connie slowed down her speed. Telling her that she must have gotten through the police check points, and was not driving not to draw any attention to herself, and the cab she was driving.

I could sense that Art's chest has really been hurting him. As I held him compress against my chest. Paying special notice to his breathing, and my futile attempt to hold his breathing at a consistent level.

Attempting to retain his excruciating pain he was suffering. While I could only lie there holding him. Helpless to do anything to ease his tormenting pain, squeezing him tightly against me.

Knowing that she couldn't move. Out of fear that the second she would release her arms from about him.

That the pain would become so unbearable that he wouldn't be able to hold it in, and it would all come out in one horrifying scream. Sympathetically knowing all I could do was to bare his pain with him weeping against his cheek sorrowfully thinking to herself.

'Never before have I witnessed such courage, or endurance that I was bearing witness too. Admiring him above all other men that I have even known. Knowing that no man could ever hope to be even half the man as the mere teenage boy I was holding in my arms.

The horrific battle of his unbearable suffering to retain his anguishing pain. That was tearing away at every nerve and muscle in his body. Never made me feel so helpless in all my life.

As his lifeless head laid collapsed into the shallow of my neck in a state of unconsciousness. That finally brought him some sort of peace from the anguishing pain.

'Oh, thank you dear God… Thank you…' I said to myself praising him as my eyes came flooding over with tears of despair. Feeling his breathing becoming stable as the car pulled to a slowing stop.

" Sue it's me Connie are you alright?" Connie called out as she sat behind the steering wheel parked at the curve, several miles from the Adoption Center

"Yes, where are we?"

"Just a block away from a gas station but, several miles away for the Adoption Center where I hope we are finally through all the police road blocks. I don't know where you want me to dive to. We just can't keep on driving."

"Connie listen to me. Pull into the station, and find out where the ladies room is. We have to get him out of this trunk. He's taking a really beating in it. Where I desperately need you to take a close look at him."

"Alright I'm going we have to get gas anyway. Just hold on I'll have you out of there shortly." She spoke out driving towards the station, pulling up to the gas pump. Sitting in the car the attendant approached it.

"Yes, Miss what will it be?"

" Fill it up please, and where might your ladies room be?"

" It's just off to the left of the station." He answered going to fill her tank." You best hurry I'm going to close up in about 10 minutes." He said filling the gas tank until it was full. As Connie impatiently waited so she could make it to the lady's bathroom.

Where he finally hung up the pump handle to approach her again saying.

" That will be $8.80 Miss."

"Sure thing." Connie reached into her purse handing him a $10.00-dollar bill." You can keep the change. If you will leave the door to the lady's room unlocked? I've been driving a long time I want to rest my eyes a bit before going on."

" You got it Miss but, I'll have to turn off the lights."

"That's alright I'm use to feeling about in the dark." Connie replied pulling the car over to the side of the station. Shouting off the headlights, and the motor. After backing the car in so that it was facing the street.

Leaning back her head to give the attendant the impression that she was resting her eyes. Watching him as he walked about the station locking the pump handles.

Then went inside the station turning off the lights. Where he then came back out to drove off.

Leaving the station unattended and the bathroom doors unlocked.

Connie hurriedly climbed out from behind the wheel, and went to unlock the trunk. Then ran to open the back door, and started pulling out the boxes, to hastily drag them towards the back of the cab, opening the lid to the trunk.

"Come on Sue I have the backseat cleaned off for him to lie on. We have to make him more comfortable while I could examine him."

Together we carried him to place him on the back seat. I went to pile the boxes into the trunk, and climbed back in behind the wheel.

While Connie ran into the lady's bathroom and pulled open the towel dispenser to yank out the roll of clothe towels. Then came back out jumping back into the backseat. Propping up Art's head placing it on her lap.

"Sue head for the lake cottage no one will ever find us there. We will pick up my Van, and transfer him over into it. Then replace the cab back at the apartment. Where we will head back to the lake cottage, and hold up there until Art gets better.

We can't take him to any hospital that's for sure. I don't need to be a doctor to know that he's hurt bad.

But, I damn well hope to be good enough where I can at least help his suffering without having to take him to the hospital.

Where if he's hurt too badly I know of a better place where I might be able to help him. Where we can hold up while he's getting better. I have a place of my own in Iowa. No one will ever find us there."

"You've a place in Iowa?"

"Yes."

"Well what are we doing sitting here. Let's go straight there." I yelled back at her while she quickly reexamined Art's eyes and chest.

" Dammit...! Sue It's a miracle that he's still alive..." She frantically yelled out re-wrapping his chest with the roll of clothe towels

"Sue we're going to have to stop, and pick up some medical supplies we don't have anything here we could really use!".

"Dammit Connie! Why in the hell didn't you bring your bag with you?! Connie he's going to make it isn't he...?"

"To tell you the truth. I don't know... but, I'll ring his neck if he doesn't... I'm so damn mad I could kill those that did this to him...! If they weren't already dead!"

Chapter 11

Are luck held out. We finally transferred Art from the cab to the van. Then returned the cab to are apartment building. Where I then called to have a tow truck to pick up my car. While Connie went shopping for medical supplies. Where things finally stabilized somewhat to a point where Connie could care for Art as best as she could. As I sat behind the wheel just slowly cursing the street trying to avoid hitting to many bumps.

"How's he doing Connie?" I ask taking a quick look back at her, as she tended to Art on the make shift bed we made up for him on the back seat.

"He's holding his own Sue but, I don't dare remove your ingeniously improvised contraption. Until I find out just how badly he's hurt but, his breathing is somewhat moral now, and the drug I gave him appears to have taken care of his pain.

We need to get him to my place where I'll be able to learn the full extent of the damage to his chest cavity. Where I can X-ray him."

"Connie give me your honest opinion. What do you think about all this?"

"I don't like it. That's for damn sure. It wasn't supposed to turn out the way it did... It was supposed to be so damn simple, and look what he put himself through just for us.

He put himself through living hell to get to us. Just to warn us where he could have betrayed us but, he also seen what we did to that girl. Where once he finds out that the head matron, and the girl are both dead. Along with the fact that police are going to be blaming him for what happened to them, as well as that they are both dead. Honestly to tell you the truth. There's no telling how he's going to react towards him being wanted for their deaths. As well as towards us as well."

"Connie we both know that Art didn't kill anyone. Where it's only going to be a matter of time before the police find out who did.

Where that oriental girl, is concerned she only got what she had coming to her. Whereas for that matron. Whatever happen had to have been caused by some accident.

This whole situation is going to need time for it all to blow over, and that will be the end of it. However the trail does ends with Art being the primary suspect, and with him lying on the ground. Obviously unable to protect himself. With that irate banshee charging at him with that knife. Implicating that someone else got to her. Where only the two of us knowing what really happened along with Art there.

Connie we are in damn serious trouble here! We killed that young girl. It doesn't matter that it was in self-defense. We just killed her. What makes matters even worse. We did it while attempting to break a fifteen-year-old boy out of an adoption center.

Do you realized what is going to happen to us if they find out who bet that girl to death?! Do You?!

"Clam down Sue. It's not going to do you any good getting yourself all work up over something that can't be changed. She dead and the only one who knows we did it is Art here, and we have him. Where we both know he's not about to go telling anyone. So lighten up some, and let's just deal with one problem at a time shall we."

"Connie if you are experiencing doubts about Art I need to knew it now. I don't want him experiencing doubts about us. Like you said.

He seen what we did to her. Where I'm sure that he knows why we had to do something to stop her. The bitch was crazy! Charging at us like she did. Wanting to kill us. When she didn't even know us, or why we were there. Hell, we had every right to defend ourselves.

So killing her isn't what is my concern. It's having to do it in the first damn place, and taking off with Art here. Literally convicting ourselves for murdering her.

There's no going back for any of us know. Not from here there's not. Where we have no choice but, to make sure we don't get caught. I'm too young to live out the rest of my life behind bars.

Where I don't want Art here feeling drawn between the two of us and what we did. Never the less even if was out of devotion towards him.

We are going to have to figure out a way so that it never comes to the point of having him chose between us, or us fighting between each other, over him, or any of us feeling threatened by the other over what happened. Don't forget that matron was also murdered. Even though the police believe it to be accidental. It's still going to be accredited as another murder. Seeing how she died during the act of committing a crime.

The entire situation as it is has drastically changed for all of us. Being involved in murdering two, people.

Which we can't undo what's been done. Where hopefully it will only be a temporary setback. For us and what we were planning.

Connie we just can't go compounding things by adding mixed feelings into it. We are all going to have to say loyal to each other, like it, or not. None of this crap! Was supposed to have happened! It's not our fault that those two others got in the way. They should have left well enough alone dammit! They are the blame not us!"

"Sue disregarding that for the time being. What I'm foremost afraid of is that when Art grows up. He's going to wind up hating us for what happen.

As for what happen. No one as caught us yet and until they do I'm not going to concern myself with it. When those who can prove we did anything are dead. I'm not about to let them ruin my life now. Not when I have worked my ass off to get where I am now in it.

Where that should be the last think you should be concerning yourself about. Where the first thing who you should be concerning yourself about is Art here.

Especially a term what he attempted to do for us. Strictly out of concern for us and not himself. Now that's loyalty for you. The one thing I'm not worried about is him ever turning on either of us."

However, Sue I'm the first to admit that his is serous. Are predicament just can't be overlooked. Not only two, people have died but, three. Where yes, we got away from the scene but, let's not forget we were seen around it by the police themselves. Well at least I was.

We did but, again didn't get away with anything. Where the police are never going to stop looking for Art here. Not when he's involved in what took place there. You know that as well as I do.

I for one, also don't want anything to go wrong. Not now after all we went through to be together. Where like it, or not three, people have been killed. Regardless who did it. We are caught up in it over our heads if for nothing else as accomplices!"

However, we can't afford letting the situation getting the better of us. Not when we have been situation in are control. Where yes, there's a lot that will most likely have to be done before we are out of this but, now isn't the time to start worrying ourselves about it.

Not when we are ahead of everything now. Where now all we've to do is to take things as they come, one thing at a time. Where Art's here is being first and foremost concern right now.

All we need to do is to make it through getting him to my place where I can take care of him. Then we will deal with what happened at the orphanage, and most likely being questioned by the police. Which you will have to deal with mostly yourself Sue. Seeing how you are his mice as you started, wanting to come visit him.

Which I don't see as to very urgent. Seeing how no one knows but that head matron that we were there at all visiting him.

Whereas we both arranged to take something off from what we do prior to coming for him to night. So that base is covered for the time being away.

So let's get his ass to my place in Iowa and get him fixed up so that we can all get back to doing what we morally do. Living are moral lives as if we don't know anything about what happened to him. In case the cops ask, or anything about what took place at the orphanage this night.

* * * *

Art couldn't help but, to overhear the conversation taking place between Sue, and Connie as he laid with his head laying upon Connie's lap stretched out on a make-shift bed made out of clothes upon the back seat, semiconscious.

"Hey you two, lovely ladies." He called out.

"Well, hello their Art." Connie looked down into his open eyes saying." How are you feeling?"

"Other than being sick to my stomach from listening to you two. Trying to solve the problems of the world, nothing at all. Connie, you too, Stuey. Shouldn't worry so much but, to put your minds at ease once, and for always.

No, I don't hold either of you responsible for what happened. I hold myself entirely to blame. Because I panicked when that hag of a matron told me that you were walking into a trap.

All of what happened could have been avoided if it wasn't for me, and my stupidity. However, there's another problem that has been overlooked.

My sister Pat but, there again I don't feel you have anything to worry about. If I know my sister she won't do, or say anything. That would harm me, as long as she knows that I'm with you, and I'm safe."

"Art three, people have died. The police are bond to question her. Once they find out it's you that's missing. As for Sue and I. We already discussed what we're going to do. This major unforeseen complications as messed up everything…"

"True Connie but, you don't know my sister as well as I do. I know her, and how she won't do, or say anything. Once she knows that I'm alright.

Whereas the last thing any of us want, is for her to come looking for me. Where she will if she becomes worried enough about me.

One of you're going to have to call her, and say what I tell you to say. Just say "Tap-dance" Then just say "I'm just fine. "

She always wanted to be a tap-dancer, that's are special code. That we would use when we wanted to see each other alone, or if one, or the other is concern about the other.

Now you best get to a phone, and call her before the police come knocking on her door, and get to her before those cops do, or I can assure you, that she will become a major problem."

* * * *

I immediately called Pat, and gave her the code word Art told me to give to her and said.

" He's just fine, we will have kept in touch." Then I hung up and went back, to rejoin the two of them. Informing them that she got the message.

"Good... That hag nearly killed me, and I'm glad she's dead. She got what was coming to her that Bitch!"

"Just what did she do to you?" I asked him wanting to know for myself what exactly happened. That brought about the tragic events that transpired.

While Art was in the process of telling us what transpired. He dozed back off into a peaceful but, restful sleep.

As I pulled up the road just across the road from a trailer lot, in amongst a parking lot of parked cars. To give Connie and I as rest where we could take a catnap before heading towards Iowa. With Connie already dozing off herself with Art's head resting upon her lap.

* * * *

Where the nest thing I knew I found my eyes opening with the sun's rays shining in through the windows of the cab. When I turn my head to avoid the sun's rays.

Instantly noticing Connie kneeling beside Art. Alarmingly jerking up! Nervously speaking up.

" What is it Connie is Art alright?!"

"It's nothing Sue I'm just giving Art another shot but, now that you are awake you can help me make him more comfortable. The shot I just gave him should make his pain minimal. By the way. Where the hell are way anyway?"

"Don't know for certain. Connie those drugs you are giving him. They aren't habit forming, are they?"

"No, not if they are administered in the proper dosage. Morphine only numbs the pain. It doesn't stop it. He's holding his own but, all this moving around isn't helping his condition any."

I rose up and went to turn on the radio to see if there was any news about what happened was coming over the news.

Hearing nothing of any significance pertaining to Art, or what happened at the orphanage. Made me feel certain that the police were still investigating what happened.

"Sue I'm going to have no choice but, to leave you here alone with Art. I need to go to the orphanage, and comfort the authorities. To make sure we won't have to deal with them, and hopefully find out what is going on.

I'm going to drive to one of those parking lots where you have to paid a machine to get in and out. Where I'm going to park on the very top level and as far out of sight I can get you. I'll try not to take too long to get there, and back.

Before I go I'll stop and pick up something for both you to eat, that will tide you over until I get back and some sort of a pot for you to do your business. I shouldn't be long.

However, while I'm gone I want you to get him a ready, and as comfortable as possible to be moved. If everything goes the way I think they will I should be back before the sun goes down. If I'm not, you will be on your own. Where I don't want you to come looking for me. Just make sure Art is going to be alright.

Whereas if you don't hear from me within two, days. Which I hope you will be at your place where you have already taken care of him. Like I said two days. Meaning things didn't turn out the way I played they would. And I'll figure out some way to get hold of you. I don't want you trying to get hold of me. Just in case the cops are following me.

However, I want you to remember what you said to me. If we don't know what happen, neither do the cops. Where there's nothing they could do to either of us. If they can't prove that we were involved.

Just get him to where your place is, and I'll catch up somehow. I feel certain that where we're concern. That we've having to concern ourselves about, but I also want you to give a lot of consideration towards your feelings about your position.

After I return I'm going to be leaving with him with or without you. As for Art here, all they have on him is that he's a runaway. It's going to take time to analyze what evidence he might have left behind..

I'll not force or impose my feelings upon you. It's going to be up to you whether you are willing to involved yourself any further with us.

Knowing that if, and when it is proven that Art here was involved in what happen. It might however also implicate you as well as myself. If we are caught together. But, I'll do all in my power to keep you out of it.

Now I'm going to chance attempting to go visiting Art. If I'm not back, and don't call within two, days. You do whatever you have to, too protect yourself. As far as I'm concern I never seen you after we left visiting him."

I went into the trunk grabbed up a change of cloth, and headed for the orphanage leaving Connie behind with Art. Going to rent myself a car.

* * * *

Where on upon arriving finding very little police activity going on around the place as I drove in, and parked in the parking lot across from the front door of the place.

Going inside up to the reception desk, asking if I could see Art. Saying that I was his mice and I wanted to settle a few things that we discuss with each other last might. Immediately implicating myself being with Art last night.

Acting totally oblivious about knowing anything about what transpired after I left the orphanage. expecting to see Art.

When I was approached by someone other than Miss Rains greeting me. Saying that Art was not available for me to visit right now. That I should call back at the end of the week to find out when he would be available for me to come visit him again.

Immediately replied. That I would be able to return any time soon. That I was leaving to go visit more relatives. Then I ask her from out of concern for Art's welfare. If something happened to him.

"She replied that she wasn't at liberty to say but, when she finds out, and when I called back she would inform me. That at present only his parents are being allowed to see him.

Then while the two, of us were talking. A police detective approached us. Belatedly interrupting us. To abruptly ask me my purpose for coming to visit the orphanage. Pushing his way in between the matron ** impolitely taking up questioning me.

Where it didn't take long before he started bickering back, and forth with me, While I became antagonistically evasive, in addressing his questions. Demanding that he answered mine first.

Ending the conflict by saying.

" My main reason for coming to see Art was because I was leaving to go visit more of my relatives tomorrow where it might be a while before I might get back to see him.

That I wanted to tell him that I would write him as often as I could. Then wanted to tell him that I was sorry. That I couldn't accept the responsibility of taking on the responsibility of taking care of him right now."

"Oh, so he was asking you to adopt him. Is that it?"

"As much as I would like to. Yes, that is what more, or less are disagreement boiled down to. I told him that I would stop by before I left to leave him some money."

I pulled out an envelope from my purse handing it to the detective. Informing him that it contained $200.00. Saying that it was the least that I could do for him. Then annoyingly inquiring again. If I could see him?"

"Not right now. Just where did you say you were going again?"

"I didn't but, if you must know I'm going overseas to live with one of my relatives while going to study. empathizing on the fact that I was a practicing psychologist, going to take up an internship with a will acclaimed psychologist.

Where I just by to visit my mother's sister Mary and the rest of her family when I discovered that Art was here, and came to find out what happened, and how I could find were the rest of his family was at so that I might visit them before I left.."

" Well leave your name, and additional information, and when we find out where he went off to we'll notify you where you can contact him. He run away from the orphanage last night, and we're in the process of looking for him now.

He won't get far. It's only a matter of time before we locate him. However, I don't think he'll be returning back here. He will only runaway again the first chance he gets. You can leave now, if we need to contact you we know where to find you."

* * * *

I left the orphanage and headed back to where I left Art, and Connie. After being gone for only a few hours.

Finding Connie still tending to Art. Gasping out a relieving sigh of relief upon seeing me emerging from the car I rented, as she stood leaning back against the side of the cab. Coming to greet me with a big welcoming hug.

After which we didn't hesitate to return the car I rented to drive to another rent a car place to rent still another vehicle. This time being a van.

Where we unpacked the cab, making up a much better make shift bed for Art to lay on. Where we moved Art into the van.

After which Connie drove the van. Following me as I return the cab.

Parking it back where it was originally park.

Whereby this time it was turning dark. Where Connie got in behind the wheel, and I climbed into the back, to position myself beside Art lying on the make shift bed where he could really stretch out to make him more comfortable. As Connie drove heading for her place.

* * * *

For over a day, and half Connie, and I switched driving. Stopping only to get gas, eat and refresh ourselves, and checking on Art's condition. Which wasn't getting any better.

Where it got to the point where Connie had to set up an intravenously solution to keep him hydrated. Where I had to feed him diluted baby food that would slid down his throat, without him choking on it.

Until Connie pulled over to the side of the road and parked. To come back to check on Art.

Once again, really becoming concern over his condition.

"How much further Connie." I nervously ask. Not believing that Art was still alive as she retied the towel constricting his chest. Stretching it tighter using belts.

"He's came to far, for me to let him die on me now. We are almost there. I just stopped to make sure he'll be able to handle the bumpy road from here.

Now keep a very close eye on him, and if you have even the slightest doubt that something is wrong. Shout out, and I'll stop."

She went to sit back behind the wheel. To slowly drive back out onto the country road. Where she hastily sped up, only to slow back down again for some reason.

As I sat beside Art. Trying to keep him from jerking from side to side, as she pulled off the road again. Onto still another bumpy dirt road. Making sure to take the bumps very carefully. Until she once again came to another stop. To just sit and look out the windshield. Speaking out saying.

"Well there it is." She spoke out, as she sat overlooking her place.

I went up to look out the windshield startlingly asking her to make sure we were parking before her place once and for all.

" That is your place...? Why it's a Southern Mansion... It must have cost you a fortune...? Just keeping it the immaculate condition that it is in."

"You would never believe how much it cost but, it's worth it because. It's all mine, all 500 acres of it."

"If you didn't buy it how did you get it?"

"My black ass amongst other things. I had to submit as well as sacrifice everything I had on a 65-year-old swamp rat of a man. Where when he died, he left it all to me. Where there was one, little hitch to his generosity. I had to bare him a child. Where again as luck had it, I managed to conceive, and give birth to his child."

"You never told me that you had a child. Now old where you?"

"15."

"That would make the child about 13 years old now."

"That it would have if he wouldn't have died at the age of 5. Where I really don't care to go into that part of my life just now."

She remorsefully replied driving down the slop of the hill. Through the open wooden gate. Onto a bumbles paved driveway, leading towards the front door of her home. Pulling to a stop in front of it.

"Sue you best wait here while I go unlock the door, and open the windows. To let some air inside the house. It's going to be a little dusty inside. It's been a while since I was last here so I best be going inside first.

You best stay out here with Art. The last thing I want him to do, is to be moving around. I don't want him waking up finding us both gone."

Connie climbed out of the van. Walking towards the double doors of the house. Disappearing inside the house.

Returning some 20 minutes later. Opening the side door of the van speaking out. " Sorry I took so long. I had to pull the dust covers off his bed. Come on let's get him inside."

Carefully we carried him into the house. Up a flight, and a half of stairs. Into an amorous bedroom where we carefully placed him down upon the bed.

"Connie this sure is one fantastic place you have her. It's so old, and colonial it's like going back in time."

"It's not all that grand. In fact, I was thinking of selling it. This place brings back memories, that are best left forgotten, besides it costs a fortune to maintain. When I last left this place I never had any intention of ever returning."

"How much do you want for it?"

"How does 3 million sound to you?"

"Three, million...?"

"Well that's what it was appraised at. However, no amount of money, could ever pay for the lives it took to preserve it.

This place is a landmark here amongst the blacks. Believe it or not. They are the one that preserve, and maintain this place. Where now I'm glad that I didn't unload it, seeing how it's most likely going to be Art 's someday."

" Are you serious?"

"Sue you just don't understand what my bringing him here means. Yes, I'm very serious."

"Come on Connie. He's only fifteen where for all you know his fascination for us, could change drastically. For you to leave this all to him, isn't the smartest thing you could do.

Sure I grant you that we have something going with him where he knows nothing about commitment."

"Sue you talk like a person divided within herself. Afraid to commit yourself totally but, wanting to, or so it seems now.

Sue none of this means anything to me. My giving him this placed represents nothing other than I'm sharing something with someone.

He's done nothing that gives me any concern to doubt his sincerity. I see no reason why I should deny him the benefits of what I have to offer him. However also keep in mind, that what I giveth I can take away, just as easily."

"Connie you made me suddenly realize how selfish I have been by harboring my own convictions I must sound like a real hypocrite?"

" You're not selfish, you are just frightened and God, knows you have every right to be but, it's my life.

You can do with yours as you please I'm just going along with what's making me feel. Not only good inside but, logical as well.

No matter how I see it. We just adopted ourselves the responsibility of a teenager. Along with all the obligations that goes along with him."

Connie went to sit down beside Art lying on the bed preparing a hypodermic for him.

"Will you be careful with that stuff."

"Who's the doctor here? I know what I'm doing."

"I didn't say that you didn't but, just be careful with that stuff. That stuff could become habit forming."

"Sue I can control the habit, it's the patient who concerns me. We are going to have to release those bras, that you have wrapped his chest with in order for me to rebind his chest properly. Doing so is going to inflict a lot of pain.

The sudden expansion could bring on excruciating pain that could induce a state of shock, or ever permanent paralysis. I've no choice but, to administer this drug."

**** "Alright damn it!" I frustratingly spoke out to her." Just get it done, and over with will you..."

"There it's done." Connie retracted the needle from his arm, raising up from his bedside." Now we'll wait a couple of minutes for it to take effect."

"Connie I hope we are doing the right thing?"

" Sue I don't like it any more than you do but, it has to be done. I know the dosage, I'm not about to let him become dependent upon it."

"Look at him Connie he looks so far out of it now. Was it really necessary to give him still another shot?"

"Yes, it was, if he went into shock. He could become comatose, and without the proper equipment he could most surely die.

I have a lab downstairs in the basement but, it's not adequate enough to handle this type of an emergency situation, and we can't take him to a hospital with the police looking for him.

Now when the drug takes effect we will move him downstairs. Meanwhile I'll go down, and get everything set. Just stay right here, and watch him."

"Just hurry will you... I don't like the way he's looking...?"

"I'm going, just don't touch him until I get back."

"I won't dammit...! Just don't take all damn day about it."

"Will you calm down...? I'm going..." Connie walked out of the bedroom saying.

Leaving me to impatiently pace the floor about his bed, as he just laid there motionless. Looking as if he was dead!

' Damn it...! Where is that women...?! What's taking her so long... I'm sorry but I just can't wait any longer...! I have to do something to help him...'

I went to sit on the edge of his bed thinking to release the restraining bras that were confining his chest. To unbutton his shirt, to pull it open.

Where the instant I saw the horrifying sight. I let out a scream so death defining. From seeing the horrid God, forsaken sight, that was covered up by his shirt.

"What in the hell...?!" Connie startlingly blurted out. Dropping the box of supplies, she was carrying in from the van.

Running up the stairs into the bedroom. Spotting Sue sitting on the edge of Art's bed. Clutching her hands against her chest. Struggling attempting to breath, as she continued to paradoxically scream.

"What is it Sue...?!" Connie panicky shouted. Running up to her side, fearfully asking.

"My, God...! Look...! Look at his right side...!" I pointed raising up his shirt, in a state of utter horror.

" It's horrible...! His ribs are gone...!" I irritatingly raved in a state of total hysteria, profusely trembling. Pointing down at his chest.

"What...?!" Connie frantically shoved Sue aside. Looking down at what she was pointing at.

"Holy Jesus...!" She disbelievingly gasped out. Noticing the indentation from the center of his rib cage down to his side. Where a good three, ribs were collapsed. Making a deep indentation in his side.

"Stop it Sue...! Damn you! Stop it...! This is no time for hysterics... Now shut your damn mouth ...! Your damn paranoia could throw him into shock. That he will never come out of!

He's bleeding inside but, it's not as bad as it looks! You hysterical Bitch...! If you dare to panic him, I'll ring you fucken neck...! Now help me get him downstairs dammit..."

"He's going to die..." I became totally distraught walking towards the bed. Struggling to compose myself. Grabbing his legs with my trembling hands. Helping Connie carry him back down the stairs.

Chapter 12

When Art miraculously woke, some eleven, hours later. The sun was shining down upon him, and the birds were singing. With the pain in his chest a discomforting annoying throbbing one, but nothing like it was before.

Where he instinctively attempted to prop himself up but, felt something wrapped around his chest. Preventing him from rising.

"Hey...!" He alarmingly shouted out." What in the hell?!" He yells out from pain. As he attempted to find out what it was holding him down. Frantically attempting to feel about himself with his free hand.

Grabbing, and attempting to pull on the cast incasing his chest. That was also bracing his left arm up above his head, extended out from his side.

Panicky hearing my voice alarmingly calling out to him. While grabbing his hand to stopping him from damaging all the work Connie did on him.

"Now you just stop that...! You must lie still, and give your cast time to dry. And keep your hands off things you don't know anything about." I grabbed his hand pulling it off the cast.

"Cast...?!"

"Yes, cast Connie and I did it yesterday."

"But my arm... Why my arm...?"

"Ask Connie she's the doctor. Now just lie still, and don't you dare try to move! It had to be done... You're not in any pain are you?"

"Yes, and No, but it's so restraining... I can't move my arm."

"Isn't that better than the pain you were in? Connie had to extend the cast down to your waist. Art you are going to be alright, and as good as new in no time but, there's something I have to tell you.

Connie had to operate on you. One of your ribs was pressing against your lung, and you were bleeding internally.

She had to do it. Your chest is being held together by pins held by a metal plate against your side inside the cast. The plate is attached to wires holding your ribs in place.

It's imperative that you don't move around too much. That's why we have you strapped down in the bed. If it wasn't for Connie you never would have made it, you were that close to dying."

"I understand Sue. Where is Connie?"

"She's lying sleeping at your feet, across the foot of the bed, she's totally exhausted. Art she works relentlessly for over ten, hours on you. She literally saved your life. You've been out for nearly eighteen, hours.

As for me I couldn't do much of anything but, stand by her, and watch her, and help her out as much as I could."

"Sue I've the both of you to thank for my being here. I was dying and the two, of you risked everything to being me back to life.

Sue the horrors of death no longer frighten me. It's the grin reality of living in this cursed God, forsaken world, that disturbs me.

I live now out of indebtedness. That I'll never be able to repay, and the only thing I can think of to say is. What's to eat? I'm striving..."

"Your what...?!" I rose up not knowing what to say to him. Feeling somewhat infuriated by his selfish remark." You are What...?!"

"I'm striving... I'm striving for affection... One does not become resurrected from the depths of hell. To be so blessed with the diving hands of Gods angles. A simple kiss will suffice."

"Oh, alright... How can I refuse you but, only one kiss?

I will not submit to your devilish ways to reap affections." I said leaning over to passionately kiss him

"Why your sneaky devil you..." Connie spoke out saying, coming upon

Sue kissing Art.

" I said no excitement, how dare you take advantage of her sympathy... I'll not give the devil is due this day...

Now why don't you just close your baby blue eyes, and get some much needed rest. We're not going to go anywhere, and you're going to have a whole life time to enjoy your new life."

"Alright but, can't I at least get a kiss good night as well? I will make me sleep a lot sounder

"Forget you young man." I spoke up cutting in before Connie could answer him." You got more out of my last kiss than you were supposed to get.

Talk about taking advantage of my womanly susceptibleness. You just can't be trusted..., and you're not going to be trifling with my affections so manipulatively the next time. Believe you me. Well leastwise, not until I'm certain that you're feeling a lot better."

"Sue I hate to change the subject. but, there's something I need to tell you about my sister Pat and I."

"Art you don't have to, tell us anything. Both Connie and I both know already, and what we don't know can wait to later. There's no rush none of us are going anywhere any time soon."

"You do...? Know could you've known?"

"A woman knows. We also know that she was only expressing her love for you. She does love you very much.

Your sister might have been your first love but, Connie and I are your foremost providers right now. You have every right to freely express your feeling, and concerns. As we have in return free to do so.

We're here for you in every respect. All that we ask, or expect is that you never prey on are feelings, for selfish reasons. Nor attempt to take advantage, or your frustration, out on us.

Connie, or I will deny you nothing but, you must also remember you are still fifteen. I know it's not easy for you to understand what I'm trying to say but, you will in time. Now try to get some rest..."

* * * *

A week past during which, we had a lot of time to talk, and to get a good insight into each other's prospective. Avoiding the major subject that would ruin the time we were all sharing together

By opening our minds as well as are inhabitation regarding each other. Knowing all too well we were exposing are inner most selves onto each other. As we lived within the confines of that one, bedroom.

Sharing everything, leaving nothing in the minds of each other to be apprehensive about. The more relaxed we became around each other.

While they allowed me to lay in that bed. Totally dependent on them for everything. As they went about doing what they had to, and saying what had to be said right in front of me.

Not hindering themselves from opening expressing themselves about me, or about themselves to a point where neither of us inhibited ourselves from establishing a liberal life style. With the other totally at ease around each other.

Where I had to admit it wasn't having all that much of an effect on me. Considering how Connie kept me heavily drugged up due to the pain I was having due to my body healing itself

Where Honestly have to admit at least to myself, that I had to be a consent nuisance to them where they were concerned. Being an immature fifteen, year old teenager as the days went on.

Where I was finding myself behaving immaturely physically. Acting presumptuously Where seeing was having a devastating impact on me, moors than the healing process. As the dosage of the drugs Connie was giving me was slowing decreasing. Where my mind became more and more objected to what I was seeing.

Whereas the mature adult women that they were. They ignored and tolerate my nuisances in a dignified manner.

Sometimes with a flick of a finger. Where others, by just letting it handle itself regardless how the situation was resolved. As we all slept together in the same bed because neither one, of them didn't trust me to be able to take care of myself.

Where even though I was getting better I was far from healed and still not able to get out of bed with their help.

Where they were going to go about hiding themselves while going about their day's business, Not only having to take care of me but, themselves as well. Where one, or the other was always having to stay with me. While the other tended to what had to be down around the house, and gathering supplies. Then having to cook in order for us to eat. Then there was the need to bathe me. Where they kept me basically in just a sheet.

Then there were those horrifying experience. When I would wake up in during the night. Waking up for a sound sleep soaking wet, Screaming out reliving the hell I went through, and survived thanks to Connie, and Sue.

Where they had no choice but to have to sleep with me. To make sure I wouldn't inflict any damage on all the work Connie done putting me back together again.

" Art." I spoke out to him lying beside him upon the bed with Connie laying on the others side of him. Just relaxing before settling down for the night.

"You know we can't hide forever. That we are going to have to come out of hiding eventually. Where Connie as well as I have been previous lives to get back to. That we just can't walk away from.

What lead both of us to start to do some serious thinking as to how we can go about it with no one, being the wiser. Where again it's going to depend on you, and how you feel about the ideas that we have come up with.

We don't want you to think that we are going to be leaving you. We are as one, now. Where that is where we hit on this idea.

"Art how would you like to become my Mice?"

"Your what...?!" You have to be kidding Sue?! Now can I become your mice. I'm a male?

"I'm serious Art no one, is going to be looking for a girl."

"A girl...?! I can't become a girl...?!"

"But, you can. Between Connie, and I. We could teach you everything there is to know about being a girl. Her habits, mannerisms, everything.

Art you might be parading around like a female but, we'll never let you forget that you are all man. Besides wouldn't you like to experience how the other half lives?"

"Sue this is crazy. You can't make me into something I'm not."

"Art I know as well as you. That all three, of us have been avoiding talking about are position the with the police. Where the fact is. That the police are not going to stop looking for you.

Where Connie and I can't suddenly up, and disappear out of sight forever. For now, we have taken a leave of absence but, by not returning back to are jobs will only draw suspicion onto us. Where none of us can afford having the police prying into a person lives.

Two, people died on the night you disappeared. We never fully discussed everything that happen where as much as we want to avoid discussing it. We can't because it's going to be over are head the rest of our lives.

Art like it or not. We have to think of ourselves first and foremost. Where neither Connie, or I can only cover out absence just for so long.

We've to create a diversion in as much as the police won't suspect us, and you can't stay here by yourself. As my Mice we can all move around undetected.

Otherwise the way Connie and I see it. It's only going to be a matter of time before the inedible well happen. They will catch you, and then us. The cops will never be looking for a girl. Which is are way of hiding you out in the open right under their noses without the threat of them catching onto you."

"I don't know Sue...? Me a girl...?"

"What's wrong with being a girl I'm a girl and so is Connie."

"Yes, but, you were born that way, where I wasn't. You look great in a dress. Have you taken a good look at me? There's no way I could ever pass as a girl."

"Sue he does have a good point there. His body structure, and physic will continue to develop into that of a male. He doesn't have the bone structure that a female has"

"Sure it will Connie. I grant you it's going to take time, and a lot of work on are part but, in maybe in six, mouths, or even a year, maybe even longer.

Meanwhile we can use the time to refine, and orientate him. While making new lives for ourselves. By the time we are through with him. There will be nothing he won't know about being a woman."

"Sue that's what I'm afraid of. I don't want to turn out to be like my brother. He likes being a woman. Letting guys do things to him, and him doing things to them."

"Art honey we wouldn't let that happen to you. No guy is going to touch you."

"Connie that's not what I'm afraid of. I would never submit to demeaning myself to that level of degeneracy. It's wearing the clothes of a women for one thing, and, how could I have breasts?"

"Art I grant you they are a few minor problems that have to be worked out but, you let us worry about it.

Art it's the only way for the three, of us to stay together, without drawing attention to ourselves, and keeping you out of the reform school, for something that wasn't your fault.

No one is going to believe you weren't responsible, or weren't personally involved I what happened.

Where like I said. We just can't suddenly just pop up with a fifteen, year old boy. Coming to live with either of us.

People will become suspicious, and start asking questions that we can't answer. If this is going to work. We are going to have to put you right under everyone noses. So they won't be giving you a second thought."

"Alright Sue I'll do it but, I'm not going to like it ... What do you want me to do?"

"Thank you Art, you will never regret your decision. Nothing just yet, it's us that are going to have to start making arrangements. As well as some telephone calls.

We have been gone for over a week now. We can't wait any longer. As it is, we might have waited too long.

We have to start getting ourselves organized to cover are assess. Now that we know what has to be done we can pull it off. As well as are initial plan as well. However, let's not get into that right now.

Art the police are no fools. We Have to stay one step ahead of them. Where all those who can connect us with you are dead.

Where I already covered Connie's, and my ass. Where showing up again isn't going to disrupt anything.

It's you that we have to concern ourselves with, and it's not going to be so bad honey, and it's only going to be until we can figure out a safe way for us all to be together. How long Connie before Art can get this damn cast off?"

"Six to eight, more weeks but, not more than ten but, I'll have to recast him in about three, more weeks

I'm going to have to go in and make sure that your chest is healing properly. Visually X-rays are going to help but, that bitch inflicted a hell of a lot of damage on you.

"That's are least concern right now." I interrupted her saying." It's getting back into our own present state of life. That is going to be are primary concern.

The web I think the best way we can do it. Is by alternating splitting are time. Maybe a week at a time between ourselves but, we'll have to be careful to reroute are flight pattern.

We can't keep driving back and forth that's for sure. I can get someone to handle my load of cases what about you Connie?"

"I don't know I'll be mostly on call from day to day. I'm interning is surgery as it is. I'm going to have to come up with one hell of a convincing excuse for my absence as it is. Where we can't forget, that I was seen driving that cab."

"Connie." Art spoke up interrupting Sue and her to get Connie's attention. "I think I can come up with some excuses that you can use.

Call the hospital and tell them that you were attacked and robbed. That during the robbery you were hit on the head, and you have been suffering irregular loses of memory.

That until just now, you had no idea who you were, or where you have been. When you found yourself laying in an abandoned field, out in the middle of nowhere.

That should cover you being seen in the cab, and you being absent from the hospital as well."

"Art what an imagination you have but, you know it just might work. In fact, I'm sure it will. I could even use having relapses, as an excuse to take even more time off.

No one could make up a story like that, they would have to believe it ...I always knew that you were a genius but, I never knew that you were an incredible one, as well."

"Why thank you dear lady of mine. Now that we have that out of the way. Let's say we eat something; I'm striving..."

"What would you like to eat?" I asked him.

"Well let's see now...?" He pondered before replying back." How about something incredibly sweet. Like chocolate along with a vanilla wafer full of honey suckle flavoring.

Then to top it off chocolate cream pie, so succulent that it would literally melt in my mouth, and for desert voluptuous berries, or cherries just for starters. I've this insatiable appetite for sweets."

"You don't want much do you?"

"You know Sue I once thought that knowledge was the food for thought but, now as I lay here between the two, of you. I find myself carrying less about knowledge. You must forgive me ladies. My veraciousness lies total in my infatuation, and affection for the two that I desire more than life itself."

* * * *

Through Art was but, a teenage boy, the attributes of his charm far surpassed our expectations. He sought not to appease himself but, to anoint, and embellish us by flattering us. Where in his attempts to do so, made him that much more determined to rise above his adolescence. As well has his handicapping disabilities, so that he could become more dependent on himself. Instead of having to depend on sue, and Connie all the time.

His naivetés over his ability to take care of himself medically. Excelled him through to want was imposing upon him to take care of himself. Where his admiration for Sue, and Connie was impeding him from contributing his share. That would make himself more self-dependent on himself. So that Sue and Connie could have less burdens to have to deal with. Which was making it extremely difficult for him for him to express his sentiment towards both of them.

Art sought not of himself but reveled in ever illustrious moment of are togetherness While weltering in the aftermath of his failures. Blaming himself for subjecting us to having to deny ourselves from living the lives we were creating for ourselves.

Which only intensified his fortitude to overcome himself being impaired and a greater burden upon us.

Even in his confined condition he never let up with us. Demanding more and more of him striving to excel beyond his own frustrations as to how he wanted to express himself.

We laid stretched out beside him knowing within ourselves the affections he most strived for to be bestow upon himself.

Connie and I both found her minds not believing what was transpiring between us and what she was finding even more incredible to believe. Was her developing feelings towards him?

Connie hated, loathed, and despised white dominance. She detested what they represented to her so much so she found their touch repugnant, and revolting.

Which wasn't the case where Art was concern. To her utter disbelief she was finding herself becoming truly involved, affectionately with a white teenage boy, and not regretting that she actually killed for him.

In all her years of dealing, and living with the hardships of the white man's doctrines and domination over her, since she was nine. Growing up in the South, was no picnic for any colored female young, or old.

Where the white men, and their sons had total domination over their lives where they didn't hinder themselves for exercising their authority upon the black culture that exist amongst them.

* * * *

Connie laid hugging up beside Art. Remembering back when she was only ten, years old, while walking from school. When Three, white men stopped her on the road to bodily forced her into their car, and forced her to submit to them.

As the three, of them took her repeatedly. Then beat her unmercifully, into an unconscious state.

Only to toss her out onto the road. Where they just left her for dead.

Where she was found by some of her own people, and was taken home. Where it took her two, weeks before she was even able to get up, and walk on her feet.

Where from that time on, she used her body, and her determination to reap her own revenge. Where by the age of fourteen, she was feared amongst the whites.

Due to the training of the old swamp rat, who befriended her when she was eleven years old. Where it was in the very bed. She was now laying in beside Art. That she held him in her arms as he died in them. Laying with his daughter upon his chest.

After which she sought to teach others, what was taught her. In the hopes that they would teach others how. Not to be afraid to stand up and protect themselves.

Until she left seeking to never to return. Where now she lies again, willing to throw all she accomplished away. Over a fifteen, year old white boy, as he laid sleeping beside her.

"Connie." I whispered out to her holding Art's head in my arms." Look at him he's sleeping like a baby but, isn't he magnificent though agreeing to go along with are idea? We are going to make it for sure"

"That he was Sue. Sue we have known each other for what now. Going on over five, years. Where during in all that time, did you ever think that we would wind up here like this?"

" Connie you're not harboring any regrets, or anxieties are you?"

"No, Sue on the contrary. I feel totally fulfilled in what we are sharing together. I've been touched by the hand of enchantment. Sue tell me that this isn't just a dream…

Even though it hasn't gotten to the point of either of us becoming intimate with him. Where I honestly believe that the only reason why. Is because of his physical condition.

Where I honestly believe as well. After knowing what I know about him now. I think would have happened already regardless of his age."

" Connie he's as real as the air we breathe. He's a devil full with a thousands desires that haven't been satisfied as yet. Who's obsessed, and is possessed at the same time even in the condition he's in even now.

Where I must admit I never expected to be sharing the same aspiration towards him as you are. Actually feeling that I fell head over heels infatuated with him.

My only regret is that someday he might find out the truth about me and wound up hating me for not telling him.

Knowing if this doesn't stop here. I shudder to think just how far I will be willing to go to not only protect him, But actually opening myself up onto him as well. Knowing morally knowing it would be wrong of me to do so.

"Sue I have done a lot of terrible things in my life as well. Things, that I never even told you about either. Things that I haven't been proud of but, I did them anyway. Without what I did never haunting me, until now. Where I myself wouldn't be harboring any regrets. That if it wasn't for his existing condition I would be allowing myself to lie underneath him right now.

"Connie we both have done a lot of things we weren't proud of, and I'm no exception either. Now come on let's get up and let him get some sleep."

I rolled off the bed walking over to join Connie, sitting on the edge of the other side of the bed, noticing that her eyes were flooding over with tears.

"What is it Connie...?" I kneeled down before her asking.

"Sue I felt him seeping within my thighs for the first time this very day. While holding him in my arms. Where thank god, I was wearing underpants. Because believe it, or not

I felt something incredible stunning happening, that infuriated me over the face that I was wearing underpants... I can't find the words to describe all that went on within me. That's how incredible staggering it was.

Sue I'm 26 years old where I can honestly say that from the first time in my life. I honestly think more for him than I never felt for any guy.

Who made me feel more like a woman as well as a person than I ever felt in my entire life simply from the mere touch of him against me. I literally felt him soaring me to such incredible heights. That I never conceived was possible. Being unleashed inside me just from his mere presence lingering against me."

"Welcome Connie. I thought that I was the only one, going through the same revelations alone. It's frightening as hell but, at least now I know that I wasn't going through it alone. For a while I thought that I was going out of my mind. I mean the mere thought of thinking about feeling that was. I utterly crazy, right?

Connie there something very special going on between the three, of us. You know what I think? I think that he's making it special because he makes us feel special. Where we don't look upon him as a teenage boy.

I swear Sue. That the second I first saw him. I knew there was something uncanny about him besides being the exact double of my nephew.

For some time now I haven't felt about him like the one, I loved with all my heart. Not like one who I could have actually fallen in love with. His magnificence is what makes him so undeniably majestic.

I'm a grown women who knows in every respect. The feeling that have been erupting for him are immoral, illogical, and against my better judgement but, yet I can't see to stop myself from suppressing overwhelmingly insatiable desires that goes way behind infatuation towards him.

Sue we both had to endured unbearable hardships in our lives from early on in our lives. Maybe that could be the connection that we are feeling that's establishing are obsession towards him. However I for one, have never felt this fantastic, or for that matter so rewarded in all my life just bye simply holding him in my arms.

Knowing that wasn't one, bit natural ever since Tommy died. Basically because I honestly felt I was responsible for his death.

Where I now fill alive again. So alive that I'm going to live for every illustrious moment of are togetherness. Just talking about him, is making my skin ripple with goose pimps from where he's just touched me.

Sue, I never wore a gurgle unless I fell the necessity to. Well, just look at what I'm wearing now. I would never trust myself just wearing thin silk panties like you are. I wouldn't let him dare get that close to me. Least of all not in the condition he is in now I won't. I can't see how you can stand it. I know I wouldn't be able to!"

Chapter 13

Where several more weeks lapsed we followed are projected plan. Into becoming a reality. Connie was back at that the hospital. I was practicing at my chosen profession. Where we both cut back on are rigorous schedules. Still keeping in mind what are initial plan was to bring Tommy back to life. Hoping that as time passed Art, would become long forgotten, and when it was time for Tommy to come back to life again. There wouldn't be any problem for him to do so.

As for myself. I schedule my patients so that I could be off every other week out of the month and off on weekend.

Taking a lot of my patient files with me to study while spending my time with Art during the weeks I would be with him. Before going back to work again.

Where Connie did like was unless something came up at the hospital that she couldn't get away. Where I would call in and have reschedule my patients until Connie could manage to get off to come replace me.

As for Art. As it turned out before Art was left to fend for himself. Three, weeks had past. During which he was healing quicker than we thought.

Where it was Connie who was the first one, to leave first while being able to extend her leave of absence for another week.

Where it left me alone with Art over the weekend. Where she took the van and returned it. To then picked up are car to use that one.

Where it was during that weekend that I had to leave Art to fend for himself. Where I flew back to reopen my office again. Sharing are car again with Connie.

Where we went out and bought another van. Not as good as the one we rented but, good enough to use for the time being.

Making it appear to anyone interested in us. That there wasn't anything unusual going on between us. As we continued to share the convertible.

Where Connie could head back leaving Sunday night where she could go spend her one week with Art. Where on the following Sunday night I would fly to Iowa.

Where Connie would pick me up to drive me back to her place. Where I would them take up caring for Art while she left, driving all night to make it back to work Monday morning

During which we were both bond, and determined to transform Art into a becoming refine female, and were we all having a ball doing it.

Where it wasn't until around the fourth week that we were able to start buying Art all the necessities that were essential for a young lady to wear. Along with all the accouterments that he would need to dress and appear appropriately dressed and appear out in public.

While we ran him through the rigorous training. That would mold him into the female that would enable him to walk about undetected. All the while he was healing. Which made it easier for us to dress him to appear out in public.

Where being that his arm was in a cast up above his head. Made it so that we still had to bathe and shave him under his arms, legs, and his face.

Where it was extremely lucky for us that Art was still carrying a lot of his females feathers to his appearance. So that the wigs we brought for him to wear blended in to the point where it brought out even more of his feminine character.

Weeks became more weeks, them mouths. Until at long last after two, and a half mouths we finally accomplished the inconceivable.

Turning a young wholesome boy into a sweet adorable sinuous sex-pot of femininity. The only drawback was having to shave his face, arms, and legs. Where we even have to give him a crew cut. haircut, so that we could glue his wig on.

We tried using his regular hair, by letting his regular hair grew out. Though his hair was getting long it was very thin, and the clue wouldn't hold the wig onto the top of his head. So we had to go short instead.

Until there standing before us, as we sat on the edge of his bed was a slender blue eyed blond, with all the mannerisms, gestures and sophistication of a glamorous refined young girl.

So cultured and refined that even to our own utter amazement. She herself actually raveled in her transformation. As she stood before the full length mirror admiring herself.

Connie and I taught Art all there was to know. Teaching him how to walk swaying her hips, how to apply her make-up, now to sit. As well as how to breath from the waist to expand the diaphragm to her chest cavity. Making her appear full busted, while holding her shoulders back as if she was baring the weight of her breasts upon her shoulders and back.

"Why you are absolutely ravishing my dear..." I spoke out inflating her vanity." You are stunningly gorgeous, and so appealing to the eyes. Congratulations honey let me be the first to welcome you to the world of womanhood."

"Sue I can't believe this...? It's really me...." He appraisingly gasped out, as he stood staring at himself as a full breasted, sleekly exquisite women. Dressed in a clinging conforming skirt, that accentuating the curvature of her figure. Being shaped by the elastic girdle he was wearing

"No... This isn't me...?!" He ranted shouting out. Running away from the mirror to plop down upon the bed, covering himself with the quilt.

"What's the matter with him Sue?" Connie disconcertingly asked, as he laid between them. Hiding himself under the quilt.

"I think I know Connie just let me handle this." I spoke out laying down beside him." Art honey it's me Sue... You can tell me what's the matter."

"It's not me...! That's what's the matter! Me damn it...! I'm not me anymore... I want to be me again... Me do you hear...!"

He continued to rant, and rave on, refusing to denounce his masculinity."

I don't want to be beautiful... My God...! Did you see me...?! I want to be myself again...!

Me damn it...! I'm not that thing in that mirror. I'm not supposed to look that way. I'm a boy

dammit! Not a girl or am I...? My God... That just can't be me! It just can't be...I'm losing my identify. I don't know who, or what I am any more...

I'm so afraid Sue... I felt myself responding as a man possessed with desire, and totally confused by it. Not being able to relate my feeling. Totally lost up looking at myself not being myself..."

"Art you're losing nothing. In fact, you have gained. You just seen your other side. We all have two, sides to ourselves. You are the lucky one, to be able not only to see but, to live them both as well.

Art this is an opportunity of a lifetime for you to see, as well as to live as both genders. You're not always going be as two, different genders. Nothing changed from are initial plan.

So use this time to learn from it, by experiencing the rewards, as well as the struggles you are now being blessed with, being a part of."

"Do you really think I'm going to benefit from being like you?"

"I know you will." I replied taking his hand in mine. Placing it upon my breast." I'm real Art you are nothing but, foam rubber. Under your dress you are wearing. Larks the stifling strife of your masculinity.

Where undermine Are's is what can exalts you as the remarkable young man you are. The clothes can't hide that which make us what we are underneath. Art I'll never let you ever forget what you represent as a person.

You didn't lose your identity you conceded to it, temporary. You are never going to stop

responding as what you are but, never forget Connie, or I will never let you denounce yourself. So revel in the opportunity of excepting your indifference and go along feeling the like man you are. Just don't let it show to anyone else but Connie, and I.

That's why we placed that protective guard there, so it wouldn't show, and if it becomes to unbearable either Connie or I will be there for you. We will never abandon you... You have to believe that.

"Sue I do so love you both. I would give my life for either of you. I know that I had to learn what you've taught me but, I can't co-exist in two worlds.

I can't be a girl not after what I've seen and shared with the two, of you, and felt being anointed from."

"Art you reacted to your biological nature. It's natural for you to do so. I admit we are going to have to work on that but, I think I have the solution that might prevent you from becoming embarrassed from it, if it happens again. We will have you wear a rubber until you become accustom to your instability by also teaching methods of self-control. Connie here is a doctor. Doctors know how to treat things like that, if that doesn't work I'm sure between Connie and I, we will come up with some other way of dealing with that annoying problem.

It's nothing for you to be ashamed of we just haven't been concentrating on dealing with that problem up to now, where to us it wasn't a problem.

Your old enough now to be aware of certain facts of life. Where we haven't brought it up. But it's been happening more and more frequently. Now that you are healing remarkably well since Connie removed that cast, and you are returning back to moral.

What you are going to have to realize now is. You are becoming more aware of what you have been being exposed to seeing where Connie and I are concern.

Along with closeness now that Connie as taken you off those damn drugs she's been having you no. To where you are become sensitive to your returning back to moral healthy teenage boy, Who's been sharing the same bed with two, women.

Where I'm not going to treat you as a little kid where certain fact of life is concern. Such as sex is concerned. Where we have been patronizing you instead of teaching you because of your physical condition. Where it's becoming apparent that we have to devote more time to teach you some self-control.

Like I said Art we all have two sides to ourselves. Of which you have not only seen but, also felt both side to us. Where you have yet to experience your other side, that obviously conflicting with your natural side. The two, side are very likely going to drastically confuse you, because we aroused your feminine side to the point where we have aroused your mescaline side, which again is only natural."

"Art." Connie entered into the conversation." What Sue is trying to say is that both sexes are comprised of internal genetically compositions that compose us.

Women are meek, compassionate and emotionally susceptible. Where men are physically, amorous in nature. Which you are obviously experiencing the characteristic of both.

Right now your body might know who you are but, genetically it's confused, and undetermined.

Your brother denounced his gender, and submitted to his unstable emotions. Where you know where your emotions lie, and so do we."

"Art." Sue once again spoke up." Art tell me honestly. Do those silken undergarments you are wearing denounce your manhood?

Even though when I see them on you. There not deterring me from accepting you as a man. Where you have come too far to be deterred by insecurity now, because I can attest to your manhood is fully intact.."

Art after all the time we've shared together I honestly can't believe that you're denouncing yourself as a person. When you are still the same person underneath those clothes.

You have nothing to feel indifferent about. Especially when it's Connie and I who knows what you are concealing. Knowing just how much the growing man you yourself are becoming.

We noticed just how susceptible you are to seeing us parading about without any clothes on, and how you react when we are laying against each other.

We are not going to let you embarrass yourself once we venture out. We are not about to now when there's no reason why you should feel insecure about a moral reaction that we can handle on the spot if it comes to that."

"Sue you are one sneaky underhanded conniving enchantress."

"That I am honey." I said rising up into a sitting position beside him." Sorry honey but, I can't let you lie there in a state of uncertainty. Now you're going to have to get up and pull yourself together, and be what we all worked so hard for. So that we can be together, and have all this behind us. Now go put your face on. We are going out."

"Out…?! Out where…?! I'm not ready yet, Am I?"

"Yes, you are. Where there's a small town about ten, from here. It's time for you to emerge out into the world, and see if out training will pay off."

"Connie are you going let this happen …? You can't let her send me out in my condition."

"He's right Sue he's bond to stick out. Just look at him. That girdle isn't going to hide anything. However, Art on the to her hand. I have to go along with Sue. We can't keep putting it off.

You're as ready as you're ever going to be where there's really no point in putting it off any longer. So do what Sue here tells you, and you damn well better not make a mess on that skirt."

"Alright damn it… I'll do it, but my hearts not in it." He rose up from the bed pulling his skirt up above his waist, walking away from the bed.

With both Connie, and I looking at each other. As if mentally conceding at the same. Where Connie called out saying.

"Oh, Art." Causing him to stop to turn around to look back at them siting on the bed.

"Yes, what is it."

"Just look at you." Connie spoke up addressing his appearance. "You are going to ruin that dress, and I'm not about to go out to buy you another one. Now come back here we know how to take care of things, without you ruining that dress."

* * * *

"It was past noon when we arrived at their destination in the small town. Where we sat parked in the parking lot of a shopping center. Concentrating on building up the courage to make Donna's first appearance out into society.

"Alright Donna." I turned to Art saying. As he sat on the seat behind Connie dressed in a different outfit. Which was now a sweater, and a pleaded skirt outfit.

"Now listen up Art. All we're going to do is some window shopping, and some browsing for some clothes. You just follow our example, and adhere to all we taught you, and you'll do just fine."

"Sue what if someone should talk to me?"

"Why talk back of course. That girdle Connie has you in will keep the pitch of your voice high. Just make sure to inhale first but, do it slowly, and just remember to breath up from your gut to expand your chest.

Those artificial breasts she devised to apply pressure against your chest, which will take care of the rest but, once inside the store.

Stay away from the jewelry, and cosmetic counters, and don't forget to keep squeezing your buttocks like you are hold yourself from taking a bowl moment. That will maintain your stride. Just remember all that we taught you, and you'll do fantastic.

"Alright Donna it's show time." Connie nervously spoke up inhaling a deep breath.

"Just watch out for the men, you're one hell of a looker. They're liable to try to come onto you. I know I would if I was one, but, I know already what you have in your pants.

"Sue I've been doing some thinking. What if this doesn't work, and I should get caught? I can't risk getting either of you caught as well.

You have taught me all you could. I've to do this alone. You said it yourself Sue I'm as ready as I'm ever going to be.

What I'm not ready for is getting either of you involved with me. I'll not place either of you in danger. Where I'm the one, the police are looking for.

I'm not going to allow either of you to be seen with me. So either I'm going to go myself, or not at all.

Sue if I fail at least I'll know that the both of you're safe. I didn't go through all I did to get caught now. I'll see you later, and if I don't. Don't you dare come after me."

Art spoke out sliding out of the side door of the van.

" If you do I'll point you out... I'm going to do this alone..." He slammed the door saying. Walking away from the van.

* * * *

While walking away from the van towards the clothing store. Art felt as though he was totally naked. That everyone could see right through, to his hidden secret.

Noticing the way all the guys were staring at him. Their eyes rays were burning against his flesh. While his body was experiencing the weirdest sensations.

Feeling himself vibrating with self-esteem, as his mental and emotional instabilities. Faded into the realm of confidence and conceit then personal vanity.

In his feminine splendor, that she was drawing more, and more attention from attracting eyes, as she swayed literally feeling herself floating above the ground towards the store.

While causing both men as well as other women all to stop. To ogle her as she pasted by them leering as if they were ravaging her. As if they were mentally striping her naked satisfying their lustful passions fantasying ravaging me.

Art never before realized. The violation, and the mental abuse a women was force to endure. It was frightening not knowing what they might do or say. But, oh... so utterly accelerating prestigious. To be the recipient of so much attention.

As well as empowering. Knowing that she could get anyone of those guys to beckon to her well.

Was becoming a real accelerating turn on. From having it in her power, of being the one, to pick, or chose to give her favor to. As she walked in entering glass door of the clothing store

Art could see very clearly, now how being a women in a man's world had its advantages but, on the other hand he could see that it also had its disadvantages.

Sue and Connie out did themselves transforming him, as well as teaching him how to use his transformation to his advantage.

To the extent that he was no longer Art but, Donna. Standing prestigiously filled with pride, and self-esteem, showing her ass as she stood before the rack of women clothing. Amongst other women obviously being envious of her beauty

* * * *

Nervously Connie and I sat waiting for Donna to emerge. Until finally Donna emerged from the store some forty, minutes later.

Spotting Donna coming walking out of the store carrying a small bag daintily carrying it on her arm, towards Connie and I. Sitting waiting impatiently on pins and needles.

Having to watch her walking care free, flaunting her stuff towards the van. Where she nonchalantly stopped before opening the side door. Making sure to cause additional anxieties between Connie, and I. Before opening the door to come sliding into the seat beside Connie before closing the door.

"Well ladies I guess I past I'm here. Let's say that we go home so that I can scream my lungs out, and get some much needed care. I sure as hell need it..."

"My god, Donna! You are on hell of a young women..."

"I damn well better be Connie. I'm one of them now. Being one doesn't make me feel all that high and mighty about myself I'll say that much. Seeing how I was made out the slut of every guys desires. Where I never felt so violated in all my life.

Where now that I know what being a women in a man's world really feels like. I couldn't see myself looking upon a woman as a man again. Now I know what the two, of you feel like when I look upon you harboring lustful intentions.

When I look upon the two, of you. It makes me resent myself for doing so too, two, so wonderful people like the two of you, asking myself.

"Now can men including myself. Look upon Gods must precious gift to them. With such depravity, and self-degradation. I've to think you both for having me see as well as feel. The degeneracy of my own kind."

"Art don't go putting yourself down. "I spoke up attempting to discourage him from feeling the way he is about himself. "You know what it is to be looked upon as a woman, only because you feel now as one."

"I don't understand Sue?"

" That's because you are not supposed to. To do so you would have to be a woman. It's not as one- sided as you are making it appear to be.

You can't live in both worlds, even though you have the advantage of having both. Where you have where others have not.

You can go home, and take you dress off, and be yourself. Where we go home and get undressed having to accept ourselves for what we done, and the frustration of what we didn't do, but wanted to even if it meant giving up what we consider are most precious asset

We are not just sugar and spice and everything nice. There's a lot more to us than you give us credit for.

Don't go putting your kind down, or placing us on a pedestal. We are as human as anyone else. It's all those do's, and don'ts, and the frustrations of living are lives amongst millions. Who are all struggling to find what the three, of us have. Where we still have to struggle to keep what we have."

"Sue whatever happened to the meaning of the word love, and just carrying for another?"

"Art love passes as the infatuation for it diminishes. Marriage becomes repetitious, and humdrum. The same women, the same man, generates the same results.

Commonality is boring, and monotonous, not to mention crazy. Doing the same thing over, and over again and again. Expecting different results is crazy by ever since of the word.

Carrying is the worst of all. We just stop caring when something better comes alone. It's the memories that it leaves behind. That are the most damaging to one, or the other.

Connie and I are good examples of that. Where it all starts with an acquaintance, them become an association, from there a friendship, and most likely evolves into a relationship. That both men as well as women are all out there putting themselves through.

Then while in the relationship where that original caring starts. For one reason, or another the carrying stops, and the relationship ends soon afterwards.

Most likely because the fascination diminished for one, or the other. Usually where it boils down to is that the relationship was just one, of convince, and that's where the commitment, resentment, and regret begins. Making it harder for the next time one, wants to get involved again with another person."

"Sue if what you're saying it true. Won't the same thing happen to us?"

"Maybe, you are no exception, and neither are we but, there's another reason that's going to make us rise above. It's called money, and the locality that binds us together.

It's called devotion we have now. Where no other has the opportunity to have, and we have what we want.

You see what holds most relationships together is sex alone. Where the want of it diminishes from the other. There goes the relationship. Unless there's something very unique established between them.

It' always been and always will be that insatiable urge that binds the sexes together. When it fails to satisfy that urge. One starts carving it that much more for the want of it. It's a curse both sexes must bear.

However, as you grow so shall we, but we'll do it together and not as one with a single thought, but the same thoughts.

Your infatuation will diminish where your concern, and oar's will never. You are but, a boy that has the love of two women.

What frustrates you about one. Will cause you to turn to the other, and we will do likewise where you are concern. I'm telling you what it's truly like.

Us women have are imperfection, the same as you guys, and they grow on each other to upset, and frustrate each other. Tempers, moods, infatuation, not to meant envy, and regret where that's just a few to start with

I grant you it's not going to be perfect between us as well but, as long as we can turn to each other. We stand a damn good chance of things working out for us. Where if it doesn't at least well know we give it our best shot.

Art you see us with your eyes, and affections for us, as well as a healthy young man should.

You can't deny those feeling where you are able to address them now between the two, of us. However you're not going to be Donna for the rest of your life. Where you are going to continue to develop, and mature into the gender god, intended you to be.

Where Connie and I are still trying to figure out the implication that are obviously going develop between the three, of us.

That aren't going to go away now that they presented a level of concern.

Where we can't ignore, or allow you to suppress, or ourselves for that matter inhibiting ourselves from satisfying.

Where now isn't the time to for any of us to get ourselves wrapped up in our own personal problems. Even though we are going to have to deal with it eventually."

" You know Sue you should paten your views of philosophies."

"What's the point? No one would listen to it. It only makes sense to those who it's applied to, like us.

At least we have a outlook, now we best be getting you back home, and out of harm's way them get the hell out of here. Where we can get involved into making new lives for ourselves."

"Sue what we are going to have to teach Donna here is how to deal with men. No one is going to get into her pants that's for damn sure. But, us. I'm serious. You have no idea just how serious I an. He's went as far as he could possibly go with me, and I love him for it. Need I say more?"

* * * *

We arrived back a Connie's place after 8 PM. Where we preceded to clear the house of our presence. During the two, weeks that followed.

With the three, of us only venturing out a few hours at a time. Building Art's confidence as how to deal with aggressive, resourceful men, making advances towards me.

Until once again we were covering everything up, and packed everything that we accumulated into the van.

Where It was half past 11 PM. The night before we were going to leave. When we finally plopped down on the bed. Coming upon Art just sitting on it, deeply engrossed in thought.

"Alright Art what's going on in that head of yours?"

"Sue it's the thought of going back. It's scaring the hell out of me. I know what the goal is that we are working toward but, all that I ever experienced was misery, hardship and despair and going to back to it is frightening...! I became what you wanted me to be. I don't see why I've to go back."

" Art we haven't played for mouths for you to turn chicken on us now. We have to establish your new identity for one thing. Then there's Connie's and my careers to think about. We can't just up and disappear, nor can you suddenly pop up form out of nowhere. Not without being someone else besides Donna.

Where going to a strange place would only increase are chances of getting caught. We are going back and that's final.

I don't want to hear any more about it, and there's no better time than right now. The longer we wait the harder it's going to get on you. We are leaving in the morning. Once back home you will adjust.

All you need is more confidence. We will stop on the way. Meanwhile we'll teach you more about how to handle grown men. By the time we arrive. You will have the confidence in yourself.

This time if you fail, we all fail with you but, knowing you the way we do you won't fail. Now Connie and I are both tired. We are going to shower, and relax for the rest of the night. If you care to join us, you are welcome to do so. Now unhook me will you?"

Chapter 14

It took us three, more days to reach Milwaukee during which we gave Art the time to reassure his confidence. That he needed to become comfortable with herself, and accustomed with his new role in life.

By hitting every out of the way town, and commodity on are way back. By the time we reached are destination Art was busting over with self-confidence.

"Proud of yourself now are you Donna?"

"I'll say I am Sue. I'm damn proud, and grateful for all the two of you have transformed me into. I'm free and independent now thanks to you. Even though I can't say that I've learn to cope but, I've learned to deal with myself, and the world, I'm now expected to live in.

I hate to say this but, I've became a real bitch.

That is totally dependent on the both of you to bring me back to the reality of what I really am. I could really get myself lost up in being Donna."

"Just never forget that we made you what you are by putting a lot of ourselves into you, That under those false breasts, and that seductive appearance, as well as that lustrous figure. You are what god, made you."

"Connie I could never denounce what god created me as, or what the two, of you made transformed me into. Where it's an accelerating felling to know where all I've to do is to reach, and be myself as I truly am.

Where there is something else the two, of you taught me. It was esteem, and admiration for that which I felt the (obviousness) of splendor, and the infuriation of finding myself not wanting to be that which I have become. While wanting to be embellished upon, by both."

"Art just what is it that you're trying to say?"

"Connie it has obviously became aware to me that I no longer belong to myself, or to any one gender. Connie I've seen, and I've also lived entwined within both, to where I know find myself just wanting to exist for the sake of existing. Feeling despise for what I am, and compassion for what I became."

"Damn you Art! You can't allow yourself to get lost up in what isn't real." I spoke up denouncing what he was attempt to relate. You are a facade, and nothing more.

Art you have come an incredibly long way, outside of yourself. I was afraid of this happening. Of you becoming immersed with your other self. You must always remember that there's no gong all the way. That you are only half of what you find yourself wanting yourself to become.

Art you are not a female. Never forget that. You don't have what it takes to be a full woman.

"Sue I am what I am. All one, has to do is to look at me. Where now I want to live each moment as what I have become.

I know all too well that I'm not Donna, Whereas Art I can't have my true identity. Where now I want to continue to exist outside the confines of the imprisonment. I'm going to be forced to live in?"

"So that's what you are talking about. Never fear sweet heart Connie here has figured out a way to give you your new identity. It's really rather simple.

All we've to do is to go down to the hall of records, and look through the death certificates to find a baby girl that died on the same day you were born, and use her name.

The rest will be easy.

Don't you understand what he is trying to say Sue. He wants to be born again. Where after we get the birth certificate no one would ever think of questioning its authenticity, let alone look into the death files.

Using that name, we can open a saving deposit box in your name. Which will give her a Social Security number actually legalizing her as who she says she is. We might have to change the name she has now but, that isn't important. When she becomes Art again, who will become initially Tommy

What is important is that she will be established with her own identity. For at least right now no one is going to pay any attention to three, women hanging out together. Where someone would sure take notice to two, women and a teenage boy living together.

We'll spend the night in a motel. Tomorrow is Friday where we are going to have ourselves one, hectic day. Establishing your new identity, after which it will be easy times for all of us. We will even be able to enroll her in school"

"Now that sounds like a fabulous idea. Why didn't he just come right out as say that. Instead of making me worry about him wanting to become like his brother"

"Damn but my neck is killing me." Connie uncomfortably spoke out saying. Pulling into the first motel she spotted, pulling to a stop in front of the registering office.

"I'll go in Connie you two wait out here I won't be long." I said climbing out of the van walking towards the office.

"Boy... this is going to be a bad one..." Connie gruntingly moaned out.

"What is Connie?"

"My mouthy curse that's what! Be grateful that you are speared from having to put up with the aggravation of that part womanhood."

"Alright I've ourselves a room, It's room 10. Connie pull the van in front of the door, Here." I handed her the key through the open window." I'll catch up with you later I have something to do."

* * * *

Connie parked the van in front of the door of the room.

"Connie you go in I'll bring the bags and lock it up out here."

She got out, anxiously entered the room to go plopping down on the bed. Leaving the door unlocked for Art carried in the bags.

Where he then shut the door behind him, placing the bags at the foot of the bed Connie was laying upon.

"How are you feeling Connie?"

"I feel terrible but, I'll live through it I always do... I've to go to the bathroom." She said grudgingly dragging herself out of bed.

" Hand me my overnight bag will you."

"Sure thing." Art reached down picking up her bag, handing it to her annoying speaking out.

" Speaking of cramps I've to get out of his confounded girdle..." He kicked off his shoes as Connie walked pass him, going to the bathroom.

While Art was in the process of wiggling himself out of his girdle I came walking into the room catching him, struggling to wiggle out of his girdle.

"My, my goodness what a surprise... Is there more, or do I've to wait for the second showing." I closed the door sarcastically saying, as he finally managed to wiggle his behind out of the girdle.

" My what a nice set of bums you have there... I would think that by know you would have learned how to get yourself out of a girdle properly? You don't push, pull, or shove yourself out of it. You roll yourself out it, after releasing the snap in the crutch of course."

"Not funny..." He frustratingly snapped back. Stepping out of the girdle. Tossing it on the bed. Then turned around to face me, scratching his lower stomach holding up the front of his skirt." So what is it that you have there?"

"Just some whiskey, ice, and a bottle of sour. It helps make life more bearable at times. A couple of good stiff drinks, and Connie won't feel anything.

As for you, you are going to have yourself a full day ahead of you tomorrow. I suggest that you get dressed for bed, and get some rest.

Now as for me, I'm going to have myself a couple of drinks, and do likewise. After I take myself a hot shower that is.

Art and I were sitting around the table when Connie came back out of the bathroom laying down on the bed, and feel directly asleep, the second her head hit the pillow.

I prepared him a mild drink, while slipping out of my dress. Then went to my suit case to get myself a nightgown to get ready to go to bed for the night. While Art sat in his silk underwear removing his bra.

"Art tell me truthfully now. How do you really like being a girl now?"

" Well, it does have its up's, and downs. However, my greatest anxiety is from feeling so incomplete I feel as if I'm divided in half. I can't see get over feeling that I'm losing a part of myself. It's like I'm constantly battling with myself with who I am. It's nerve-racking as hell not knowing what to do."

He removed his bra tossing it across the room onto one, of the easy chairs at the table. Scratching his chest.

"I'm raveling in the realm of my manhood, yet I've to face the perils, trails, and tribulations as a woman. Finding myself feeling threaten by those like me fearing the most. Afraid at times of going out into the jungle out beyond that door.

Where now knowing how you, and Connie are having to survive in it. Sure doesn't makes me feel very great about myself.

Where yet I find myself wanting to be adventurous like I'm some sort of a freak of the human race.

When I go out dressed like Donna. I feel threatened, abused and literally raped by every man, and in competition with every woman. But then again like moments like this. Seeing how voluptuously gorgeous Connie and you are. Not having to struggle over hindering myself from being effected physically by what I see. Makes me feel so hypocritical

Where I'm just as much a women as the both of you are practically in every respect. Sue I want to be all you want me to be for all are sakes but, when Connie or you hold me in your arms. You make me feel so anointed but, harboring so much despise for myself.

"Art being a woman isn't glamorous or prestigious by any means. At times I find myself wishing that I was a man. Just so that I could dish out some of the punishment that they so ignorantly dole out upon me.

Men as well as women have their vulnerable points. Man have strength and their masculinity to hide behind.

Where women have only their femininity to protect them. Where us women have are one

very detrimental flaw. It's called. "Emotion "that enables men to prey, and manipulate us.

It's the very thing that they use to manipulate and dominate us. It's what they use to maintain prevalence, and to achieve their ultimate goals. Where none have ever really experienced what you are experiencing and it's emotionally effecting you.

With us, it's that damn mothering instinct in us, that makes us so susceptible, and passive. We don't only see the man, but the boy, and his mischievous nature.

It's are internal affliction syndrome that invokes our mothering nature. To nurse, pacify, and make his owes go away.

Or that compassion curse that make us women feel we can change them. So we open ourselves up to them, to which they in return take the utmost advantage of. Where one would think that is bad enough. Where if that wasn't all we had to deal with.

We have ourselves. Are ever so precious adorable selves. Which is are righteous chastity that torments us, far more than any man ever could.

Art the only way I could possibly answer all your question is by saying. Some things must remain secretive between the sexes, and in the realm of ones, own sensitivity Where we are all individuals are we not.

It was once said. That one should never set precedencies, but those one would place upon

oneself. Where never denounce yourself for what you see, or feel but, what you feel with your heart. and return the compassion that was given.

That's where it all first starts with one's expectations, and the uncertainty of them being a great letdown, or being exceeded. Which incites contemplation, which blinds mostly everyone to a great extent to what heightens one's susceptibilities, and senses.

You think you know but, you don't beforehand. Then when one finds out it's to later to rally matter all that much. That is unless it met, or exceeded one's expectations

"You're being evasive."

"No, I'm not. You just haven't listened that's all. If you were I would have answered you question in the only way, I could.

It's not what you put into it. It's what you both shear during the act and derive from it. Making love isn't all physical.

In fact, it's more mental than it is physical. If it was from the feelings derived from it. It would always be the same. Are adjustable where it takes very little effort for them to become accommodating. Even if all the man wants is selfish lust for himself.

Which so many do so, because they are egotistical conceited jerks. However, there are those exceptional few. Who make a women feel so very proud to be the recipient of their adornment?

In all earnest I really can't describe how it make me feels other than to as. That it feels incredibly divine with the right person."

"Sue you know I love Connie and you both with all my heart."

"If you didn't honey, and we didn't also We wouldn't be here together right now. However as far as I'm concern actions speak louder than words. That word love is easy to say when one, wants to manipulate it of get something from someone else. Where it takes no words to love someone to get all one desires from a simple hug.

Now I think that's enough talking for right now. I can feel that the drink I had is catching up to me. Where I think what we both need to do is to get some sleep"

I walked over towards the bed climbing up on it. Laying down beside Connie to stare up at the ceiling, waiting for Art to come laid down beside me.

"Sue just one more question. Why is it that the two, must beautiful women in the world, never got married? Any man would be proud to have either of you for their own?"

I turned my eyes attention on his eyes staring at me. Admiring ever detail that his ogling eyes could behold. Seeing him struggling with himself from reaching out wanting to follow his amorous desires.

" Alright Art I'll tell you... Damn, I should learn to keep my big mouth shout... You are such an inquisitive devil..."

"I'm all ears Sue."

"That's not all you are." I sarcastically replied. Feeling the fingers of his hand hesitatingly foundling my side. Just below my bra covered breasts. Pondering whether I would be allowing myself to submit to his hands presence.

"Art all men want a beautiful woman but, they don't trust them because. We are go to have around as a status symbol to inflate their male egos. The prettier she is, It's a sure thing of the attention she'll attract.

Men love to date gorgeous women mostly to show off to their friends, or business acquaints to make them envious of jealous.

They love nothing more than to have sex with us but, they don't want to take on the responsibility of being the only man in our lives.

Because all too many time, we do draw trouble, and must men love to brag, and boost about how big and trough they are but, when it comes right down to it. Very few rarely stand behind what they say.

Especially when it come to them getting themselves hurt defending our honor, and their masculinity, like I said before. We do attract a lot of suitors as well as considered expensive to maintain.

So in order to avoid a physical consultation. They rather lavish us with expensive gifts, so that they could show us off, have sex with us a few times then move on.

Most likely to go marry some common, or plain women down the block, or next store. Now they are the ones who have it made, not us.

Where They are always the ones that get it all. Where we are the ones that has to hump are butts off. To get what we want. While having to settle for all those conceited slobs that think they are god's gift to women.

*Condemnation hasn't been very favorable, or flattering towards attractive women, and rightfully so.

I mean look at the way we are presenting ourselves. To say the least not with very much dignity, especially the way we expose ourselves around you. Along with the way we act, and compromise ourselves with little, or no hesitation were you are concern. In regards to what we hold most scared to us.

Look at Connie, and I and yourself. Do you think for one second that we would knowingly expose ourselves if we felt uncomfortable, or in any way doubted your sincerity towards us?

I grant you a great many women have degraded themselves by knowingly placing themselves on display, allowing themselves to be exploited.

Because they mostly lost any regard for themselves, or for the plain and simple reason, they just gave up their ideals.

That's not the case were Connie and I am concern, nor is it because we feel that you are bond to us. It's because you love, honor, and respect us along with the fact that you just don't want to use us to satisfy yourself selfishly.

You linger hesitating not knowing weather, or not to pursue your endeavor. To fondle my breast reluctantly just pressing yourself against my upper thigh.

Knowing that we have never restrained you from pursuing to venture further before. In itself expresses your concern over imposing yourself upon me right now.

Where I fear not of your amorous desires, so why should you fear me denying your advances? When are relationship has long surpassed the embarrassment or constrains the inhibit ourselves from each other.

I don't believe that I need to say more. If you aren't ready to acknowledge yourself, or ready to overcome your own apprehensions that's up to you, and you alone. Where I do find it unnerving at times. Why you should even care to want to torment yourself, when you knowingly know you will never turn yourself away from perusing expressing your desire appease us in the only way you feel you can.

Now getting back to answering your question. Why should men marry us when they have it made already. Simply put, there's millions of gorgeous women like Connie and I who you hold in such high esteem.

Look at Hollywood, the Riviera. The worlds filled with beautiful women. It's a meat market out there. That so few what to buy, but sure don't mine sampling.

Those dastards will lie, cheat, and manipulate us. To get us to believe that we finally found our mister right.

Only to suddenly find out. That he's already got a wife, and a half a dozen kids, or is bisexual, or impudent, or some sort of perverted degenerate creep. Leaving thousands like Connie and I, and a lot fewer eligible men for us so called especially glamorous women.

Because There are so very few men that are straight, or available. That are truly out there searching for the women of his dreams.

Where all it would take is one bad experience with one, women to widen him up. To change his attitude to one, of vindictiveness. Were we being all out there competing against each other. Until after a while both sexes just simply give up. Or say to themselves. "They are just feed up to care anymore."

When I was fourteen, I had such dreams about love, and romance. Where I became very susceptible to affection. Whereas it turns out that my dreams were virtually shattered while in search of being romanced.

Where at first it was a kiss. Then just a little foundling, then more than a foundling. Where it just meant giving up more, and more becoming more involved, and more passionately stimulating. Where it became more obsessively insatiable.

Where I was finding struggling to suppress myself any longer. Where once that barrier was eliminated, it just didn't stop. Leastwise not with me it didn't.

The more that word "Love" came out of their months." You know I love you...Please let me show you how much I love you. I need you so desperately, I can't live without you. When we are older we'll get married I promise... That's how much I love you.

Promises, and more promises. Then after they got what they wanted. It's more promises to another gullible naive girl.

I opened myself up, and gave, and gave, and gave, and they never stopped taking. You wanted to hear why, and now you have.

As incredible as it must sound. I've no doubt where you're concern. I don't feel any sort of the hesitance with you.

With you I just want to feel alive, respected, and admired for me. I reach out taking his hand in mine placing it upon my breast." There now I received the suspense of indecision. Now it's up to you to take it where you want it to go from there.

"Sue I never realized that being a woman. Especially a beautiful one, was so hard."

"That's putting it mildly honey. You are finding being a gorgeous woman as a glamorous adventure but, it's far from that.

As you will discover. We didn't do you any favors by putting a dress on you. Where I wouldn't have, if there was any other way.

But, there's a bright side to being beautiful. It's not all humps, dumps and grinds. Being ravishing does have its advantages. If one uses her assets while she has them.

She could come out financially solvent. Men would spear no expense to receive our favor. Extravagance is a blank check, with your name on it, and believe me they will pay handsomely. It took more than brains to excel me to the level where I am now.

It's really hilarious when you stop to think about it. It's hysterical in fact, now that I look back on it all."

"What is?"

"Watching all the madness going on about us. Knowing that not one, single women would ever take notice of what the three, of us are sharing together.

Honestly Art, I hope and pray with all my heart that your feelings for us will never fade. As our looks, and our bodies will with age."

I rolled over onto my side hugging myself against him. Knowingly knowing where that was going to place his attention on besides my breast. Looking into his sparkling blue eyes speaking out saying.

"Now let's get ourselves some sleep." Knowing it wasn't going to stop here.

"But...?! He bewilderingly blurted out.

"Now Art dear. You did say one last question..." Being abruptly stopped. "Well why didn't you say so..."

* * * *

We woke early the next morning Connie was in the bathroom taking a shower as I open my eyes. Startlingly not finding Art lying beside me.

Startlingly I jerked up. Only to find him fully dress standing before a mirror on the wall directly in front of me applying his make-up.

"Hey... what time is it?" I propped myself up against the headboard of the bed asking.

"Hi, sleepy head it's eight, AM. Time for you to get up. Connie's in the shower. How am I looking? She vainly turns around to posing for me

"You're looking gorgeous as usual." I rose up out of be walking toward the bathroom totally naked. Where upon entering, stepping into the shower with Connie to wet myself down with the warm water socking my hair.

* * * *

It was past ten, AM when we finally made it out the door. I went to return the key. While Art packed the bags into the van, and Connie pulled the van up to the office. To wait for me to checkout.

" Well sugar how are you feeling this morning?"

"I'm feeling as if I could take on the whole world. It's you that I'm concern about, I don't like seeing you unhappy. I wish there was something I could do for you."

" You're honey, just being here with me makes me feel better than I look and it's all worthwhile."

"Connie I know that I haven't been the only person in your life. I also know that you are harboring some mixed feeling over the color of your skin. I just want you to know that if I ever lost you because of your doubts. It would leave me as a shell of a person.

I'm not just saying that from out of infatuation for you. I'm saying it because I honestly do love you. I could care less what color you are. All I care about is your love for me"

"Art don't you also love Sue?"

"Yes, very much. Connie I only have one, heart to give. I can't divide it between the two, of you. Because I wouldn't know what half to give to each of you. No more that can I just reach out to one, and not the other.

I want to share everything with the both of you. Not being able to deny what I'm feeling for the both of you. Where the both shares no equals, or better than the other. Not even amongst each other. I'm sorry Connie for not being able to make any sense. The words come out of my mouth different than I want them to."

"Art what the three, of us are sharing is nothing less than a miracle. It contradicts the nature of things.

What we have achieve between us is in complete defiance of the laws of nature. There's no jealousy, no rivalry, and no emotional vindictiveness.

I can't believe it myself but, it's really happening but, I don't know if it's humanly possible to be able to share the same feeling with the both of us, nor how we can we share oar's with you.

It's going to be that difference, that is what is going to make what we have together stronger. Competitiveness is the natural way of things. That what make us different is also going to make us desire more than one over the other. Where apparently that isn't happening with us.

Where again making what is going on between us incredibly unbelievable to comprehend anyway one might look upon it.

Let's face it. It's gone beyond physical attraction. You have seemed as well as we all have shared more than the closeness of our bodies.

We have totally opened ourselves up as well to each other where not even are own bodies have formed a barrier of discontent between us.

Where not even are ages, or color. Where not ever are own personal preferences have entered into what we are embellishing ourselves with. Where I honestly believe that it's the solid continuity that constantly keeps bringing us back together from out of wanting to be together.

You're right I have known other men in my life, and yes, there were a few that I really felt something for.

However, there was always that feeling of insecurity, and emotional instability. Whereas incredible as this must sound to you.

The very second I laid my eyes upon you I sort knew where my destiny truly lied. Something inside me just snapped and I just knew we were destining to be together.

Then when I held you in my arms, and incredibly felt what I never felt before in my entire life.

Where I felt your embracing touch sipping into my heart.

That was the defining moment, when I felt your despair, aspirations, and compassion, all being adsorbed into me.

Where I found myself I raveling in the splendor. In more than just your eyes lighting up like a beckon. Literally fulling my soul with adornment

You penetrated me more than humanly possible to do so.

Which to this very second has never left me. To the point where I dreaded the thought of being away from you for even a second. Can you believe that. With me at my age.

Art I couldn't help from being woken up last night. Though I wanted so much for it to be me instead of Sue. I honestly felt no jealousy, or despise against her.

However, you have to realize that you can't continue to struggle patronizing us. Like it or not we are two, grown women and you are still a young teenage boy. You are going to need to just let things happen when they happen and stop trying to encourage them to happen. Moderation not spontaneity is going to have to be practiced here.

As much as I would love to share myself with you every chance I could get it's not going to do either of us any good by over doing it. I totally realize that feel you can handle the both of us but, in reality you can't. Least of all at the pace you are attempting to expressing your desire for us. There's other way of showing how much to love us.

I wish it could be different. But what you are attempting to do goes total against the nature of things. Fascination, is not easily suppressed but, ones physically ability to exert oneself consistently will eventually take precedence over one's desire to do so.

All I'm saying is, take it a bite slower that's all. We are not going anywhere, and believe you me there's no way either Sue or I will ignore you.

Where again I'm getting the feeling that you are attempting to us sex to compensate for something you could be fearful about, or lacking to fill the void.

I want you to know that you can come to us if anything is what so ever bothering you. I'm not one, for giving advice, so take what you want of it, and get rid of the rest. Regarding Sue, and I.

Never say anything that you don't honestly feel, or mean. If something truly goes against your real feelings. Regardless how frustrated, or upset you might become don't try to conceal it by using other means.

Words are going to be the hardest for you, as well as us at times. Words are easy to come by but, extremely hard to forget.

They can inflict reprehensible damage as well as arouse emotional enlightenment, and expectations. Sometime words can even be more satisfying than even I can imagine.

Like to begin with, I might want to tell you. That I'm a woman, not your mother. That I'll let you know. As I hope you will when things aren't right. That we are going to argue, and disagree about a great many things, and tempers are going to flare up. That's because we are all humans not robots.

If we hinder ourselves from getting out are frustrations in the open. Doing so could destroy our lives together.

One can only compromise, or tolerate for just so long. We all have our personal convictions, and standards where if infringed upon will result in a consultation. So learn were the others sensitively lies, and ignore bringing them up if at all possible.

Art I realize that it might appear that we are continuously lecturing you but, it's the only way for us to get you to understand us, and also for us to find out if you're harboring any inhibitions against the way we look at things.

You are now just as much a part of us, as we are of you. Where the time will come that all we might have left once your sexual fascination, and curiosity diminishes, and we find out that all we have left will be just us.

There are going to be limitless obstacle for all of us to overcome. Like after we finish what we stated out to do too begin with. Regardless how well, or badly it might turn out for us.

Hopefully we are all going to want to continue to develop and, and establish other interests that might intertwine with our existing life styles we established for ourselves.

That might drift us apart from each other while developing along with others interests, or just getting involved in us just living are new daily lives.

That we are going to have to trust, as well as continue to confide in each other. That trust is going to be essential where we are concern.

If for any reason that trust is lost, or stops and doubts settles in. It could be the beginning of the end of everything we are trying to avoid now and even later on down the road.

That's why it's essential that no of us succumb to jealously, doubts, or regret over what has already transpired between us now as well as in the future.

Where it's trust that is mostly important to are feeling towards each other don't ever change towards each other.

Art Sue, and I are answering all your concerns. Hoping to elevate any, and all doubts you might be having. Because we are concern about you. Where we want you to do likewise as well.

We don't want you to hold anything back from us, regardless how offensive you might think it might be.

We have to work it out, or it will just boil up until the pressure becomes unbearable and it blows out of portion.

Art I couldn't help to overhear some of what you and Sue where talking about last night. If I think that understand what you said. Is that you don't look upon us women as women but, more so as just another person.

Totally disregarding who they are unless they are closely associated with you. Where you are also look upon us as, above you.

Where Sue, and I already know you are striving to accelerate yourself up to our level. By attempting to exceed your level of maturity, physically, morally, and emotionally.

What I have to say about that is. Forget it. You might know the expressionism of a women but, you'll never become one.

What you don't know is that a woman can be a hundred different women all in one. Her compassion is intuitive, as she is fabulous, or inspirational. Whereas her impulsiveness that has no limits.

Art since the beginning of time men has relied on their brute strength. Where us women had to rely on are wits, and conning. You can put on the facade of femininity but, the realm belongs to us women.

Where men see only what they want to see, and take that which we will, or will not give but, you'll never know why. We give of ourselves even if you continue to copy us.

There's such a thing as going beyond the extreme. You are prefect just as you are now, and you don't have the necessities of what it takes to go beyond where you are now.

Basically because you have no business knowing what goes on inside us. That's never going to happen where you are concern.

Sue and I brought you up to the point where you are now for one, reason only. By what I understood about what you were trying to get out of Sue.

Was that you were contemplating going beyond being yourself underneath that dress. That's never going to happen. If I have anything to say or do about it. If you get my meaning?

If you don't. Let me enlighten you. I'll never let you …. No, on second thought." She abruptly said. Catching herself before she said to much.

Where Art caught the jest of what she was implying and didn't want to continue the conversation on any further knowing that she was becoming upset.

"Connie do you think we will ever have got out of this?"

"I honestly don't know, and it is nerve-racking to say the least. The uncertainty most especially. Art you know of me but, yet nothing about me, or my previous life, and barely nothing of my present life.

Art life never did me any favors, nor do I regret what I had to do to survive. Life holds no certainty for any of us other than right now UT, you can be assured that I'll do everything in my power to see to it that we do secede.

I want to say that what life has in store for you, as things are now. Are going to change, one way or another. However as hard as I want to I can't forget that three, people lost their lives, and you came close to dying yourself.

Even though you told us what happen that brought it all about. There's no way you can prove any of it.

Sure it appears that Sue and I can possibly walk away but, we have committed ourselves to you. I grant you things progress a lot further than they should have but, that can't be changed either

now, and it did bring us all closer together. Where I honestly believe that was only to be expected.

What isn't going to be accepted is us continuing. Knowing it's normally wrong for us to do so. As for me I harbor no regrets and I'm sure Sue doesn't either.

She's right about what she said last night. She's hoping the same thing I'm concern about. That your interest in us doesn't change as we grew older.

Where we have to live with the normal guilt that you are still only fifteen, years old. Who is now sexually involved with two, grown women.

I know what you are feeling about the way things are. That's only moral for any guy to think. What I want to know is. What you really are feeling about what you are sharing with us."

" It's fantastic! In one respect. Where in another overwhelmingly inconceivable. I never thought I could ever get any closer to anyone as I did with my sister. But, I exceeded my expectation just by coming to know the two, of you.

I know what you are thinking that my love for the both of you is due to the sexual nature we have come to establish between ourselves. Where yes, it was at first.

Where it's now progressed way behind that. I can't honestly have explained that. Other than to say. I don't need the sex to assure me how I can't describe my feeling for the both of you.

I'm the first to realize the age difference between us. As for the sex. I feel that I don't need it when all it takes to fill my heart with overwhelming joy, and fulfillment is just being with you, or simply just being able to reach out, and touch your hand.

Just knowing that you are close to me makes me want to live for your sake and not my own. That without it. It wouldn't matter if I lived or died. I hope I express myself to where you could understand how I feel about the both of you?"

" Well for me you did that's for sure As for the sex part I'll worry about that when I'm too old for it to matter but, only for right now. Now hush here comes Sue."

"Well here we go. Is everyone ready?" I said climbing into the van." Alright Connie let's go. Are first stop being the courthouse.

* * * *

Four, hours later we all came walking out of the courthouse with Donna's new identity with Sue holding a copy of her birth certificate with Sue speaking out saying.

"Damn… I need a drink… What I don't put myself through for the affection of a man but, we got it that's all that matters…"

We all climbed into the van pulling out of the parking lot. Breathing out a sighing breaths of relief. Feeling certain that Art wasn't detected as well

Where all the while he was right under the very noses of half the police office, lurking about inside. With all those cops staring directly at him.

"Well we did it… We got what we went for." Sue spoke out saying, handing Art his birth certificate to hold onto.

"Hey…" He blurted out." Wait a minute … This makes me out to be 17 years old?!".

" Sorry hon, that's the best I could do, where you don't look a day over eighteen, Look at it this way at least you wouldn't have to worry about dealing with going to school.

Once we're out of this mess we'll concern ourselves with your education. One step at a time honey. Slow and easy does it. Now that's the way I like it

Next stop is to open you a saving account to establish your identity. From there on we will have to see about getting you a driver's license. You wouldn't by any chance know how to drive do you?"

"I drove several time when Pat came to visit me. As for the test, that's no problem, all I've to do is look at the book once."

"Sue, Connie spoke up." I think that we should go to the DMV first before going to the bank."

"You could be right Connie. If she makes it through there, she's a shoe in from there on out but, I want you to wait down the street from the DMV. Just in case we get caught, at least you'll be safe I'll come and get you if she passes her written test

Donna no matter what happens no running. Somehow I'll figure out a way to get to you. I don't want you hurt, or dead. Do I make myself clear?"

"Yes, but, only if you get away yourself. Both of you have risked your lives enough for me. If neither of you dare to come back for me! I'll ripe my clothes off, and expose myself to the whole damn world. I mean it Sue if things go bad get the hell away from me and never come back!"

"We hear you Art." Connie spoke out saying. Pulling over to the curve beside the DMV." Just get out, and get your butt back here."

Art and I climbed out of the van and went into the DMV.

"Holy cow... Sue.... Look at that line of people? It's going to take a week just to get up to the desk."

"Just take a number, and relax. They have to take care of us before they lock the doors. Just don't forget if you have to go to the bathroom go into the women, and not the guys, and for Pete-sakes use the stall, and always stop to make yourself look presentable before leaving.

Art went to get a number, them went to get one of the hand books to read while waiting. It took him less than a few minutes to page through it before he sit it down.

"Come on? No way... You couldn't have read it that fast?"

"Who needs to read when all I've to do, is look at the pages. I got it trust me. I'm not about to forget I got this..."

Thirty minutes, later Donna's name was called. I accompanied her up to the window where a slightly heavy set women was sitting behind.

"Yes, what can I do for you today?"

" She's come to apply for her driver's license." I replied speaking up for Donna." She's seventeen, and my niece. Who just arrived from England to spend time with me where she was born."

"I will need someone to sign this certificate of liability before she can take the test."

"That's why I'm here I'll sign, I'm her Aunt."

"You do realize what your signing means?"

" Yes, I'm fully aware she's an excellent driver she's been driving for years over in England. She even has her own car but, she had to leave it to come live with me. Her parents were killed in an automotive accident recently."

"I'm sorry to hear that. I could issue her a temporary license all you have to do is to show me her overseer's license."

"She can't do that. When she move here, she had to turn in her license but, she can pass both the written and driving tests.

"You know..." She questionably looked around." You know I don't think that will be necessary."

Writing out Donna and temporary driver's license." Just don't mention this to anyone, it could cost me my job. " She handed Donna her driver's license." Welcome back to America."

"Thank you Miss." Donna joyously said to her." I'll never ever forget you for this." Donna said walking away from her window. Walking out the door down the street towards the van Connie was waiting in. Climbed in.

" Well that didn't take too long what did you do use your feminine charm?"

"No, Sue lied like hell, and got me a temporary, without having to take any tests. I can't believe that I wasted my time going through that damn manual. Sue here could get a blind person a driver's license."

"Why thank you sweet heart I'm glad to be appreciated. Now on to the bank Connie before Art here causes me to have a nervous breakdown, or are luck fails to hold out."

* * * *

The bank was a breeze. Once again I went in with Donna. Opening her a saving, and a checking account. Leaving me as her only living relative, and beneficiary. Walking back out to join up with Connie waiting in the van.

"Alright Connie let go home we are done for today."

"Home it is then." Connie pulled out from the curve. Heading for their new home that they brought to surprise Donna with.

Feeling certain their lives were once again being complete where they had everything to live for at long last. Relieved to say the least, that their worst day was finally over. Thinking of going to the post office later.

"All I can say ladies is that I'm damn glad this day is over. All I care to think about now is getting out of the dress."

"Not so fast girl. You are going to have to keep that dress on. To make sure that all your new neighbors see all us new ladies who just moved into the neighborhood. Where we just brought ourselves a new house."

"A new house." Art bewilderingly snapped back." What new house...? Neither of you ever told me anything about a new house...?"

"Why are new house, that we brought for your homecoming." I replied." A new house, a new beginning, and a whole new life for all of us to live happily ever after."

"I don't know what to say Sue…?"

"Then say nothing."

"But I've to… This girdle is killing me. That leather patch Connie attached to it isn't helping me any either."

"What…?! That's only there to prevent you from exposing who you are under that dress… Why are you getting aroused…?"

"I think that I know Connie. He's gown so rapidly in such a short period of time. That the excitement of him maturing is getting to him."

"Ladies would you mind terribly if I ask you a very big favor." Art uncomfortably spoke out.

"Sorry love." I spoke out." It's going to have to wait until we get you home."

"Sue you don't understand what the favor is. It's going to see my sister."

"Your sister…?!" I alarmingly blurted out." What are you crazy?! The cops have to be all over her place, just waiting for you to show up there."

"Yes, Sue me, but not Donna I just have to see her."

"Art why do you want to jeopardize all that we worked for now?" Connie spoke out asking him." We will go see your sister but, when it's safe to do so. Damn it Sue say something…!"

"Alright Donna." I answered for Connie. Knowing that there was no way they could keep him for seeing her. Also knowing that he had to find out sooner, or later that truth about his sister.

" But let 's call her first, and let her know that we're coming. At least that way we will find out if she's even home, or not. I'll call her.

I'll just tell her that it's Me. She'll knew who I am, and give her the code word. That I just got back into the city after vacationing with some friends, and that I was just wondering if it would be alright if I could stop by to say Hi.

There's a pay phone over there Connie." I pointed it out to her causing her to pullover for me to call.

"This is absurd Sue...!" Connie frustratingly spoke out.

"I know Connie but, there's no time like the present to make a clear slate of things. He's gone through a hell of a lot, to get this far Beside he has to know eventually."

"I've to know what?"

"That you'll have to find out for yourself. We can't tell you nor will me." Connie pulled over to let Sue make the damn call."

Connie pulled over I got out to call Pat. Knowing that once Art found out about her. His respect for her would turn into loathing, and disgust. That she was whoring herself out in order to make a living.

I didn't want to make the call but, I had no choice but, to do it. If I didn't our lives as well as Art's would lead to ultimate disaster. If he would venture out on his own to get to her.

Chapter 15

"Hello Pat...?" I evasively spoke into the phone. As I heard a female voice answering my call on the other end.

" Pat... it's me Sue. I hope that it's you and not one, of your friends, and you are not still at your tap-dancing classes."

"Why Sue... My Goodness how nice it is to hear from you. It's been so long since I've last heard from you. I was beginning to wonder if something might have happened to you."

"I'm just fine Pat. My vacation was just perfect. How's everything been going with you?"

"I suppose okay. You know the police are still looking for my brother. He's probably in Tim-Buck-Two, by now. He would be a fool to show up around my place." She skeptically answered back. Warning Sue that it wasn't safe to come visit. Hoping that she would catch on to what she was trying to tell her.

"Pat the reason I'm calling is to ask you a big favor. I was wondering if I along with a couple of my girlfriends could possibly spend the night with you?

I sublet my apartment, and they won't be moved out until tomorrow, and I'm kind of short of funds at the moment."

"Well, I guess it will be alright but, only for one night. You realize that I've personal problems of my own, I can't take on your problems as well. You will have to be out by morning in either case. Tell your friends that they are welcome but, I don't want any problems. I hope that you understand where I'm coming from?"

"I understand fully, and thanks. I assure you there will be no problems we'll see you soon." I hung up saying going back to the van.

* * * *

'Two other girls hah...' Pat said to herself.' Sorry dear heart but, you should have never of came back.'

Thinking that Art had to be with them, and most likely getting it on with either one, or both of those two, sluts where she wasn't about to let them get away with having her brother.

Knowing that he belonged to her, and her alone. Where now it was time, that she got him back where he belonged.'

* * * *

"Well Art we're almost there." I turned to him saying." So let's not blow it. Just act morally, and we will be alright. No one should give us a second thought, so don't act to suspicious, or nervous.

Honey listen to me. We have tried to help her out but, she refused are help." I spoke out lying to him. Knowing that we have been paying for her silence. Since the day we went to talk to her. Hoping to prepare Art for the unexpected happening.

" We will help her out if she would let us but, we will not support her for the rest of her life. She's your sister not oar's, and we don't want to come between the two, of you. Where you have no idea what she's been up to since the last time you seen her. Just remember you are with us now. Meaning you have to trust in us no matter what."

"Sue what are you trying to say?"

"I don't want to say anything right now. It's not our place to tell you, that Pat alone must tell you. If she doesn't them I guess we will just have to leave it up to you, and your own judgement. Alright we are here." I spoke up informing Art, as Connie pulled to a stop at the curve in front of an expensive looking apartment building.

"Alright Art this is where she living." Connie spoke up shouting off the engine.

"Hey this isn't a bad looking place. She's not doing too bad for herself, judging from the looks of this place. It must cost her a fortune to live here.

I must say living on welfare now days is not at all that bad as when I was forced to having to live on it.

To tell you the truth Sue. I'm finding this hard to believe it could have changed this much. The last time I saw her she was really having trouble getting enough money to live on. There's something wrong here…?"

He skeptically spoke out looking uncomfortably back and forth between the two of us as if having second doubts about going to visit Pat.

"You two, know something don't you…? She's not living on welfare is she? You can't do his to me. You have to tell me the truth about what's going on here.

You can't let me make a fool out of myself, by not knowing the truth about what's going on with her. She's my sister I love her… now what's going on here…?"

"Honey we were hoping to spear you this but, you would find out eventually anyway, where I guess now is as good as time as any." Connie turned to him saying.

" But it's for her to tell you not us, and it's you and you alone who must stand in judgement. Now come on let's get this over with."

We left the van, and enter the apartment building. Walking up to the elevator taking it up to the second floor.

Where for some reason I sensed an uneasiness, as I got onto the elevator. I felt irregularly peculiar about what we were doing. That whatever it was. Was just sitting there waiting for us to enter when the elevator doors open.

"By the way Connie how's your stomach?" I ask knowing that she was feeling the same thing I was.

"Need you ask Sue?"

"No, but, I thought that I would anyway." I tapped Donna on her head getting her attention. Placing my finger across my lips.

Signaling to her to keep quite while Connie and I looked around the elevator. Then pointed to the control panel at the thirteen, light was lite up, as well as number two, and the building didn't have thirteen, floors only ten."

" Sue I hope that we aren't placing too much of an imposition on your friend Pat. I really don't feel right about imposing on her like this.

Maybe we best go check into a hotel, and just say hi, and goodbye to come back, and see her again some other time? I got the impression that she was trying to tell me something when I was speaking to her on the phone.

However, I don't think so we will be imposing upon her. Knowing her the way I do, she wouldn't have agreed.

However, Connie if you still feel uncomfortable after you met her we will think of an excuse and do what you suggested. This is being floor...

" I spoke out saying as the door open. "Come on you two, her apartment is right down the hall it's 222." I lead the way down the hall skeptically looking around.

Anxiously anticipating some door to suddenly spring open, and to be comforted by someone up until we came to Pat's door.

Where Art anxiously couldn't wait. Reached out pushing the doorbell button. Stepping in front of us, impatiently waiting for Pat to answer the door.

Where when Pat open the door. She startlingly became literally shocked by seeing Donna standing before it, disbelieving what her eyes were seeing. Knowing the instant she saw who she was.

"Oh, Jesus...?!" She shockingly gasped out. As her stunned eyes ran disbelievingly up, and down her brother standing before her. Dressed like a girl that was nothing less than ravishing to her bewildered eyes.

"Hi, Pat.' I spoke up breaking the silence, addressing the shocked expression on her face." It sure is nice to see you again, may we come in?"

"Why of course..." She dumbfounding replied. Opening the door.

Signaling for us to hush. By placing her finger across her lips.

" Yes indeed come in. I was expecting you."

We entered, walking directly into her living room. As she remained behind to close the door. Them came to join us. As Connie and I sat on the sofa, and Art stood waiting to give is sister a heartwarming hug.

Where Pat took the initiative. Immediately taking him into her arms. Hugging him with a heartwarming hugging embrace constricting him against herself, as she whispered out softly.

" Be careful what you say, it's not safe."

"Pat allow me to introduce you to my friend Donna. Where you already know Connie here."

"You must excuse me Sue I wasn't expecting you to arrive so soon I'll make you some coffee."

"That sounds great but, you don't need to put yourself out for us."

"No, it's no bother... Would you like to give me a hand Donna?"

"Sure I would be most happy to."

"The kitchen is right this way, please follow me."

Art followed Pat through the swinging doors into the kitchen. The second they were on the other side of the closing swinging doors.

Pat went frantically crazy. Hugging, and passionately kissing him, with her luscious lips, while her aggressively soft inquisitive hands, were all over him. She was so overwhelmed to see him that her emotions went berserk.

Art struggled to free himself form her embrace. Walking over to the sink turning on the faucet. Then speaking out saying.

" Slow down sis. It's me, I'm here, and I'm alright. Just give yourself sometime to calm down somewhat."

"I can't...! My God...! I can't believe it's really you...! I missed you so very much . Oh, my darling... You mean so much to me... I love you so very much…" She emotionally started crying rushing up hugging herself against him again.

"Come on Pat you need to settle down." Art spoke out pulling himself out of her constricting arms.

" We're going to have all the time in the world to catch up. For right now I want you to tell me what's been happening where you are concern."

"Honey the police are really out to get you for killing all those people. Even after all this time, they still have my phone tapped, and this apartment bugged.

They even have the elevator bugged, and they are constantly following me everywhere I go. Hoping that I would lead them to you. It wasn't safe for you to come here… I tried to warn Sue but obviously she didn't catch on. To me trying to tell her to stay away."

"Hey Pat." I shouted out from the living room. Hearing someone ringing the doorbell.

"Someone is ringing your doorbell, do you want me to answer it?"

"My God Art…" Pat panicky gasped out." It's has to be the police…! You shouldn't have come here…! Now they will arrest all of you…!"

"Just calm down Pat, and relax no one's going to get arrested. Just act moral, we will handle the rest. Now just go answer the door, and get that terrified look off your beautiful face. I'll be out with the coffee in a few minutes, now go on."

"Alright dammit! I'm going! I hope you know what you're doing I sure as hell don't…!" She nervously walked out the kitchen door, past Connie and Sue sitting upon the sofa going to   answer the door.

Stopping before the door looking out through the peephole spotting familiar faces on the other side speaking out saying.

" Yes who is it?"

"It's your neighbor down the hall." Joe a plain clothes detective replied back. Saying from the other side of the door, Standing with his partner Jack.

"I was wondering if I could speak to you about a very important matter. I wouldn't be disturbing you if I didn't think it wasn't important."

"Alright." Pat replied. Knowing for certain that it was the police but, still opening the door evasively.

Just enough for her to see out noticing the badges they were flashing for her to see.

" Shit...!" She annoyingly blurted out." I wish that you would stop hassling me... So what is it this time...?"

"May we come in?" Joe asked. Forcing his weight against the door, pushing Pat aside. So he could barge his way inside her apartment. Heading straight for the living room, with his partner following in behind him.

"Hey...!" I startlingly shouted out." You can't come busting into here like this!" Jerking myself up into a standing position before the sofa.

"Just calm down lady." Joe forcefully replied." We just stopped by for a visit." He stood before Connie and I. With Connie still sitting calmly on the sofa but, looking startlingly shuck up by their presence.

Only to aggressively rise, and take up a defensive demeanor. Standing beside Sue authoritatively speaking out.

"Alright that's quite enough...!" Connie alarmingly shouted with enraged anger." Just what is going on here...?! Who the hell are you two, guys?!"

"Police lady." Jack authoritatively replied back." What's your name lady?" He directed his eyes on her standing before the sofa. Looking somewhat dumbfounded as to what was going on.

"Just hold it right there!" Connie irately spoke back." I don't know where you get off barging in here but, you damn will better have a warrant to do so!

If you don't I think what you have just gotten yourselves into one, hell of a mess. Not to mention a lawsuit!

If you don't come up with that warrant to justify your invasion of these premises. I want to see it right now!"

"Lady this girls brother killed three, people." Joe answered her demands saying.

"I don't want to hear your reasons! I want to read them...! I'm not accustomed to having my privacy being violated. Where I happen to be a part of this actions you are taking here. Even through I'm only visiting. You better be justified to be here!"

"Alright coffee coming up." Donna spoke out emerging from the kitchen carrying a tray in her hands. To become abruptly stopped by noticing two, men standing in the living room.

"My goodness... nobody told me that we was going to be more company." Donna walked over to the coffee table, placing the tray down.

" I'll go get some more coffee cups."

"That won't be necessary Donna." Connie spoke up saying. Stopping her form leaving the living room." They were just leaving anyway. Weren't you...? That is unless you are planning on arresting someone here?

I hope you realize that I could have you both arrested for forcing your way in here the way you did, or at the very least. Have you both brought up on charges, on illegal trespass, and invasion of my privacy.

The only thing you have going for you is that this isn't my place of residence but, I'll soon rectify that."

She reached down picking up her purse reaching into it pulling out a $5.00 bill, handing it to Pat.

" Here Pat is my $5.00 dollars I'm paying you for rent for tonight.

Now gentlemen and I say that loosely. I'm now a resident here, and I strongly suggest that you refrain from taking any further action upon my character, as well as my premises.

I don't knowingly know why you came busting in here but, if there's anything here that would violate my civil rights to privacy.

I strongly recommend that you get out of here immediately. Whereas for my guests. They don't have to show you anything. I already know them, and we know nothing....

Where on the other hand you have shown nothing other than your ignorance of the law. Along with gross miscarriage of justice. By barging in here without legal authorization to do so. Now am I getting my point across to the two, of you, or do I need to call the police?!"

"Holy shit Joe!" Jack his partner nervously blurted out.

"You have that right officer." Connie reprimanded him yelled back." And you are in it right up to your ears. Now show me that warrant!"

"Connie." Pat spoke up taking advantage of her position, to really hit the cops where it hurts.

"Connie did you know that everything you said was being recorded? They have my placed bugged."

"They do, do they...? That takes a Federal warrant... I demand to see it right now! If you don't mind, and I mean right now...! She authoritatively demanded.

"Miss can I speak to you privately out in the hallway? I think we can clear this matter up. But, first just give me a few minutes to discuss this matter over with my partner Joe here." Jack lead Joe towards the door then out into the hall.

"Jesus Joe...!" Jack uneasily whispered out." We have got are assess in serious trouble here. We better call the captain. She's right dammit, and she knows it!

"Are you crazy Joe?! The captain will have us pounding the beat for the rest of our lives. Let's just get those bugs out of there until after that bitch leaves...

Hopefully I'll be able to persuade her not to pursue to pressing any complaints, or charges against us, the illegal action we have taken without having a damn warrant. The warrant we had expired a month ago"

"Alright Jack but, just remember this wasn't being idea. "

"I hear you dammit! Now just shut-up and let me do the talking." Jack annoyingly replied walking back into Pat's apartment.

Infuriatingly walking back into the living room coming upon Connie standing before the sofa with the others.

"Alright lady we'll do it your way. We will destroy the tape and shutoff the bugs. Now that is settled. I would like to talk to you in private, please follow me."

He leads Connie into Pat's bedroom closing the door behind her as she entered. Making sure to let the expression on her fact let him know that she was very upset about the situation she was placed in.

"So what is it that you want to talk about." She turned to face him asking him point blank.

"Listen lady I don't know who you are and I don't really much less care. What we care about is three, people who were murdered. Where we have reason to believe that women Pat. Who you came to visit, was involved in her brother's disappearance. Who is the one behind the murders.

Whereas f I wanted to press the issue. I could arrest you, and get away with it for infringing on an ongoing murder investigation.

As well as interfering with a police officer in the line of carrying out his duty. I'm trying to avoided a legal fist fight here, so just don't push it.

Continue to do so, and I will haul all of you in, and let it be fought it out in court. I'm just doing my job as far as I'm concern. Where you will be dealing with my ignorance of the law.

Whoever even though I'm not supposed to divulge this information. Where in order to curtail you pursuing any further action. That could impede this investigation I'll tell you this.

The authorities are pretty confidant of the boy's innocence of one of the deaths. That her death was caused by accident, because she stumbled from an object the was in front of her, and tripped.

We also determined that it was most likely Pat's brother who she stumbled over. Now I can't fill you in on the rest of what happened. Regarding the other victims but, he's also been somewhat exonerated of all charges but, of one of them. Where the other still remains to be unsolved as yet that he was involved in. That needs answers to resolve

Do solely from a witness who calmed she saw what happened to another one of the victims. Who waken out of a sound sleep, hearing a lot of shouting and yelling going on outside. In the front of the adoption center.

Where she claimed to have seen someone lying on the ground, and two, shadows running towards it. When someone else appeared charging towards the two, shadows.

Where she said that those two, other shadows. Rose up in defiance of the person lying on the ground, and attacked the other shadow charging towards them.

Where a brief fight ensued, after which the two, shadows went back. Picked up the person lying on the ground, and carried whoever it was off. Where she said they loaded him into a waiting car and drove off.

This witness was the one who called the police. Everything appears to fall into what the witness saw but, only up to a point

Where we have every reason to believe that Pat was one, of those shadows. Being that her brother is the one who disappeared that very same night. Where she can't account for her time on the night he went missing.

What we can't account for is the other victim. The one who was carried off. We are going on the assumption that Pat, and her brother were the ones who attacked that girl who came charging towards the two, who were tending to the one laying on the ground.

That it was Pat and her brother who killed the girl who was attacking them, or maybe the one laying on the ground.

Where the answers to what really happened have yet to be determined fully. All way knows for certain is that three people were killed and maybe even a fourth, and her brother Art is still missing.

The theory is. That something went array. Where Pat, and her brother planed for him to escape that night but, something happened that caused the death of the third person, and maybe a fourth.

The young girl was carrying a knife but, it didn't have any of her brothers or her blood on it. However, the blade did have the blood on it that belonged to a man who was chopped to death from a meat cleaver. That had the young girls finger prints on the handle who was killed by the two, two who attacked her.

If that one who was carried off is still alive there is a chance that the truth might come out. Where it's obvious that Art's sister Pat isn't going to say anything, so that leaves Art himself. Where it's only a matter of time before we catch him.

I mean he's only a fifteen-year-old teenager with no place to go expect for his sister. Where he has yet showed up trying to get to her, and she isn't attempting to get to him. Which is telling us that there's more involved in what took place."

"Why are you telling me all this?"

"Well there is also another theory that's being looked into. By what we seen. It also appears that the boy Art himself was badly hurt internally.

It does appear that he did jumped out a window, and vomited up a lot of blood. Where he could had been the one, who was carried off.

Which leaves even more unanswered question to complicate things as they are now. One being who were the two, shadows, if one of them wasn't his sister Pat.

Then if that's the case and as badly as it appeared to have been hurt. If he was lucky to have made it through the in his condition. Again places his sister as an accomplice, and still the prime suspects to all those who were murdered.

Placing the material witness in collusion to everything along with Pat as the primary accomplice, and if Pat isn't protecting him. One of them is going to make sure that he can't testify against her.

(The other scenario is that the kid is out for revenge. 4 other people have been murdered in the past 2 mouths. All those witness are placing him at the scene. A good half a dozen witness witnessed the head matron come crashing out the study window and described the event as the first witness who called us. They said that they saw someone stumbled out the broken window and dragging himself until he fell from being severely hurt.)

Trying to cover all bases, we are going on the assumption that Art could have someone else who is aiding him to recover from his physically injures.

Overlooking a critical factor. His meant condition from having to endure everything that went on mentally.

For all anyone knows. In his mind he could still be reliving the horrid events that took place that night. Where he could be out contemplating attacking helpless people blaming them for the beating he took. Least ways it's something to take into consideration. Where until he shows up alive, dead, or otherwise it would be amidst on the police department par, not to prevent anything from happening if at all possible.

There's another thing that warranting concern. The girl that was murdered was killed using an advance form of Martial Arts. Where nowhere in his, or his sister record were they ever known to be trained in the Martial Arts. Let alone a high advance method of procedure.

Where all the police have is his sister Pat to go on, and certain procedures might have been overlooked. We have to many unknown suspects and not enough people to go around.

Now are you beginning to understand why we are monitoring his sisters every move, and why we came barging in the we did?"

"I understand that much but, what you're telling me just make any sense?"

" Tell me about it but, it doesn't make any more sense, than the three, of you showing up here, and what also doesn't make any sense.

Is why you picked Pat's place to come to. Instead of not just check into a hotel, and where is it that you know Pat from anyway? The three, of you don't add to Pat's way of life. It's as simple as that."

"If you been listening in over the phone you already know why. Where to put it bluntly that $5.00 bucks I gave Pat was my last $5.00 bucks.

We really over extended ourselves on are vacation. Where come tomorrow I'm going to take out a loan. To tide us over until I get back working full-time again at the hospital. I'm an interning doctor at one, of the hospital here."

"So who's the young girl with you?"

"She's a distant relative of my very close friend Sue. Who we brought back to visit us here in the States. Where Pat is a friend with Pat and we were desperate. There are you satisfied now?"

" For now I am but might I suggest that the three, of you find somewhere else to spend the night, and stay as far away from this place, and Pat if you possibly can.

There's an ongoing police investigation going on here. I strongly suggest if you don't want to get further involved in it. To just say clear.

I hope for all your sakes that none of you are involved in any of this. Believe me I'm going to find out if you are.

It could be that I am overlooking something here. Where there could be that there's more involved here. Than just her brother, and that's what's not making any sense at all.

I mean the way I'm seeing his importance. Is that he just doesn't fit in himself. Other than maybe being a victim himself. Where it could be that what we are dealing with is adults matters, and if that's the case.

That kid has more to fear than the police, and the longer he hides. The worse it might become for him, or it already did. "

"Well don't let me stop you from doing your job. So if you're quite through with are conversation?" Connie walked back towards the door opening it going back out to join the others.

"Connie is everything alright?"

"Yes, Sue everything is just fine..." She replied walking the two, officers too, and out the door closing the door behind them.

To panicky run over to the wet bar pouring herself two, shot glasses full of whiskey. Gulping them down one, after the other. Without stopping to take a breath of air. Attempting to regain her composure."

"Donna I want you to come with me." Pat took Art's hand saying. "We won't be long ladies, just make yourselves at home." She leads Art off into her bedroom. Closing the door behind them.

"Connie I'm rather reluctant to let her go with her. I think Donna's feeling somewhat confused right now. Not to mention frustrated about the whole situation. Maybe we did wrong by coming here? Where to tell you the truth I don't like that damn bitch one, bit."

"Hush." I alarmingly whispered out to her. "Are you forgetting that the walls still might have ears... If you ask me those cops gave into easily..."

Chapter 16

"Well Donna how do you like my bedroom?" Pat uncomfortably spoke up evasively asking Art. Not sure if the cops turned off the bugs feeling certain they had one, of more hidden in her bedroom.

"I love it, it's so much you..." Art went to sat down on her bed.

"Why thank you Donna, it makes me very happy that you have notice my feminine side. It's been so long since anyone has taken notice."

She sinuously walked towards him. Sitting down beside him on the bed. Looking over towards the mirror on the dresser at the bulbs encircling it automatically lite up when she turned on the light using the light switch to turn on the overhead light..

Where Pat anxiously placed her loving lips upon Donna's, passionately embracing them. Using her hands to glide his hands. Rekindling his memories of how wonderful she felt to him when she allowed him to explore her hoping to resurrect his past remembrance of her femininity.

Whereas she anticipated Art's enchantment, became that of arousement. Where she took it upon herself to lean him back, where she rolled over on top of him, whispering into his ear.

"Oh, Art... how I have longed to hold you in my arms again. I want you so very badly... You fill my heart with such joy knowing that your love for me hasn't diminished...

I want us to become one again. I need to feel our souls coming together as one. I know you want to... I can feel how badly you want to united with me again...

Honey I thought that I would never see you again but, now you are here, and back in my arms again...." She seductively slid her hand up under his dress, onto the silk panties

" I want to feel your strength surging through me, beckoning onto my inner being. Inspiring me to want me to anoint you again. It's been so long since we been together. Oh my darling Art... you are my life... Without you I would surely die...

Take me, caress me, bestow your stifling might upon me. I want to feel the revelations of being inflamed with burning wanting desire for all I have been desiring for so long."

She seductively swooned into his ear, sensuously enchanting him, provocatively stimulating him using her body. Encouraging his hands to become more amorously assertive

* * * *

"Sue you better be right about all this. We both know what they are doing behind that close door together."

"Connie we both know that this day would have to come. He has to find out for himself where his real feeling lies.

We both know how she's paying for all this. He alone will have to accept the grin reality of her transgression of being so free with her affections onto other guys.

We both read the reports concerning him. As well as his whole families. Can you tell him that she's not his real sister, that he's with?

Let's face it we are no better than she is. The only difference between us, and her. Is that we are giving are all. Because now we feel that we love him.

Where before it was because of my obsession, thinking of him as my nephew Tommy, and because of what happen we became sensitized to each other. Where again, because of the closeness we share where it evolved from there.

I don't like him being with her. If you want to know the truth. I hate that bitches guts. But the best way for her to win him over, over us. Is by us getting in-between the two, of them.

Believe me Connie if I know Art as well as think I do. She's going to show herself for what she is. Believe me it's going to show him just what she has been doing with herself.

She's going to show just how much she loves nothing but, money, prestige, and material possessions, and how she goes about obtaining it.

That is where his love for us is going to prevail over the love for his sister. I'm not stupid Connie there's reasoning behind my madness. There's no better time to find out where we really stand with Art.

I for one, want to find out if are coming together going to turn out to be total lost. I must admit I would have preferred to wait longer but, now that I think of it. It's best that it happens now. This way we will both know where we stand."

"Sue you do realize if he decides against us that it's going to open up a whole new can of worms. If we are going to be able to continue to keep ourselves going with are future plans. Not to mention all we have did for him. Besides the fact that he knows all about us.

I for one, don't like having anyone hanging anything over my head. If we can't trust him to be faithful to us, how can we trust him not to tell all about us?"

"Let's not jump ahead of ourselves shall we…? I don't know about how you really feel about Art but, I know how I do, and how he feels about me.

Believe me Connie I honestly don't feel we have anything to concern ourselves about. You haven't confided in him as much as I have. I know that are closeness goes a lot deeper than you can ever imagine, in every sense of the word.

Connie there's a lot of difference between a hole, and us. Where I'm counting on him to notice the difference right off. If I'm wrong. We will deal with it them and not before. Beside there's nothing we could do to prevent it from happening anyway."

"Sue I'm not denying how he might physically feel towards us. What I'm thinking about is his loyalty. His sister knows how to manipulate him to her will, where we are still trying to convince him of our feelings towards him.

Believe me when I say that he's feeling very insecure where we're concern. There isn't a day that doesn't go by, that he doesn't keep attempting to ensure himself that we are not going to get fed up with him, and abandon him.

He's more than confused he's outright terrified over us leaving him. Where all he will be left with is Pat. Hole, or not. She will never turn him away. Where he feels certain of that with he, where he doesn't with us.

Sue telling, and showing him that we are devoted to him. Is lacking something that we are not supplying him. That will convince him of our sincerity and devotion for him.

Where I strongly believe that it's are age difference, and he's becoming too dependent on us not abandoning him. That's keeping him skeptical.

I hate to admit this Sue but, I'm starting to have some doubts where Art is concern. I don't want to give him the impression that I have to vie for his affections. Either he wants to be with us, or not. I can't even believe that I even mentioned what I did over a fifteen-year-old kid. Do you have any idea just how crazy that sounds?

None of what has transpired since I met him makes any damn sense at all but, yet here I am head over heels totally involved with him."

* * * *

'" Oh, Jesus…" Pat laid stretched out upon the bed beside Art, lying beside her. Gasping out a gratifying sigh of relief.

"Do you've any idea what you've just done to me…?" She rolled over on her side raising herself up onto her elbow. Looking down into his sparkling eyes staring into her's.

"Yes, Pat I do, and I didn't like what I felt. You seemed distracted, and yet so preoccupied with applying expression.

As if you were trying to convince me, as well as yourself. That what we were sharing together really meant something. Other than putting yourself on exhibitionism. Just what was it that was going on with you, and between us?

I know what we were supposed to be sharing, but I'll be damned if I know who you were sharing it with, it sure didn't feel like it was me. Like it did when we were in the car."

"Why whatever do you mean...?" She slyly replied back." Why are you looking at me like that...?" She uneasily asked, discretely glancing her eyes towards the dresser mirror them back on to him again.

"Come on Art. You have no idea what you are talking about. What was happening was as real as it gets. I don't know what it is that you are expecting it to be like. I haven't changed any. I'm the same as I was before. I can't see how it could feel any different...?"

"Pat why are you blocking me out of your life?"

"Why would I do such a thing...? Why can't you be grateful for what we just shared together any other guy would?"

"You've been seeing a lot of other guys haven't you...? Someone has to be paying the rent for this place. I'm not stupid. I know that you couldn't afford it living on welfare."

"What do you want me to say without hurting you?"

"You are hurting me, as well as yourself. Along with our feeling towards each other, by trying to deceive me.

No matter what I'm still your brother. I know everything that's transpired between us including the compassion as well.

Which I will never forget. You forget I grew up feeling all your moods, frustration, but most of all the sensationalism of your divine reverence. What I was feeling was anxiousness, over empathizing on making gestures"

"Why should it matter so much?" She defensively snapped back. "I have never forsaken, or denied you anything nor will I ever.

Things are different now Art, we are both much older now. That what we have shared together between an incestuous brother, and sister for years in not anymore. It has gone far beyond that.

Where it was me giving and you receiving. With me receiving more than I got in return for doing for you.

Where you have to admit That I never received anything for devoting myself. For not letting you to turn out like your brother.

I've never faltered in my devotion towards you, nor could anyone ever take your place in my heart, because I love you.

I grant you that it's never went this far but, I'm glad that if finally did. If only to prove how committed I am to my love for you is.

Where again it can never be anything but sex between us, so why make a big thing out of it. You got what you wanted out of it, now didn't you,

Like I said it's only sex. Where I fail to see how you can feel it any different from the last time. There's no way."

"Pat if you love another don't forsake that love, or infringe upon it to patronize me. Be faithful to yourself as well as to him."

"But I don't love anyone but you. I never could, don't you understand that? All any other guy is to me, is security. So that I could rise above the slums of poverty that I was entrapped in.

So what if they are my way out, and nothing more.

It's you I love with all my heart there isn't no other. You are my primary reason why I'm doing what I'm doing...

I hate myself for doing what I've to do but, it's the only way I can ensure that I'll never lose you again.

Art it's going to be me who is going to be providing for you from now on. You belong with me... We always shared that special bond between us.

Even when we were kids I cared, and catered to you. That went beyond the limitation of being brother, and sister. I don't know about you but I'm finding my way a lot more appealing than using my hand, now don't you agree? "

"Pat I have nothing anymore. For you to ruin, or denying yourself for me. From living your whole life over me. Would be meaningless.

Nothing going to change the fact that I'm your brother, where you need someone to rely and depend upon, and to make a life for yourself with. Witch can't be me.

It can't ever lead us out of bonds. That restrict us, from going anywhere with are feeling towards each other.

I harbor no regret, or remorse over what we just shared together. Other than I wish that you would have told me first. Rather than having me unknowingly finding out for myself.

Your lying to me, by faking emotions, that we never shared before between us.

Where your feelings that were once affectionately smoothing, and compassionately appeasing.

Felt like nothing more than just a form of compliance. Makes me feel there's something going on with you that you're not telling me."

"I know honey, and I was so hoping that you would never find out. I should have figured that it was going to turn out this way.

You being with those two, whores! but maybe it's for the best this way. At least I got to hold you in my arms once again. I just want you to know that I'll always be here for you.

I never expect you to be unappreciative when you did find out, just how far I was willing to go to show you just how much I loved you.

It never dawned on me, that doing what I did. Wouldn't be the most special thing I could do to show you how much I love you. Because those whores took that opportunity away from me by being the bitches that they really are...

I swear Art if I find out that those bitches did something to turn you against me. I'll see to it to make their life a living hell.

Art you haven't been screwing them have you? Is that how you found out that I have been selling myself to guy? You only went all the way with me once. For you to have ravel in doing so again could only mean you have come more familiar with having internal sex.

Damn you Art this is going to damn far! I'll not allow them to us you because they can't find anyone else to screw!"

* * * *

"I can't stand this any longer...!" Connie frustratingly blunted out. Gulping down her drink angrily walking from the wet bar towards the closed door of the bedroom.

Causing me to panicky jerked up running towards the door before Connie reach it. Blocking her from irately charging through it. Grabbing hold of her arms, holding her at bay nervously speaking out to her.

"Connie... Just back off a second before you open that door, and pull yourself together. At least prepared yourself for what you might see.

You don't know what you might see, and you might not be able to handle what you do see. Now just give yourself time, that's all I'm asking."

"Alright Sue." Connie inhaled a deep breath of air. Gulping down her aspirations." Your right we can't afford hysterics over nothing... and that's what she is nothing... I have myself together now. So come on open the damn door, and let's get this shit on...."

"I opened the door without knocking. To take it upon myself to enter the bedroom. Startlingly founding them sitting on the edge of the bed. As we stood just inside the open doorway.

"Well don't just stand there." Art spoke out." Come on in."

"We didn't mean to disturb you." I spoke out. Struggling to compose my anger. Noticing Pat's clothes wrinkly disarranged, as well as Donna's. As we walked over to join them. Sitting down beside Art on the edge of the bed.

"We became concerned. The two of you've been in here for some time but, I see that the two, of you are obviously hitting it off just fine.

However, I think that it's time for all of us to have ourselves a talk. It's obvious that we do have ourselves a predicament here that needs clarifying.

Donna I think it's time for you to take that shower now." Connie suggestively spoke out saying." The three of us have to discuss something in private. Now go on and do what Connie tell you."

"Alright I'll go but, the three, of you just remember something. It's not for any of you to decide anything. That might pertain to my life, and how I want to live it. I alone will decide that." He defensively rose up walking towards the bathroom closing the door behind him. Instantly pressing his ear against the door, wanting to hear what the three, of them were talking about.

"Sue I best go in and help her." Connie rose saying walking towards the bathroom door. Opening it finding Art already taking a shower when she entered.

Silently sitting on the toilet closing the door to wait for him to finish. Leaving Sue and Pat alone in the other room.

Art turned off the shower and pulled the shower curtain open to startlingly see Connie sitting on the toilet holding a towel upon her lap.

"Connie!" He startlingly blurted out not expecting to see her. "I didn't know you were in here with me." He spoke up as she rose walking towards him preceding to wipe him off.

"Connie what's going on between Sue and Pat?"

" I don't know, and to tell you the truth I could care less. My only concern is you but, I don't mine telling you. That I don't like what went on between you and Pat one damn bit. However, I also know that you had to get her out of your system, you have haven't you?" She looked him straight into his eyes asking."

"Connie she's my sister, there's no way I could ever get her out of my system. As for what we shared together I'm not going to deny that you're not right in what you are thinking.

Where I realize that it is something that I never really openly discussed with either you, or Sue. Mainly because I didn't know how to address what we shared together. Connie may I ask you a question?"

"Sure."

"Connie what is it that you see in me. That you don't see in any other guy? Look at me Connie there's nothing exceptional, or outstanding about me.

Where I'm not about to say that I'm not taking the utmost advantage of our relationship for I am. Where the irony of it all, as selfish as it must sound on my part. I don't ever want it to end."

"Art we choice you above all others because you are very special to us. Where all we have said, and shared together. Should have given you the answer that you are seeking. That is if you were listening.

Art loving someone isn't as easy as the word makes it sound. It's a very significant word that has a great many interpretations, as well as values but, for those that are truly in love words are meaningless.

The word love can't be defined mainly because no two, people share the same values or the same revelations from all they are feeling inside, just being with the other person.

That's what makes it so utterly fantastic, and accelerating. Because it's the imbalances that never really come together. With each one giving, or dominating the others obsessions, and expectations to want to unite in a common bound.

That never seems to be ever reached but, miraculously comes together. Where it is always the nerve-racking lingering aspirations of insatiably wanting more of each other. Where the more they strive the further it become to reach.

The strife, frustrations, and aspirations that one feels inside themselves is what draws one, together with the other. There's no answer as to why, or when those who become smitten with love. Where they themselves don't even know why.

I could be standing across a crawled room full of people, and I would still be drawn to you. By the magnetic force that binds us together.

I can't speak for Sue but, for myself I know why I have chosen you above all others. However, I am apprehensive about my feeling. Mostly about what I am feeling in the relationship. Especially to those I just described to you. Over how I came to them.

To be openly honest with you I didn't want, or expect them to happen where you are concern. For versions reasons that I already addressed with you.

Like I said before. This whole thing is totally crazy to begin with. I never expected it to get this far. Where there again a lot has developed that made it inedible to come about but, not as far as it has I'll admit that.

Hell I'm a grown mature woman who should have known better knowing. That this has been tried before, and that it was virtually impossible for it ever to work out where we are concerned. However, it's like I said. Something happened, and everything changed, and here I am like it, or not. I can't honestly say, that I'm in love with you."

"Connie, Pat's going to be getting married."

"She's what …?!" Connie ecstatically blurted out." Honey are you serious…?!"

"Yes, or so she told me. I know that I hurt you by doing what I did with her but, I had too. I had to find out where my real feeling really did lie.

Connie that which I thought I truly felt for Pat. Wasn't what I felt for her while she was holding me in her arms.

Yes, I love her but, what's so confusing about my love for her is. That I love her as my sister but, yet I feel so distant from her.

Oar's was a love that was never meant to last. It should have never been to begin with but, it was our way of life. That created it but, it's just not the same any longer.

She's changed… She feels cold, and disconcerting. Not only sexually but, emotionally as well. Like there's no life existing inside her, and she just does what is expected for a woman to do

Connie I have only known three, women in my life. Where through my feeling do differ between you, and Sue. I feel blessed by the divining hand of God himself. Just being close to either one of you.

I don't have to touch, or be held in your arms to be assured of my feeling towards you. Just being near you is all the insurance I need.

Connie I felt nothing with Pat. It just wasn't there for either of us anymore. It was all so meaningless, and unpleasing. Where I actually found myself struggling to get it over with..

Connie there was something about her that made me feel very comfortable. We shared a lot together but, it never went as far as it did today.

Yes, I was wanting it to happen but, it felt nothing like…?"

He questionably pondering searching for the word to express how he felt, and just couldn't find it.

* * * *

"Sue what is Connie doing in the bathroom so long with him?" Pat frustratingly asked.

Looking towards the closed bathroom door.

"I guess she's just trying to give us some time for us to talk."

"Sue I don't see anything for us to talk about. As long as the two, of you honor your agreement. You're not thinking about backing out on it by any chance, are you?"

"No, but, a few complications have arisen since we lasted talked. As you are obviously seen one, of them."

"You sure did a fantastic job I must say that. So what else has changed?"

"Pat we all have a great deal at stake here. Even are frustrations being high as well as or hopes but, until the dust settles down. We are all going to be at nerves end. Pat one, amongst three, doesn't go around."

"Now I see what you are driving at."

"No, you don't. Someday you are going to marry, and have children of your own. Where you are going to find very little time, if any to devote yourself, to very much of anything.

Where we on the other hand have nothing but, time to devote to our lives. What I'm trying to say is sharing is one thing but, total commitment is entirely a different matter."

"Sue I understand what you are trying to tell me, Where I hate to say it. You are absolutely right. You see I'm planning to get married very shortly.

That's why I took it upon myself to make a few alterations to my relationship with Art. To ensure our long lasting relationship will continue. I think I'm pregnant Sue.

"Pat are you sure?"

"Sue I was never more sure about anything, as I am about that. I'm pregnant alright. Tell me Sue what are you plaining on doing?"

"Nothing much really. Other that take care of my mice. Who I discovered just lately she going to be heading my way very soon.

Where I will eventually relocate somewhere else. Someplace outside the city where I can settle down after I'm married, and maybe have a few kids of my own.

I just have to see how everything turns out. One can only hope that things turn out for the best for all concern.

Sue let 's face it. This way is never going to work. There can only be one us. So how are you going to handle the competition?" Pat asked looking over towards the closed bathroom door.

"Sue I don't mind telling you that I don't like colored people. I owe her my gratitude but, nothing more. It makes my skin crawl to think of her having anything to do with Art."

"Now hold it right there! She's my friend I'll not tolerate anyone talking about her in any derogatory or slanderous manner! Just keep your personal opinions to yourself alright!"

"Hey, alright... I'm sorry. Jesus. I wish I could figure out from which direction you are coming from."

"My own! I'll go after what I want but, I'll do so with respect I'll not downgrade, or demean Connie. So back off her! The last thing you want is me losing my temper!"

Chapter 17

While all the manipulating, and controversy was going on in Pat's apartment. Jack and Joe were totally oblivious of any of what was being discussed. due to the fact that they were in the process of packing up their gear, and already disconnected all the hidden microphones in Pat's apartment.

Reprimanding each other for taking matters into their own hands. Berating each other over their stupidity, bickering back and forth. Blaming each other for going off have cocked barging in like they did.

"Damn you Joe! We will be lucky if you aren't canned for your stupidity. If that bitch goes to the captain. We will be lucky to only get busted back to a dog catcher!"

"My fault?! You actually have the gull to blame me for your blatant disregard for procedure! When it was you who go yourself all wound up, and went barging out the damn door. Darting over across the hall.

Knowing that I would have to follow you... I'm your partner, as well as your backup. If the captain gets wind of this. It's all going to be your damn fault, Asshole...!"

"Alright so I might have gotten a bit anxious but, you could have used a lot more decorum, in the way you handled things.

That bad cop routine doesn't work on everyone I'll have you know. You're the one, who blow it not me!"

"Just fuck off... Dammit!" We will simply tell the captain that we closed up early because nothing was going on, and if she shows up complaining. We will simply say. She must be thinking of someone else. No one else was there when we were, and that Pat bitch isn't going to say anything that's for damn sure. With all of what we have on her.

Hell, we will let him figure it out by playing ignorant, and let him figure it out. It's my guess He'll forget about it right after she leaves. So just finish packing up, and let's get the hell away from here."

* * * *

"Spare me the threats Sue they don't work with me."

"I'm not threatening you. I'm only saying that you don't put my only true friend down in front of me. She's more of a sister to me than you are to Art. That being said let's get back to his, welfare shall we."

"I guess that I own you that much after all you have done...., and seeing how I'm in no position to do anything else right now."

Connie, and Art came out of the bathroom. Where instantly Connie felt that something was wrong as they walked toward Sue, and Pat sitting on the edge of the bed.

" What is it Sue?" Connie nervously asked.

"We have to talk Connie. Just the three of us, privately. Let's go to the kitchen where we can talk in private. "I spoke up answering her with a disgusted tone to my voice

"Donna I want you to stay here until we come back. I mean it now this conversation is just for the three of us." I lead them out of the bedroom into the kitchen where we all sat around the table.

"Alright Pat it's obvious that you have something on your mind that you want to get out. Just between the three of us, so let's hear it." I started the around table conversation saying.

"Look you both know what I do for a living. It's what pays the bills around here, and let's face it. This is never going to work out.

I mean come on, let's get real about all this. You two, are grown women what could you want with a mere kid.

So I was thinking about, how we could all stand to make a small fortune here. That is if the three, of us would only take advantage of this golden opportunity you now presented regrading Art."

"Now just hold on one, second." Connie stopped Pat from saying anything more. As if already knowing what she was going to suggest.

" Pat you're not suggesting what I'm thinking you are about to suggest, are you?"

"What if I am Connie? How can it hurt him? We do it, and we are still alive. Where none of us look any worst for ware from doing it.

Besides thanks to the two, of you. He's more women now than he ever was a man. After a couple of time. Hell, it will become second nature to him.

Just like it did for us. Hell his own brother doesn't seem to be having a problem. He utterly gets off on being some guys bitch."

"You mean that you would actually sell out your own brother and turn him into a homosexual...?" Connie disbelievingly asked. Not believing what she was hearing.

"Look Connie I love him just as much as you both do but, I'm not about to go rotting in no cell for him. I'm not selling him out. He's going to make out on the deal, as well as we're."

"I think that we will just tell him about how you are so eager, and willing to sell him out to other guys." I threateningly implied"

"Go right ahead Sue tell him. He will never believe you. I'm is sister remember, and I can make him believe anything I want him to.

Where I've been with him a lot longer than either of you two, have. Where let's not forget that I have the same thing you two, do neither of you

Where I can give him everything you have been giving him. As long as he get it he's not going to give a damn who he gets it from.

He'll hate you for telling lies about me. Which you will wind up losing him anyway and you can't touch me. Where if you did, and he found out.

Which he will. He'll never forgive either of you. Neither of you have any choice but, to go along with me. Where let's not forget. Even though I can't prove it but, the fact that you are with him. Is enough to tell me that it was one, or both of you who were involved in killing that oriental girl.

Whereas even if I'm wrong just by suggesting it to the cops, would cause them to suspect one, or both of you.

I have you by your short hairs and you know it. Hell, I'm not saying that you still can't get yours from him. Hell, go for it. If that what turn the two, of you on."

"Pat don't force us into an uncompromising position." Connie threateningly said." You have no idea of what lengths we would go through for him."

"Don't threaten me Connie. I don't frighten so easily. Beside Sue here already tried that, and as you can see. I'm still here. Especially when I know that I'm in the position of authority.

His ass is no different than mine he'll get used to it. Now come on let not keep him waiting."

She authoritatively demanded walking towards the kitchen door them out it. Leading Sue and Connie out into the living room. Where she sat down in the easy chair, and Connie and I sat on the sofa

" Sue I want you to get back, and stay with Donna. Connie, and I have to speak alone."

Sue left going into the bedroom. Finding Art sleeping soundly, laying upon the bed as she closes the door behind her. Walking towards the bed. Going to wake him up.

"What's happening...?" Donna asked. Only to snapping out of his slumber inquisitively asking." Is there something the matter......? "

" Honey I need to get you, and Connie out of here...!"

" Then what are we waiting for... Let's go..." He grabbed my arm attempting to pull me up off the bed.

"No, Donna." I pulled him back down suppressing his state of urgency. Only to hear a massive explosion sound. Then feeling the floor shaking ramblingly beneath my feet.

With Pat, and Connie coming bursting in through the bedroom door. With Pat frantically shouting.

" Thank God... you're alright...! As Connie slammed the door shout, then stood placing her hands against the door, feeling it for heat.

"Shit...!" She alarmingly shouted out." There's a fire...The door is hot... Everyone back away from the door, and stay away from the windows ...!"

She went about hastily covering the bottom of the door with the blankets from off the bed. Hoping to keep the smoke out long enough until the fire department got to them.

Where they were actually three, stories up counting the lobby. Too far up to jump without getting injured. Where Donna was still dress as a woman, and not fully healed from her previous ordeal. Where as if he attempted to jump he could wind up killing himself. Along with exposing that he was wearing a disguise, and not a girl but, a boy.

Whereas luck had it. Within minutes Connie could hear sirens approaching getting louder. and louder.

Causing her to feel certain that they were going to be alright. As she took control over their situation. Telling everyone to get down on the floor below the windows.

Knowing that the glass could shatter at any time from the heat of the fire burning outside their door.

Where Sue then jerked up, and ran into the bathroom. Turning on all the faucets, and clogging the drains. To let the water flood over down onto the floor. So that it would sock the carpeting, hopefully prolong the fire from burning through the door. Then went back and joined the others carrying shocked towels with her to cover over Donna.

Where a demanding knocking sound came against the door. Then someone voice shouting." Is there anyone in there?!"

"Yes...!" Connie yelled back answering the voice." There's four, of us in here."

"Just stay calm we will have you out of there in no time. Just don't open the door, and stay low to the floor."

Instantly Connie recognized the voice Carl's. "Carl is that you...? It's me Connie."

"Connie...?!" Connie it's me Carl... I'm here. I hear you! Just stay calm, you're going to be just fine..."

"Carl what in the hell happened...?"

"Just a minor mishap nothing to become concerned about. We have it all under control, or soon will have. Just stay put."

"Alright Pat just what's going on here?! There's something you're not telling me dammit! I just fell to sleep for a second, and all hell breaks loose."

" Art believe me." Pat frightfully cried out." I didn't have anything to do with any of this...!"

"Do with what...! Come on out with it Pat."

"Stop it the both of you right now!" Connie infuriatingly shouted out. Stopping the chaos going on between Art and Pat shouting back and forth at each other.

" Both of you need to shut your damn mouths. Before they put us all behind bars Dammit! Nothing else is important right now. Than us getting are assess the hell out of here Dammit! So stop your damn fucking auguring!"

A loud crashing sound startled everyone. As two, fire fighters came busting through the closet door beside Pat's dresser.

Exposing a hidden room behind the dressers mirror with a camera sitting on a tripod. Pointing directly at her bed, that was indulged in flames.

"So that's what you were going to use to persuade us to go along with you..." Connie infuriatingly said, whispered out at Pat. Hoping not to draw any attention to any of them.

"Go along with what...?" Donna skeptically asked.

"Not now... Later..." Connie irately snapped back. Pulling Donna up onto her feet. After which Sue went off searching with Connie. Searching Pat's secret room.

As the fire fighters continue to put out the flames not paying any mind to the arguing going on between everyone else.

"Hey...!" Pat alarmingly yelled out." This is my room. You have no right to search through my things!"

"Calm down sis." Donna grabbed hold of her shoulders. Holding her back as she attempted to get free. To stop Connie, and I from searching what remained of Pat's secret room.

" Sis I don't know what you have been up to but, they wouldn't be searching that place if they thought it didn't involve something about us. Until they find out you are staying right here with me...."

Connie and I shockingly found out. That it wasn't only the camera that was burning. As they stood looking into the smoke filled compartment still burning but, there was also shelves full of films canisters as well. That the fire fighters were spraying with water trying to put the flames out.

"Ladies you are going to have to move away." One of the fire fighters yelled out.

Shoving them back away from the burning compartment. Back to where Donna was restraining Pat. Then going back to fighting the fire.

"Donna." Sue pulled her aside." Now isn't the time to tell you what your sister was attempting to force us to do to you.

However, it should be very obvious when all you have to do is to take a look at what was going on behind that dresser mirror. To give you a damn good idea of what she was up to, where you were concern."

"Pat tell me that what I'm hearing isn't true."

"I don't have to tell you a damn thing!" She defiantly rebelled. Shoving Donna back away from her. Not giving the fire fighters a second thought. That they could overhear what she was yelling back at Donna about.

"You're all such fools...! Do you think I'm in this alone...? Do you...?!

You don't know who you're dealing with!"

"Alright the fires out." One of the fire fighters yelled out. Interrupting the argument that was going on.

" Just stay away until things cool down some. We need to go check out the rest of the apartment. Just remain here until we let you know it's safe for you to leave."

He disappeared stepping back through the hole they made, from the other side of wall into the closet.

Which it didn't take Pat more than a second to go back to yelling at Donna. Defending her position against the accusation Connie and I made against her.

"Why shouldn't I take advantage of his only asset...?! Let's face it ladies the both of you sure as hell are to get yours!

You two, morbid deranged boards are going to get yours ...! What's the matter ladies can't you handle a man...? Is that why you resorted to molesting children...?!"

"Shut up Pat!" Art infuriatingly shouted out at her. Nervously looking around hoping that no one was listening to what she was yelling out about? Connie, and Sue.

" Just shut you rotten disgusting mouth!" He annoyingly spoke out in a lower tone of voice.

"You're not going to insult your way out of this. Now just shut up before I forget that I'm your brother, and ring you damn fucken neck! What are you trying to do get us all arrested?!"

"No Art." Connie interrupted his aggressive mature." We don't need you to defend us against the likes of her.

Listen to me girl. What you said might be true but, with one exception. We know where are heads are at. We don't have to settle for anything we don't want to! Where you have to tolerate your revolting pathetic self!

You give your ass for nothing, where we give it with meaning, and compassion. You want to gain profit from it. Where we just give for the sake of giving from out of affection with sincerity.

Are whorish ways, as well as our affections are taking us someplace. Where yours is getting you nowhere but, deep and deeper into you own animosity. Over hating yourself for what you are."

"Shut the fuck up your black bitch!" Pat obstinately yelled out. Startling us all! Causing us to panicky look over to the open door of the closet, and the large hole opening coming through the other side of it.

"That's enough!" Art infuriatingly shouted out. Grabbing up a blouse laying on the bed. Wrapping it about her mouth, gagging her.

When shoving her back against the wall beside the bed out of sight from the bedrooms still closed door. Irately mad enough to want to slam his fist in her mouth.

" Now that will shut you the hell up! Come on let's just get the hell out of here!"

"We Can't." Connie reprimanded him saying." There's no way to insure her silence... She knows all about you. If she would sell you out for a cheap film, what is she going to do when the police come talk to her?"

"There's no way she's going to do that!" Art irately snapped back saying." She's an accessory to murder. If she so much as says a word I'll see to it that she spends the rest of her life imprison right along with me. I saw what she did to that poor girl. I saw you murder her right before my eyes. So go ahead and tell the cops.

I'll say anything to insure you do dear sister... And what I don't know I'll make up. There's no way you could explain us being here with you. Without implicating yourself. Believe me this is far from over sis.

If those film are what I think they are you're going to be so damn busy explaining them to the cops. Let along to the people you were making them for. Let's not forget those people you are obviously using to pay the rent for this place.

The way I'm seeing it my dear, and loving sister. You are in no position to do a damn thing but, to keep you big revolting month shut! "Art preceded to untie the gag, and walked her out of the bedroom.

While Connie and I preceded to gather up as many of the unburnt films as we could. Shoving them into are overnight bags. Before going out to join up with Pat, and Donna.

In what was left of the living room. As the fire fighters went about making sure that the fire was out.

Where other went about investigating what could have cause the explosion. Discovering that it was the camera itself that started the fire from overheating. Which started an electrical fire, that shorted out an electrical outlet that was overloaded in the kitchen. That created the gas explosions from a defective polite light on the stove.

"Alright you two." I softly spoke up getting their attention. " Let's just put a hold on what's going on between us until we can do it in private."

"Private my ass! Pat defiantly rebutted. Once again not caring who was around to hear. As Donna reached up grabbing hold of the back of her neck. Giving it an aggressive threatening squeeze.

"Don't do it... I don't have anything to lose here sis. Keep it down or I'll see to it that I will make you regret the day you were born...!"

"You are fools..." She quietly replied back as Art continued to squeeze the back of her neck.

" If you think that you're going to get away with this you're not! Maybe you will where the cops are concern but, not from the syndicate you're not.

They will follow you no matter where you would go. That's who those films belong to, and they are worth a fortune to them.

If you think the cops are bad. The cops are just babies compare to them. They have eyes and ears everywhere.

It's only going to be a matter of time before they catch up with all of you. Where you can be damn sure I'm going to tell them who has them. So you damn well better give them back before it's too late.

Don't kid yourselves. All of you should have taken me up on my offer. The three, of you are all losers! I'm going to be the only one, who's going to survive this. If you don't change your minds now.

I will can get you out of here, and away from the cops. I have the connections. Now is going to be your last chance to save your hides.

I will even use my influence with the syndicate to get Donna here set up in her own place, as well as the two, of you. It's not such a bad life, once you get used to it."

"You don't frighten me Pat. Connie stepped forth getting up in her face saying. "I cut my eye teeth on those degenerate morons.

You have no idea just how ruthless, and unscrupulous they know I can be. You make sure to tell them that I Connie Price the swamp girl took them."

"Did you say Connie Price the swamp girl from Ohio? That Connie Price...?!" Pat disbelievingly gasped out fearfully asking.

"So you've heard of me have you?"

"Who hasn't...?! Why you are a legion... Art do you have any idea who this woman is...?! She's a notorious exterminator. An extremely vicious, diabolical killer, who terrorized three. notorious crime families.

Her along with ten others eliminated over 100 hundred people. Bringing the syndicate down to its knees.

The more men they sent out after her. The more she would mail them back in boxes marked

"dog meat."

Her and her she devils. They would come out from nowhere, and disappear into nothing like phantom evil demons straight out of hell.

Killing with their bare hands, leaving only one, alive to tell about what happened. Killing their way right up to the head kingpin himself. When she then she cut off his fingers up to his knuckles, on both of his hands.

In one, night they killed over twenty-five men without a single one of them firing a single shot... My, God! Art she's Connie Price...!"

"What are you talking about? That can't be her. Connie is nothing like the person you are speaking of."

"It is her dammit! She can't be anyone else but, her. No one else would ever acknowledge herself as being her.

I don't know how it all came about but, it had something to do with a plantation, and a baby girl that started the uprising...

Art all but one, were black girls at the time. The one that wasn't. The head boss married. Where afterwards she remained with him. After they made a pack to end all the killing.

Art that was just over four, years ago. You can't stay with her, not after what I just told you about her. She's a killer of the worst kind!"

"Pat nothing Connie has done would matter in the least. I will accept her fate as if it was my own."

"Damn you Art! She's going to get you killed! Don't you understand that?! She's a demon possessed with the damnation of hell itself inside her...

You foolish, blind headed dope! She's not worth your life. She's a mentally disturbed sadistic killer...

What makes you think she won't kill you when she gets tired of you? You know too much about her for her to let you live now. She can't let you just walk out of her life just like that! You can't be that big of a fool?!"

"Pat no one lives forever. Every moment I spend with Connie and Sue is like living an eternity of shear happiness. Say what you want about her. It matters not to me. If she is who you claim her to be. I rather have my life in her hands than in yours.

Pat I look upon you, and I feel loathing and disgust for what you have become. If others in the human race turned out to be like you. We all might as well end are suffering here, and now, and all cut our own throats.

You think of nobody but, yourself, and you prey like a vulture gorging yourself on the decayed flesh. Of those that show any signs of emotion for you. It's not I that has to live in fear. Where the way I see it. It's you.

I don't fear death I was resurrected from it. I only exist for right now.

There's no tomorrow there's only now.

If you, or anyone dares threaten to take away from me. Any precious moment of my existence I will rise up from hell itself. As vindictive as the devil himself to reap my revenge.

You make her out as she is the most terrible person who every walked the face of this earth. Well fuck with me, and she'll be nothing equal to the wrath I will lay down upon you, or anyone else. Who would dare harm a hair on either of their heads...! An I making myself clear...?!"

"My, God...! They brainwashed you...! You didn't seem to mine me imposing upon your principles when you were getting yours from me?"

"Pat you have never impose upon me, until now but, you have been doing so to yourself all your life. You yourself made the hell you are (wailing) in now.

You hate Connie and Sue for having the one thing that you fear the most." Free will" Where I must admit I always have been dependent upon you. Where you never let me down, again until now.

Where we have come a long way together but, we never really came close to one, another. Where what we really shared was our fears.

We hide ourselves within that fear. Using what we shared to hide ourselves in thinking that it gave us a reason to want to survive.

All of which has brought us to where we really belong. With us going are separate ways. It's not going to be good-bye but, fair well. My place is with Connie, and Sue that's where I belong now because I emerged from that fear to find happiness."

"Connie you know what's going to happen as well as I do." Pat sympathetically cried out to her." Are you willing to accept the responsibility for his life?"

"Art she's right about me but, I didn't like to have to kill... There's just so much I haven't been able to tell you about myself."

"I don't care dammit! I swear if either of you dare to leave me now. I'll walk out that door stake ass naked! I know what I'm doing.

Why can't you see what's she's trying to do? She trying to turn us against each other? If you let her do that. So be it but, don't except me to remain like this. Without any hopes of living again...

Shit...! Now who the hell is that...?!" Art angrily blurted out hearing someone call out Connie's name.

"Hey you in there it's me Carl..." Carl entered the living room. Coming to tell them that it was all clear, and the fire was out. As they all stood taking amongst themselves with the entire place in a shambles

"Sorry about the apartment but, it was a lucky thing that you were all in the bedroom when the explosion took place. Someone could have been seriously hurt.

The nearest that we can figure is that an electrical movie camera caught fire, and the electrical wiring heated up, and started another fire in the kitchen. Where the gas from the stove caused the explosion.

The renter of the apartment will mostly have to stay but, the rest of you are free to go find some other place to spend the night."

The Three, of us look directly at Pat not knowing what she was going to do or say.

"Yes, you best be going. Sorry you can't spend the night but, as you can see. It's not possible now. By the way you three." Pat spoke out getting their attention." I think it's best if we don't see each other for the time being.

It's been nice seeing you again Sue. I will call you the next time. Take care now, I wish I could say things are going to be alright but, as you can see I'm most likely going to have to find myself another place to live.

By the way Sue I wouldn't be moving back to Ohio I hear it's going to be unbearable to live there."

"Thanks for the advice Pat. I will take it under consideration. You take care of yourself now. Come on you two, we best be going. We had enough excitement for one night."

"Hold it right there everyone." Phil demandingly spoke out holding is badge out in front of him. With his partner Jerry standing behind him blocking the door saying.

" FBI no one is going anywhere just yet. Back inside all of you." He stepped in forcing are group back into the apartment.

"Sorry for barging in on you like this Carl but, it's official business." Phil walked pass him saying, up to Pat." Are you Pat Miners wife of detective Frank Miners?"

"Why yes, I am… What's the matter …? Did something happen to him…? He's alright isn't he…?!"

"Well he's alive but, he's far from being alright. He's under arrest for soliciting prostitution, extortion, and amongst other things.

We would like for you to accompany us down to headquarters. Without having to place you under arrest. Just for questioning you understand.

It appearing that he has implicated you, along with others as being in league with his illegal activities. One of having connections with him being a hit-man for the syndicate.

Are the three, of you involved with this woman here?" He turned his attention on the three, of us asking."

" It's alright Phil I can vouch for them." Carl stepped forwards speaking up for us." I know them all personally. I can assure you they had nothing to do with any of her and her husband's illegal activities.

We had this woman under police surveillance for some time now, and we were fully aware of her husband's involvement with criminal ties. I'm totally up to date as to why they were here I'll personally vouch for them"

"Alright them ladies the three, of you can leave but, try to be more selective of your friends next time. This one here came from the button of the bad apple barrel, she's going to be going away for a very long time."

"'Thank you." Sue spoke up leading us out of the apartment, and out of the apartment building. Walking us down the street past all the activity going on about it us. Coming to a stop when we reached the corner.

"Now what Sue?" Art asked." Isn't there something we can do to help her?"

" Art honey, we are in our own troubles up over our necks now. The police are one thing, but the FBI...? There's no telling what they have on your sister.

There's no way we can't risk exposing ourselves more than we already have. She's made her bed now, let her lie in it. Don't forget she tried to set us up as well, to sell you out.

She no more your sister than I am. Blood is thicker than water and that girl has none of yours running though her vanes.

She's out for herself, and no one else. She's demonstrated her love, and devotion towards you expressing the way she feels about you."

"What if she tells on us?"

"Let her no one's going to believe her. The authorities will only think that she's trying to lie her way out of her own mess."

"Sue where are we heading how?" Connie annoyingly asked trying to change the subject.

"Back to are apartment where we should have gone to begin with. We could all use some peace, and quiet and a good night sleep. We're still paid up to the end of the mouth. We'll go to are new place later on, after we're sure nothing more is going to happen..."

Chapter 18

"Alright Pat I'm here now." Cliff, Pat 's attorney was sent to represent her by the syndicate. Sat beside her on the sofa. Who arrived only moments after Connie, Art, and I left Pat's apartment.

Cliff was a high priced criminal lawyer who represented a lot of the low end criminals. Assign to act in the syndicates best interests. Who was also representing Pat's husband Frank.

Phil's plan was working perfectly. Allowing Pat's attorney to talk him out of arresting her. However during which, he put the squeeze on her about him knowing about her husband's actives with the syndicate. As well as informing her that he is getting very close to locating her brother Art.

While during having the apartment searched they came upon several ledgers that were hidden under some loose boards under the bed but, they were in some sort of code.

Along with several burnt canisters of film that he didn't inform her about. That were now being sent down to the bureau. Before he left her apartment along with the fire fighters, and the investigative group of police officers. Leaving her alone with her lawyer.

"Alright Pat now you can tell me what really happened here."

"Cliff what's going on with Frank?"

"Not now Pat. He's not the issue here where you are. Now tell me, or I'm working out that door, and leaving you on your own."

"Alright dammit! I tried to set up a con with two, of my girlfriends, that I had spending the night here... Cliff it all happened so damn fast. By the time I realized what was happening it was too late for me to do anything but, go along with it. Hoping that until I could contact you. I could stall them from taking anything out of the place before you arrived.

How was I supposed to know that a damn fire as going to break out from the camera hidden in that compartment behind my dresser, and caused an electrical fire in the kitchen, and the damn stove exploded."

"Alright I understand how that could have happened. However, what's with those two, girlfriends of yours?"

"Well, they are not really my girlfriends I meet the one, named Sue when I went to visit my brother at the Adoption Center.

Where out of nowhere she called, and ask to spend the night. I had no idea that she was going to bring some black girlfriend of her's along with her.

Well that Sue is a real looker. All I was trying to do was bring some fresh meat into the organization but, it backfired. Besides that one as got an ass on her, and knowing you the way I do I just know you would love to get it on with her."

"Knock it off Pat and get to what went down here, and stop beating around the brush dammit!"

"Alright… damn lighten up will you Jesus. The reason for the cops and the fire fighter for being here should be obvious. That damn stove blows a hole in the kitchen wall.

As for the cops. They weren't the cops but, the damn FBI. Who came with the fire fighters, and that damn detective made it known that they are still looking for my brother. Where by the way he's saying it? They are getting damn close to finding him.

Whereas you know he escaped from the orphanage. Where he's being sought as being the prime suspect being involved in three, deaths that occurred the night he runaway.

Cliff that's not all, there's still more. That black bitch not only found but, also went into the compartment behind the dresser.

Because those damn fire fighters came breaking through the wall of the closet and exposed the camera. Where the nosey bitch went in, as well as took a bunch of the unburnt films.

I demanded her to put them back, and she won't. Even after I told her who those films belonged to. That's when she gave me a message saying that I should tell you. Cliff she told me to tell you her name. She said her name was thee Connie Price... Cliff she also told me to say. That she'll be expecting a visit."

"That's just fucken great...!" Cliff irritatingly spoke out." And now that bitch is here, and has become involved ... That sheds a whole different light on this entire situation! Lucky for her. Not from us she won't.

Now what's this again about the FBI. Did the cops, or the FBI find anything else. Like maybe something hidden underneath the floor underneath your bed?"

"I don't know anything about any of that stuff. You know Frank better than I do. I only married him to front for the organization like I was told to do.

You don't suppose he could have been a plant, and it could had been stuff on the organization. Hidden aright under my very nose, no less?

It sure smiles like he might be. You know as well as I do that once the FBI starts to come after someone, that they don't give in until they get who they are going after, Where I heard that detective say . That they are keeping Frank under wraps where no one can get at him?"

"Well it's a sure thing that they are obviously up to something. That I'm sure of. However, you just let me handle it. Where from here on out, just don't be saying anything without having me with you. I mean not a single word."

"Cliff what about those two, whores. Are you just going to let them get away with what they took from us?"

"I don't know yet. I'm going to hold off taking any action until I find out for certain what we are going to do about them.

We might have to bring in some outside help, to deal with them. Where that won't be so easy once they hear who they will going after.

That is if in fact she was the real Connie Price. That was in fact the woman you had here. Where I'm hoping that's not the case."

"What's going to happen to me now?"

"Nothing. However, consider yourself on a paid vacation for the time being. We can find a replacement for Frank, and start up all over again. Just stick to the roles and you'll be just find.

However Pat I have to admit. That if it wasn't for your track recorder with the organization, you would be too hot to handle. If you get my meaning. Just stay the hell out of trouble. I best be going now, here."

He handed her several hundreds." Go find yourself a place to say, and get in touch with me. To let me know where you are. Don't go wondering off on me now... "

He walked towards the door, then out of the apartment. Leaving knowing that she wasn't worth the risk of having around to the organization. Knowing that her days were numbered.

* * * *

" Amah..." Art cuddly moaned out, laying in between Connie and Sue on the bed in their old apartment." How this is he life..."

"Just be quite and go to sleep." I spoke out to him nestling up against him. Hugging him in-between Connie and I. Watching his eyes close whereas his mine obviously was refusing to let him become restful. As he kept restlessly tossing, and turning, and squirming about in

a state of unrest. Obviously his mind wasn't letting him stop from thinking about all that happened.

Little did Connie, and Sue know that his mind wasn't letting going of the thought of Connie actually killing someone before, and then again because of him. Was deeply preying on his mind. Then the thoughts of his own sister turning against him. Wanting to sell him like he was a peace of meant.

Only to find out that his own sister was actually involved in a criminal syndicate. Was startling to get to be far too much for him to bare mentally.

Them him contemplating that the syndicate might actually come after Connie herself. Was just too much for his mind to bare.

"My God…!" Art cried out frightfully saying." Where, or when is it all going to end…!" As he jerked himself out from between them yelling out.

Jumping out of bed. As if blaming himself for everything that happened, and is still going to continue to happen. Where he was helpless to do anything about preventing it from happening. As if his mind was increasingly attacking him persecuting him for all that happened. Mindlessly walking over to the window.

Opening it to stand before it. To just stare out aimlessly into the darkness of the night. As if struggling to try to find something. That would make his being mean something, besides hardships, dismay, and total anguish to everyone he came to love in his life, including himself.

Causing himself to think that he was doomed since the day he was born. Persecuting himself for bringing death, and damnation down upon those he loved, including his own mother as well.

"Oh, Jesus…!" He startlingly jumped back. Alarmingly blurting out, feeling something coming around his waist. Shocking him out of his minds train of thoughts.

"Hey… Calm down its only me…" Connie spoke out to him.

"Oh, Connie…" He pathetically cried out. Spinning around in her arms, grabbing her around her waist. Frightfully squeezing her with all his might up against him.

"Hey… What's wrong…?" She consolingly asked. Looking into his eyes. Knowing something was seriously troubling him.

"I'm so scared Connie. So very scared… I love you so much, and look what my love for you makes you do…? Look what I'm doing to you… Too both of you?

I'm ruining your lives because of me … I destroy everything I love… I'm destroying yours… Can you ever forgive me…?"

He sorrowfully pleaded. To suddenly stand, pushing her back away from him speaking out affirmatively.

"I don't want to love you anymore…! Do you hear me…?! I hate you! I hate you both...!" He deliriously screamed out. Stepping back further out of her arms.

"You're a Niger...! A Niger... Whore...! You are both sluts... I hate you ...! Do you hear me?! I hate you both...! I can't let this go on any longer...!"

"Holy Shit...!" I alarmingly yelled out. Being awaken from out of a slumberous restful sleep by Art's raving.

Jumping up out of bed, running up to stand beside. Connie standing before him, as he braced himself back against the wall. Panicky stretching out the palms of his hands baring Connie from approaching him. Diligently staring aimlessly at her.

"Sue... What's happening to him...?! Look at him ... My God! Sue look at him..." Connie frantically asked. Panicky looking at Sue in desperation, not knowing what to do.

"Just calm down Connie. I think that I know what's happening to him. He's blaming himself for everything that's happened.

I thought this was going to happen eventually. He's having a nervous breakdown becoming distraught..."

"You are bitches...! Get out of here...! You revolt and disgust me...! Go back to the gutter where you belong... Get the hell out of my sight!!"

"Connie we have to bring him out of this... Go turn on the shower, and make it ice cold. Now Dammit! Move it dammit!" I shouted out at her, causing her to run towards the bathroom.

"Alright Art." I authoritatively spoke out to him." I know what you're trying to pull with this act of yours.

You want us to hate you ... Why should we. When you are doing such a great job of hating yourself?

You know something? You are pathetically revolting. You are a selfish egotistical bigoted hypocrite...! You are disgustingly sickening... Do you hear me...?! Sickening...

You mind is so wrapped in your fantasy world. It can't relate to what's real. Because you can't accept your life for what it is, or life as it really is.

You are running away from yourself, and the life you have for yourself. It's not life that's persecuting you it's you persecuting it.

That's right cower, cry, throw your tantrums. Like the misfit that you are. Go ahead Waller yourself in hate and self-pity.

No one's going to hate you, and you are not going to hate anyone, or yourself... You are blaming yourself for all that's happened to you. When there's nothing to blame yourself for, because you have fond out things. That are disrupting your fantasy world. Where you are having to force yourself to accept the truth. That goes against how you want to picture your life to be.

You want us to hate you, because you think you are at fault for everything that's happening to us but, you're not. When no one is.

We had a plan, and still do. Nothing is gone it's still going to happen. You just have to give it time.

The ones who are responsible are people like that matron, your father, and your sister. Then having the misfortune of being continuously victimized, and persecuted by society. That you are letting yourself get all caught up within you... Come to me Art..." I called out to him with open sympathetic arms. Seeing Connie hastily emerging from the bathroom.

"Art honey Connie and I are here for you. We know that you love us as much as we love you. We aren't going to let anything happen to either of us. You have to believe that.

We are what's real. We never lied to you,

You are just upset right now. You are just succumbing to an overabundance of frustrations that you are not prepared to handle mentally.

Trust me Art it will all pass. You need to talk to us so we can help you deal with what is bothering you. You can't continue to keep holding it inside. It's not going to go away by keeping it all locked up. We all have to share ourselves with each other and open ourselves up to each other to release the pressure that is mentally tormenting us.

We can't speak for you sister, nor can you feel guilty for the path she chose to follow in her life. She has to live with it. It's not yours to live with where you have to live for yourself, and us... That is the path you chose along with us.

Come to me Art. Don't let yourself bare the burdens of the past, when you have only to live for a bright future with us..."

He came forlornly walking into my arms. I walked him into Connie's waiting arms. Where we both walked him into the bathroom. Where all three, of us walked into the running shower together.

"I've him Sue he'll be alright now." Connie spoke out taking control of him, closing the shower curtain braving the ice cool water that was beating down upon his head, and shoulder.

As I stepped out of the shower to get out of my wet clothes and dry myself off. Then went back out into the bedroom, to sit on the edge of the bed to think about how everything was beginning to effect Art's mind, and mental condition.

While noticing Connie coming out of the bathroom leaving Art alone in the shower, drying her hair with her socked shortly pajama's dripping wet.

" He's doing alright by himself now Sue. I best get out of these wet clothes, and get something dry for Art to put on when he gets out."

We both sat on the bed waiting for him to come out wrapped in towels. Totally at a loss as how we were going to handle what just happened. Basically because we never expected what happen to ever happen. Thinking what happened between his sister and the three, of us. Was to traumatic on me for him to mentally handle.

"Connie we are going to have to keep him secluded for a while longer. He's beginning to become emotionally disoriented.

What he needs is rest, and peace of mind. It's all just too much for his mind to handle. I'm amazed that he handled it this long.

We're going to have to keep him in a peaceful environment for the time being. He can't take much more, before his mind could snaps. Where his body is barely healed from the physical beating that he took."

Art came walking out of the bathroom drying himself off passively speaking out. Saying "I'm out now. I'm so very sorry... I don't know what came over me...?"

"We do." I replied looking up at him." Now get out of those wet clothes, and into some dry ones. Then back into bed." I sternly but, sympathetically spoke out. Taking advantage of his consoled attitude. To establish who was in authority and holding myself responsible for what happens. Hopefully attempting to relieve him of the burden of holding himself accountable.

"Yes, Sue." He sorrowfully replied shamefully. Reluctant to look at us, doing as I told him. Then climbed back into bed.

"You are both mad at me for what I said aren't you? I wish saying that I was sorry would erase the memory of it all but, it won't. So I won't even bother...Good night." He rolled over on his side turning, burying his face down into the pillow.

"Oh, no you don't." I annoyingly spoke out pulling him back over onto his back. Here take this... It's a sleeping pill, you need your rest, now take it."

He took it from my hand, and swallowed it down." There I took it. Now are you satisfied...?" He rolled back over onto his side, this time kept his face exposed.

* * * *

The next morning Connie and I let Art sleep. I knew the sleeping pill I gave him would keep him out for a good 12, hours.

While we took turns watching over him. We moved things around getting things ready for the movers, packing things up to be placed into the moving van. That we wanted to carry ourselves along with us.

Where the apartment came mostly furnished so we had very little that had to be move by the movers. Where we didn't want Art to be disturbed.

When I was sitting on the edge of the bed when Art unexpectedly opened his eyes sooner than I anticipated he would.

"Well and a good day to you... Have a nice restful sleep did you?" I greeted him asking.

" Boy did I ever..." Art** stretchily woke himself saying." What time is it?"

" It's almost 4 PM."

"4 PM...?!" He startlingly jerked himself up blunting out." Why did you let me sleep so long.? Where's Connie...?" He looked around the bedroom asking appearing to be unnerved about not being able to see her.

"Calm down there's nothing to become alarmed about. Connie's over at the other house getting things in order. Have you forgotten that we were supposed to be moving today?"

"I guess I forget." He replied leaning back against the head board of the bed." Sue I'm so

terribly sorry about last night. I just don't know what could have gotten into me?"

"I do, and it will pass but, you've to learn not to become so excited over the least little thing. I know we have gone through some very trying, and difficult times but, they are all behind us now.

As for what you found out about Connie, and yours sister. It's best that you found out now rather than later. Now forget about what you learned. It's baggage you don't need to carry around with you. What's past is past."

You are going to have to learn to understand, that there is something in all our lives that we feel are best forgotten, and best left unknown to anyone but, ourselves.

Art you have to live for the way life really is, not what Connie and I have been bestowing upon you. By us doing so isn't helping you rationalize the condition we are having to deal with. In order for you to concentrate on the fact.

That we can't allow ourselves to become invoked in someone else problems. Here doing so could and most likely will distract from our own problems.

We can't let ourselves forget the seriousness of our own plight where we can't afford to lose touch, or becoming traumatized to the point where it will endanger are on welfare.

You know as well as we do that we have been catering, and patronizing you by. Over protecting you from being discouraged, or resentful towards us because of all that's happened.

Where we can't continue to keep you in a glass bowl, from what you might hear, or still going to have to deal with from others. Last night is over, and we're still here.

Where this is a new day that none of us knows what lies ahead of us. So let's just try to keep it under are control and not let it get out of hand like yesterday did.

"I don't know if I can forget and start anew Sue. Where after last night there's no telling what's going to happen next. I'm not about to forget what I said. The stench of my words still cling to the roof of my mouth. Especially where Connie is concern."

"Art I realize that you are concern about what happened last night but, your primary concern should be us, As well as the fact that you're here with us, because we want you to be, not because we have to be together. Especially all that has happened seeing how everything has become all distoraghted all out of proportion.

I don't know if you realize what happened to you last night but, what you had was a nervous breakdown.

The tension is getting to you because you are refusing to except what you are hearing. Not giving any consideration to whether it's true or not.

So I suggest that you just stop thinking about everything, and just let Connie and I handle things for the time being, yourself, and us, and what is going on in our lives for right now."

" Sue people have died because of me. Where how many more will be made to suffer the same fate because of me?

I grant you they might have deserved to die but, I was still responsible for them dying I'm just not worth the two, of you ruining your lives over. What if Pat follows through with her threat, by telling that syndicate she's working for about us and what we have that belongs to the syndicate?"

"Hey... I'm back..." Connie shouted out entering the front door of the apartment. Closing it behind her yelling out.' Hey... Is anyone home...? It's me Connie..."

"We are in the bedroom Connie." I yelled out to her.

" Well look here... He's awake..." Connie spoke out standing in the open doorway of the bedroom.

" Now isn't that just like a man to lay around all day. While the women of the house do all the work. So, how are you feeling love?"

She asked walking to join Sue sitting on the bed beside him sitting down beside her. Smiling at Art acting as if nothing what so ever happened where I was concerned the night before.

"Terrible Connie, just terrible... Over all that I said to you last night I'm going to hate myself until the day I die for all I said to the both of you.

Connie I know how I must have really hurt you but, I wanted the both of you to hate me. I didn't care if it was killing me inside."

" Hush, Art. Let's just forget it sugar. We know why you were saying what you were. I don't like what happened any more than you do but, you're not at fault.

Just remember the only thing you are guilty of is loving us. However you have to remember that it's a jungle out there. Where one must do what one has to do, in order to survive out there.

However now the answer to that question not only affects you but, on us as well.

Where you are concern. Regarding weather ,or not we hate you for you doing what you did, and said last night. In as far as the answer is going to reflect on are future happiness."

"Connie I know what I said last night. Like I said before, my words will never leave my mind, or elevate the scares they are going to leave upon my heart. Where I honestly do love you both with all my heart.

Where yes, it's very important to me. That you don't hate me, and that you do believe that I mean every word I say to the both of you. Where after saying what I said how can I expect you to believe anything I say to either of you."

"Love all you need to do is to look into my eyes to see what is in my heart for you. Go ahead look into my eyes sugar and see for yourself. Where there's no need for you to bother telling me. I already know what you are seeing.."

Art looked into her eyes breaking down emotionally as his eye filled with tears of remorse over what he said.

." Connie please forgive me, and believe me that with all my heart and soul I honestly do love you.." He reached out to take her in his arms saying. Attempting to pull her towards him to kiss her.

"Oh, no you don't." Connie spoke out holding him at bay arm's length away. With the palms of her hands against his chest." You're not going to get me all excited. Now just keep those loveable hands of you to yourself."

"You don't believe me..."

"But I do. Why do you think I told you to keep your hands to yourself? I will melt like butter in them, from wanting you to. Now don't you think it's time for you to get up and get dressed?"

"I guess you're right, I can't lay around here all day. So if you ladies would be so kind to excuse me I must be getting dressed now."

"Come on let 's leave him alone." I said walking out the door.

"Yeah, sure." Connie reluctantly replied raising up following Sue out the door. Closing it behind her.

It was nearly 7 PM before they finally packed the rest of their things into the van, and were heading for their new home in the outskirts of the city. When Connie pulled the van into a parking lot of a restaurant saying to the two of us.

"I need the two, of you to go inside a have yourselves something to drink I've to make some phone calls. I'll join you as soon as I finish, now go on.

* * * *

Connie waited for Art and I to go inside. Before going to a pay phone to make her calls. Looking back at the restraint to make sure they were inside. and couldn't hear what was being said.

As she hastily dialed ate phone number and impatiently waited for someone to pick up the receiver on the other end. Where as soon as she heard another women's voice speaking on the other end, she immediately spoke into the receive saying.

"Hello Mother... Yes, this is Connie. I'm sorry to call you at such a late hour but, it's important I'm at phone number 555-5566. Where I need to say."

(The moon is on fire... Send help but, stay out of sight until you hear from me through the messenger.

I'm in Milwaukee Wisconsin I need Virginia to call me the number I give to the messenger. Tell her it Swamp girl. That I'll wait until I hear from her, unless something comes up. That if she doesn't hear from me after three, day from her contacting me. I won't be able to contact her, and to send them all back home. The number I'm calling from is 555-4643. I'll wait for five minutes. Send the pigeon.)"

Connie hung up, and stood by the phone waiting for Virginia to return her call. Hoping that contact could be made right away.

The phone rang. Connie picked it up, waiting to hear the voice on the other end, and the recognition word again, before impatiently speaking into the receiver.

"Who am I speaking to?"

"It's Virginia Pride." She replied back giving the recognition word. "

Swamp" Letting Connie know that it was her, Virginia she was speaking with. Them saying." I've got your message."

"Connie instantly spoke into the receiver saying. "(The wolfs are howling at the noon. Its hell night... That can only be stopped by one phone call. Come quick I'll call Mother to let you know when the time is right.)"

"Are you sure...? You are actually going to wage war against the syndicate again...?"

"They took away from me once. I'll not let it happen twice. There will be no stopping it this time once it starts, we'll speak again.

I don't want a consultation between us but, I'll stand to defend what is mine to the death. Tell them I've no desire to die, or to kill again. This is not of my doing. Tell them that, if it's to stop before it starts.

You must warn yours, and make sure of their welfare. I'll call mother in three days, be ready but, do nothing that will alert anyone of your presence. Tell all you choose not to join. I harbor no ill will. This is my fight."

Connie hung up, going inside the restraint to join Art and I. Sitting in a booth waiting on their order of drinks to arrive. Looking directly into my eyes making sure to get my attention

"Sue I want this done, and over with once and for all. That swamp rat taught me well. You needn't become involved."

"Connie you also taught me well not to know what you are telling me. I agree enough is enough. You know I'll never desert you... If it's meant to be so be it. I tried to do ate right thing but no one is letting us be."

I replied back answering her. Hoping that Art would be obvious of what we were talking about. Hoping to avoid him getting himself all distraught again.

"Thank you, I knew I could count on you. Let's just hope there's no need for it I will give them a change. It will not be of my doing but, theirs."

"What are you two, talking about?"

"Nothing that need concern you, now drink up so we can get you to our new home shall we."

* * * *

Jesus H. Christ. Ralph startlingly blurted out sitting parked in a van. Assigned to monitor what he was lead to believe was Connie's and Sue's apartment building. That unknown to them they already vacated earlier that day.

Across the street along with several other FBI agents.

Acting on the assumption that a woman by the name of Connie Price was of special interest to Phil, after he overheard her name. Being associated to a notoriously sought after phantom women.

Who once battled the syndicate. That wound up costing the lives, that was believed to be 50, or more of their solders.

Being mentioned at Pat's apartment, by Pat herself. Who could have no way of knowing what she might to the syndicate.

Ralph being a very close associate of Carl. Sat thinking to himself, about getting hold of Carl by phone. To tell him what was going on.

"I best get in touch with Carl like I promised I would." As he sat outside Connie's apartment building." Speaking out to his partner about his intentions." I best go call Carl now, just sit pat until I get back."

"Why?" One of the FBI agents asked. What are you seeing out there…? Give me those binoculars…" He snatched them out of Ralph hand. Looking out the window of the van through them. While Ralph left the van going into the drugstore on the corner to make his call to Carl.

Chapter 19

" Yeah, Carl this is Ralph you best get your ass down here in front of Connie's apartment building You're not going to believe what's going on.

I counted six, black sedans parked in front of it. Which are nothing least than syndicate vehicles if I ever seen them.

The nearest I can tell. They're still inside the building. Where we haven't gotten a chance to get inside as yet. Not without not being seen but, the lights are still on in their apartment."

"Holy shit...! Carl alarmingly blunted out." What's going on there! A full scale war...?! You best get on the radio, and get some back up down there! I'm on my way!"

Carl slammed the receiver and headed towards the door.

"What's going on Carl." Terry his partner asks. Jumping up from his chair behind his desk to join Carl. Hurriedly heading towards the door.

"A blood war that's what." He panicky replied." There's a half a dozen cars parked out front of Connie's, and Sue's apartment building. Who happen to be very close, and dear friend of mine.

Where Paul, and some ass hole FBI agent. Are acting on a statement made by some syndicate prostitute. Who's place just blow up, and started on fire. Who's place they were at when it happened. Where that slut mentioned a name relating to Connie herself thinking that it would get her ass out of trouble.

If those thugs dare try anything with Connie, or Sue, all hell is going to break loose...! Those fools don't have any idea the hell they will be walking into! Especially with Connie."

"Hey, relax getting yourself all wound up isn't going to stop anything if it's going to happen. Even if you get there before the shit starts.

Besides what in the hell do those guys want with those two, anyway? What name was it that came up anyway." He asked following Carl hurriedly rushing to get to his squad car.

"Connie Price that's who! "Where think it has something to do with that slut Pat who brought up her name.

She's the sister of that kid who disappeared from that orphanage, where those three people were killed. Where she's involved with those syndicate guys up to her ears!

I should have never of let them just walk out, without some sort of escort. I just knew that she had something to do with her brother escaping. I just never gave it any thought that she had a sort of pull with the damn syndicate. That could be the very reason why that kid hasn't gotten himself caught as yet."

* * * *

Terry alarmingly spoke up excitedly. Reporting what he was observing to another FBI agent who came to join him in the van, while Ralph was gone going to call Carl.

"Hey Glen I'm glad you showed up. As long as you are here, you best come have a look at this. We are going to need to call the chief in on this shit.

Look for yourself. There's half of all the hoods in the city parked out front of that apartment building across the street. We are going to have to block off the area for blocks... Before whatever is going to come down, comes down. There's something big going on here."

Another black sedan pulled up beside the first sedan parked in front of the roll of other sedans parked directly in front of the main lobby doors.

Where after sitting idling. That sedan pulled off, with the others following behind it. Abandoning the front of the apartment building.

As Ralph returned back to the van, climbing back in behind the wheel. Watching the caravan of sedans dispersing from about the apartment building.

When Carl pulled up. Pulling into nothing but, a totally empty street in front of the apartment building. Looking around in total disbelief wondering just what in the hell was going on. Not understanding what in the hell just happened?

"Dammit to hell! Just what in the Sam-hell is going on here...?!" He emerged from the car shouted out. Walking up and into the apartment building. Going up to Connie's apartment. To find it empty.

Causing him to run back down to his car to call in a APB, giving the description of the vehicle they were driving. Making it imperative that they were located.

"Damn it Terry it doesn't figure...! Why would the syndicate come here? She's a blasted interning doctor. She wouldn't have anything to do with the likes of them.

It just doesn't add up...?"

"I know, let's pull in that slut Pat and find out. I'm sure she has something to do with what's happening here. If I heard you right. We best not leave it without knowing for sure just what is going on. I got the impression that your friend Connie isn't someone to be messing with. Just what is it that you know about her anyway.

* * * *

The Three, of us finished bringing the rest of the boxes into the new house. We were all upstairs in the master bedroom relaxing.

When I walked out onto the balcony for some fresh air. When I noticed several black sedans parked down the street. Just sitting there. With the windows darkened so no one could see inside. Instantly getting a chilling sensation running up her spine. By noticing the way that they were parked facing in are direction

"Oh Connie." I nervously called out to her." Can you please come out here for a second?"

"Yes, Sue what is it?" Connie stepped out on the balcony joining me asking.

"Look but don't look to hard I don't want them to notice." I discreetly pointed down towards several parked black sedans.

" I think we have company. A lot of company... Maybe you best get Art somewhere that he will be safe. We don't want him getting involved in this. If this is going to be involving us. I'll say here an keep an eye on them."

"Alright dear heart." Connie walked back into the bedroom speaking out to Art." We need to get you to bed.

It's getting late, and we have a long day ahead of us tomorrow, now let's get you into the bathroom so you can take yourself a long refreshing shower. Then get you dressed for bed. I want you looking your best come tomorrow."

She walked with him into the bathroom, shutting the door behind him. Shouting out to Sue.

"Sue get your ass back in her right now."

"Why? They are only cockroaches." I flipped them off standing before the railing letting whoever it was know that I was aware they were out there watching us.

Then while walking back into the bedroom to join Connie. Something told me to stop before entering, and look up towards the roof.

Where I Spotted two, dark shadows that looked like heads peering down over the edge of the roof. Then two, more silhouettes appearing. Climbing up the sides of the wall of the house. Literally clinging to it while climbing up it as if sticking to it as they shimmed up towards the roof.

"Oh, brother..." I nervously spoke out. Stepping back inside the bedroom." Connie I don't know who's larking about out there but, I hope for their sake they are friends of yours. It would sure be a few less for us to worry about..."

"Where did you see them...?" She skeptically asking. " It doesn't seem possible that they could have found us, and get here this soon."

"Two, on the roof directly above my head. Then another two, climbing up the wall of the house. Who are you talking about when you say they?"

"Damn... Them I told them to wait... It sure sounds like them alright. Dam it all Sue the last thing I wanted was another blood bath..." Connie ran out onto the balcony shutting out.

" Enough...! No more...! I don't want to do this. If it can be avoided..."

Just then a squad car pulled up in front of the house. Where none other than Carl himself climbed out, and proceeded to walk towards the front door.

Amidst the sedans pulling away from the curve. While Carl stood before the front door. Anxiously knocking on it.

"Now how in the hell did Carl find us here?" Connie spoke out going downstairs to speak to him. Leaving me staying behind to guard the bathroom Art was in.

* * * *

"Why hello Carl what brings you here...? and how did you find out where I lived to begin with?"

"I'm a cop remember. Now I want you to tell me what's happening here."

"Why nothing as you can see. Leastwise nothing that I can't handle."

"You have to be kidding me. You had half the hoods in the damn city sitting out front of your apartment building.

Connie you forget I know you... I mean it Connie, and you know I mean it. I don't want another blood bath. Least of all not happening here in this city. If you are going to do something take it elsewhere. I don't want to deal with the body count.

I want you, and Sue, and your other friend to come with me down to the police station. Until I find out just what's happening here. Don't make me arrest you, or place you in protective custody. You know I will do it. Now start talking dammit!"

"No, thank you I'll pass, and you can't arrest me. I'm quite aware of what's coming down around me thank you. However, thank you for your concern."

"Connie this isn't going to happen here. Let the police handle it. We know it has something to do with the girl Pat. So let the police handle it...

Don't let Ohio happen all over again... I don't want to be the one, who will have to stop you. You promised."

"Carl you must do what you have to do?"

"Why Connie?"

"That's a good question. However, I will tell you this. It's not of my doing I'll tell you that much."

* * * *

"Oh, Jesus Christ...!" I startlingly blurted out jumping back ready to defend myself. Alarmingly seeing two, hooded apparitions, coming barging into the bedroom from off the balcony through the balcony doors.

Separating as if taking up a defensive position. Dispersing themselves about the bedroom. Armed with weaponry representing the extent of their training in the Martial Arts.

Recognizing who they were. I relaxed my defensive position, standing before the bathroom door.

Recognizing one as Mickey and the other being Bridget. Two, of Connie's warriors fully dressed for the purpose of inflicting death.

"Hello Sue." Mickey spoke out positioning herself beside the door jamb of the balcony door." We were in the neighborhood, and came to visit, where's Connie?"

"She's downstairs answering the front door. It's that friend of hers that cop, by the name of Carl."

* * * *

"Carl I promise that I will call you if I need you, and I don't. I really must insist that you say goodnight, and stay out of this.

I'm really tired, and I have to be at the hospital early tomorrow, so unless you are here to arrest me. I must say good night"

She closed the door walking away from the front door. Walking towards the staircase. Only to be stopped by the phone ringing. Causing her to stop to answer it. Picking up the receiver placing it to her ear. Listening to what was being said on the other end.

"Yes this is Connie Price speaking to whom am I speaking?"

"Yes, I understand you. If you must you must. It's been nice speaking to you I'm sure we will be meeting very soon. Just remember This doesn't have to be, and nothings gone so far that it can't be forgotten."

* * * *

Alright Terry I tried." Carl climbed into the squad saying slamming the car door." Let's go, we can't do anymore here."

"You can't be serous? You are leaving them totally unprotected…? You saw those cars sitting here when we pulled up."

"Unprotected my ass! You have no idea of who's already there. You damn right I'm serous… As long as no innocent civilians don't get hurt. I'm going to let the shit fly where it may."

"Carl I don't know what's going on in that head of yours but, you can't let this go down. You will really be sticking your neck out a mile on this one. You are a cop, you can't ignore any potential danger, or knowingly knowing that someone will wind up getting killed.

You could lose everything you worked for, even your pension. If you knowingly allowed any of those women to get hurt, or maybe even killed. You are talking syndicate here… Paid killers."

"Terry you always wanted those rats out of their holes. Well they are out now. We will let them play their game. Let's just hope for their sake that they know what they are playing with.

The way I recall it. They sure as hell didn't the last time, and they lost their Assess.

Which is no place for us cops to be getting involved in. Why the paper work alone will take up until I retied just to write out.

Where it's going to be more beneficial for us to pick up the trash left behind and deal with the left overs where they will be at their weakest.

There number alone tells me that they are underestimating Connie's potential, and seeing how Sue is still with her. They are going to need a hell of a lot more than they have.

We can only hope that it will be stopped before it starts. If it isn't it's going to be hell's eve night

I mean it Terry hell is putting it mildly. When the devil himself wants no part of any of this."

"This is station commander Roger calling car 17 come in car 17... Dammit Carl pick up the damn Mic."

"I'm here Commander, over..."

"Carl put your ears on. We had a tap on the phone like you requested at that Pat's place However the conversation was cut short by two, nitwits shutting off those bugs at that Pat's place.

We need time to hook up a tap on the phone where you are at now. vet all lost dearly and regretted leaving the job undone. You've only to give the word and the moon children will rise again."

" Mickey you've it. I'll not let them again take away from me. That which I treasure more than my own life."

* * * *

Terry pulled the car to a stop at the curve just down the street from Connie's place. Across the street from it so to observe the entrance. As still other black sedans keep cursing the area and parking about the place.

"Dammit…" Carl frustratingly blurted out." I wish I knew what in the hell was going on in that damn house?"

"Carl." Terry replied to him." Isn't it best that nothing is going on? Like you said once it starts they'll be no stopping it.

It's obviously that whoever is inside those sedans know that we're here. There not blind, and yet they still keep coming to just sit and wait. Ignoring us, like not carrying one way or the other about us still sitting here.

Hell, Carl there has to be some 20 or more men larking about here just sitting around doing nothing. Just waiting on one word, or for someone to do something stupid, for all hell could break loose.

Where it's obvious that whatever they are waiting for hasn't come yet. Someone is damn scared about something, and it isn't us that's for damn sure.

You know what I'm thinking Carl. Even though I was just a rooky cop walking the beat. I recall something like this coming down exactly similar to what's happening here, that so many solders congregated like this but, that was over 5 years ago."

"I remember too Terry. It was a full scale war. Hoods, thugs, and pushers were being bumped off all over the city but, then again for some reason. All the killing stopped, and didn't start up again, where it's my greatest fear.

That if it isn't stopped this time. It might not ever stop, and there's no telling how many innocent people will become victimized by it.

Family members, friends, even associates were being targeted. Whole criminal families were killing each other. Thinking one was turning against the other.

I was in the middle of it all. Watching scores of people dying, and couldn't find out who it was doing all the killings between one, family and the other. Where all I was doing was running around filling body bags."

"Carl you sound as if you know who was behind it the last time?"

"If I knew Terry it wouldn't matter. All I know now is that it could be happening again right now, and you know something else. I could care less, and if you were smart you would do likewise.

Terry what I'm about to tell you I want off the record officially. I want you to keep this strictly confidential just between us..."

" You've it Carl come on lay it on me..."

"That's alright Terry, on second thought it I think it's best to say nothing right now. If I'm right hopefully maybe, we will all be going to be able to sleep easily tonight.

"Car 17 come in." John the dispatcher voice came over the Mic." We have a hot line piped in straight to your dispatch radio."

"I've it Terry." Carl picked up the Mic. saying." I hear you, is commander Roger's in on this?"

"I'm here Carl." He replied back answering his question... Hold on the phone is ringing now. She's picking it up now...."

"Yes, this is Connie. Who am I speaking to?" Connie sternly spoke into the receiver.

"You may refer to me as Clay." A male's voice on the other end of the phone answered her back.

"I'm empowered to speak with you if you chose to negotiate. I've the power to call it off, if we could arrive at a reasonable settlement.

Look out your window if you doubt my authority but, mine you it's only temporary, and time is of the essence as well as your compliance to are demands..."

"Sue go to the window, and see what's going on?"

"Sure thing." I said walking over to the window looking out it." Connie it appears that they are pulling back but, leaving their headlights on, while parking in a different location."

"They're what ...?!" She uneasily replied." Alright I'm listening" Connie congenially spoke into the phone." Just what are you up to...?! And who the hell is this...?!"

"Your executioner that's who. You really don't think you could get away with it intimidating anyone this time did you, or that you were the only one that possesses the knowledge, and the abilities of those special techniques? Where let's not forget. You are alone and I'm not?

Where however it is in your power to stop the inedible outcome. Where you could avoid a lot of bloodshed. By settling this just between ourselves.

The winner takes all. You know where the abandon Mission is, near the curry. I'll be there waiting for you. You have 4 hours to get there. Your decision will determine if those headlights go out, or not.

I strongly suggest that you don't disappoint me. I've someone here that wants to speak to you." He handed Virginia the phone.

"Connie Its me Virginia... I'm sorry but, they got to me before I could get to you. I'm to tell you that if he wins. All of us well have to swear are allegiance to the syndicate. Where Pat will be taken care of.

That if he losses. The fighting will end. We will all be allowed to go on living in peace but, this must be the end of having any further involvement with them."

"Tell him that I agree Virginia, and I'll be there. I should have known that they would pull something like this." Connie hung up the phone.

"What is it Connie?" I nervously asked her.

"Yes, Connie what is it...? Mickey asked.

"All of you listen up. I've something to tell you. I'm going to have to leave soon. They have Virginia, I must go alone, and only me.

Mickey I want you to tell the others when they arrive to go back home. Where if I win a one, on one fight with this Clay character it's over. However, if I loss. All of you will have to take a vow of allegiances to the syndicate.

Mickey if I don't return I'm counting on you to handle things. However, in either case. It will bring an end to all this."

* * * *

'Oh, no you don't...' Art spoke out to himself. Overhearing what Connie was saying on the phone. From over extension on the night stand beside his bed.

Hanging it up sliding out of bed, going to the balcony. Where he climbed down the drain pipe down to the ground. Where he stood looking around for the van. Where he hastily ran over to it and climbed into the back. To hide behind a pile of empty boxes and covering himself up with a packing blanket.

* * * *

"Sue I want you to stay here with Art. If I don't return never let him forget that I love him. With any luck at all I should be back before he realizes that I was gone. Mickey you did bring my things with you, didn't you?"

"Yes, everything is sitting upstairs in that spare room Sue here put us into."

" Thank you, now Mickey I want all of you to stay here with Sue. Just encase they don't live up to the agreement. I best be going now..." She walked towards the stairs going up them.

* * * *

"Holy shit... Carl...!" Terry startlingly spoke out." I can't believe what I just heard...! What in the Sam-hell does she thinks she's doing...?! She's walking right into their hands... No wonder they all pulling back. We have to get out to that damn Mission."

"Hold it Terry. We all can't go converging on that place. That place is going to be crawling with syndicate solders.

Even though this is a golden opportunity to net them all, and possibly break the back of the whole damn syndicate. Not to mention the promotions we could get for doing it. We are going to have to pass up the chance of a lifetime."

" Forget it Carl. "Caption Roger's voice came over the Mic." There's no better time than right now to clean house, and if you don't want the credit I'll take it.

We have the situation under are control dammit! Where we have the upper hand over all of them. If only one, person dies we could nail them all at once.

As long as we stay in control, and don't do something stupid. We could take down most of the rackets in the entire city.

Come on you two, you just can't pass this up?! She's going to get her's anyway. Why shouldn't we benefit from her stupidity?"

How does assistant administrator sound to you, and Terry how does captain sound to you? Once I'm promoted I'll promote the both of you?

"Roger does have a good point their Carl. We are getting nowhere fast as it is, I'm for going along with Roger's"

"Terry are you sure you want to do this? What he's suggesting is complicity to conspiracy to murder. If it comes out that we purposely let her get killed. We could become accessories to her murder?"

"We won't Carl. That's the terrific thing about it. If I wasn't sure I wouldn't have even suggested it. Don't forget we are the police." Roger's entered into the conversation stating his position.

"Carl you handle your end just by staying out of it, and I'll handle my end from here. Only the four of us knows what's going on. Just hold your position and I'll get Phil's men to back off, and just let it go down totally oblivious of it happening.

I've always been distant for big things. We all might be in law enforcement but, there isn't a single one, of us that isn't ambitious.

Believe me Carl this is are big chance. Let's take it, and rid the city of those dastards in the process..."

Chapter 20

Connie pulled the car off the road. Driving into a wooded area about a half a mile away from the mission. Shutting of the headlights then the motor.

"Well girl." She spoke out saying as she climbed out from behind the wheel. Carrying her powers with her to a remote isolate spot where she could prepare herself for what lied ahead.

" This is it. I never thought that I would ever have to put on my powers again."

She kneeled down upon the ground placing her shroud before her that cover her weaponry upon the ground.

To **ceremoniously symbolically adsorb their possessive strength. Placing her forehead down upon the shroud.

Giving her mind, and her body openly ritualistically, waiting in mental prayer for the sign to become anointment possessing with her inner strength from the weapons anointing powers. Knowing that her powers had to ingratiate her, if they were to endow as well as serve her.

Upon receiving their anointment. She then opening the shroud. Spreading her weaponry out upon it.

Then one, by one she offered up their strengths raising them above her head hoping to absorb their universal powers. Allowing their powering energy to be absorbed though her arms into, and throughout her entire body. Taking possession of it energy sources.

To meet her emissary battle until all that was going to be blessed upon her became an extension of her being.

She bowed kissing the shroud that protected her powers. Giving her gratitude for all that she received. Not knowing to what extent she was anointed with. Leaving that up to the gods who sought deliverance upon her.

Then rose to put on her armaments, and stood giving her gratitude for all she was adorned with along with all their teachings, and philosophies they bless her with.

Extending her hands to the heavens. Summoning the wisdom, and conning of her God, who she served for his blessing. To do him honor. Mentally preparing herself for the inevitability of death.

* * * *

Art sneakily watched her preforming her ritual peering out the side door window. Where he only had to blink is eyes once, and she virtually vanished.

He then sought to get out of the trunk to go after her. Blindly running off into the woods not knowing where he was heading.

Only to be hurtled to the ground by a pouncing force. Coming down upon him from above. Only to feel a left threatening razor sharp blade of a knife pressing against his throat.

As he looked on horrifically, into two, pitch black eyes, staring down into his. Forcing him to look up into the eyes of death. Peering out from a concealing black hood.

"Damn you...! What in the hell are you doing here?!" Connie infuriatingly asked him." I could have killed you dammit! Now did you get here...?! Answer me damn you!"

"I hid in the van..." He fearfully answered her.

"Why you stupid Asshole... Why didn't you stay with Sue...? I can't have you wondering about!" She angrily said dragging him over to the tree, she jumped down onto him from.

To tie his hands around the tree trunk, and them his feet together. Then stuffed a peace of clothe in his mouth. Where she then proceeded to tie his head back against the tree trunk, securing the gag in his mouth.

"Now you just stay right here! I'll be back shortly." She said darted off. Leaving him. Feeling assured that he would be safe until she returned.

* * * *

Where is she damn it...?!" Clay impatiently asked nervously pacing back and forth." She said that she would be here... So where in the hell is she...?! Are you guys ready...?"

He uneasily asks, while nervously looking around actually counting how many there were. Noting their positions, he place them in. Making sure that they were all present and accounted for. Positioned in their hidden locations about the inside. and outside of the abandoned Mission, speaking out to remind them of the instructions he gave them.

" Just don't forget, that at the first sign of me losing. Shoot the Bitch." I want her dead before we leave here.

"You're one, rotten Bastard...!" Virginia spoke out, with loathing, and disgust for him. I thought you said that you were an expert?"

"I am scumbag! I just don't like losing. Larry get outside, and make sure all the men are in position. I want that tramp dead, and I don't care how she dies. She's not going to get away with pulling her shit this time! I'm going to be taking her head back on a platter to show everyone who's the real master around here."

* * * *

"Holy shit... Carl!" Terry nervously whispered out to him. As he laid beside him in hiding with him and some six, other police officers, dispersed about the hill top. Just above the Mission.

" I should have known that you would never go along with Roger. I hope for both are sakes, you know what in the hell you are doing...?

There must be at least 25, men down there. It's a setup, just like you figured it would be. Do you think that just the 8, of will be able to handle them?"

"Terry dead men don't talk. Are men knowing what to do. The second she goes down we open fire. They won't stand a chance in hell. Beside I don't think that there's going to be too many left by the time she gets to that Mission."

* * * *

"So there you are, you little runaway." I said as Mickey and Bridget along with two, others came upon Art tied to a tree stump. As Mickey untied the leather strap holding his head back against the tree, then removed the gag from his mouth.

"Sue... How did you find me...?"

"I didn't, they did. I only did what Connie asked me to do. Which was to watch out after you. By all right I should leave you the way I found you. To teach you a lesson."

"Sue... You won't believe what she's turned into... She nearly killed me!"

"Listen to me boy." Mickey spoke out to him. Standing beside the tree standing guard over him.

" You are damn lucky that she didn't! She's not with us anymore. She's with her destiny."

" Mickey." Bridget called out to her." She went this way."

"Sue you take the boy back to the car. We are going to make sure it's going to be a fair fight. Whatever you do don't attempt to follow us. We will be on are guard now..."

* * * *

"Well? Is everyone in place." Clay nervously asked Larry the second he entered the Mission door.

"Relax... Nothing could get past them, not even a ghost."

"Good, now all we have to do is to wait for the lamb to come to the slaughter."

* * * *

'Damn it...!' Connie annoyingly said to herself. Coming upon Carl along with about 6, other men, deployed about the hill. Overlooking the Mission.

'What in the hell is he doing here? I don't believe this.... 'She looked around for a way to get around them.

Spotting one, where she could slip through. Working her way towards a clump of bushes. Getting as close as five, feet near a couple of Carl's men. While working her way down the slope of the hill towards the Mission.

Only to come upon still more men deployed in hiding about the Mission. When she spotted two, men hiding in a clump of bushes some 12, feet in front of her.

Knowing that she had to attack silently and swiftly. She slithered like a cobra, on her belly holding two, needle sharp darts in each hand. Coming up behind their backs.

Where she sprung up hurtling the needle sharp darts into their temples. Jerking up pulling them down onto the ground muffling their mouths.

Turning to spot another leaning with his back against a tree trunk out of sight of the Mission. When she drew a shuriken and hailed it. Catching him right in the larynx of his throat. Causing him to fall, clutching his throat into the bushes.

Using her weaponry, she worked her way about the Mission. Picking the men off one, and two at a time.

Using a blow gun with poisonous darts. By using the tree tops, and the dead to lure them over close to her. Separating one, from the other. Without drawing very much concern from others close to the one, she was after. When she came upon spotting Mickey, and several others taking up her polite.

* * * *

"This waiting is getting on my nerves...?" Clay nervously spoke out pacing the floor." Where in the hell is she...?!

Larry get back out there and check on the guys. The rest of you keep your eyes on those windows."

"But there's nothing out there." Larry questionably answered him back.

"Damn it! Just do what I tell you...!"

"Alright I'm going.... "He said walking towards the door opening it. Only to be hurtled back across the floor crashing against the far wall. By a darting piecing arrow impacting right through his chest staking him to the wall. With his legs hanging above the floor.

"Alright...!" Clay frightfully shouted out becoming totally disorientated, and distraught over the shock from seeing Larry being hurtled backwards. Then handing from the wall in a state of utter panic. Frantically shouting out.

" She's here...! Get the damn fucken Bitch...! " As the sound of shattering glass cause Clay to panicky spin around in readiness.

As still another one, of his men fall to his death. With another arrow lodged in his right eye.

As he turned just in time to see. Still another man being impaled by a dagger. Coming crashing through the glass of a window into his mouth.

Shoving him backwards to staggeringly stumble. Firing blindly from his finger being frozen on the trigger of his automatic rifle. Dropping down onto his knees then falling dead backwards down onto his back.

Panicky Clay hid behind Virginia using her to protect himself. As she sat in a chair with her hands and ankles tied. Holding his knife against her throat paradoxically shouting out.

" I'll kill you Bitch...! You lied to me...! This was supposed to be a fair fight...! Not a blood bath... Come on you Slut... Let's get it on...!"

He dragged the chair Virginia was sitting in. Backing himself up against the wall behind him. Assuring that on one could come up behind him. As he kneeled down behind her.

"I'm here Virginia Just like I promised I would be." Connie entered the door of the Mission saying.

" You're no warrior Clay.

Why you are nothing more than a frighten child. Far lesser hit a man with any honor. Who hides behind a bonded woman...

With your men not around to be able to help you ... You are all alone, and totally afraid to even die honorably.

I stand here ready to defend my honor with my life, are you prepared to do likewise...? Stand clear of the women you are hiding behind, and meet me with honor."

* * * *

"Dammit...!" Terry angrily whispered out as he stood in hiding with a group of his men in amongst the bushes. A short distance from the missions open double doorway where he heard multiple shoots being fired repetitiously. Noticing that nothing was happening, nor was anyone moving about.

'Hey, come on here. He startlingly stood disbelievingly speaking out to himself...' No one is that damn good...!'

Becoming totally dumbfounded saying to himself. Having already spotted several dead men lying about the area. As he joined up top gather still more of his men together. Nervously speaking out to those who joined up with him.

" Come on guys what are we doing just standing here?! Do you want just one women take all the glory? Let's go help her."

He nervously shouted out. Spotting someone standing in the light of the open door way. To go   charging directly towards whoever it was.

Taking matters into his own hands planning on catching, and arresting whoever it was standing there into custody for murder. Hoping to make himself out the hero of the day. Heroically shouting out.

"Come on men, lets got those fuckers...!" As he went charging out of the bushes. Charging down the slop of the hill. Firing several shoots in the direction of the person standing just inside the open doors with the rest of the men follow him.

"No...! No... Stop...!" Carl jerked up onto his feet screaming out. Panicky at them. Helplessly seeing Terry and the men following him. Falling like dead flies down to the ground. Then rolling head over heels rolling down the hill Being hit by flying arrows, shuriken, and razor sharp darts being lodged, and protruding all about their bodies.

Where Terry came to an abrupt halt. Being the only man left standing at the basin of the hill. With two, arrows lodged in him. With one in his chest and the other in his upper back. With

Disbelievingly turning to looking back up at Carl. Standing at the top of it.

With a pitch black shadow popping up from out of nowhere directly behind. Holding a large sword. Slashing the razor sharp blade out at him. Catching him across his stomach.

Dropping Terry to the ground onto his knees clutching his stomach with his hands, As he then dropped face first down onto the ground.

Whereas, as fast as the ghostly shadow appeared. It disappeared into the darkness of the night as three, other shadows appeared.

Taking up a standing position about the basin of the hill. In amongst the dead police officers lying about the basin.

"No...!" Carl panicky yelled out. Seeing his close friend and partner laying dying on the ground. Paradoxically not thinking about himself. He ran down the slope of the hill, towards Terry Dropping down onto his knees Picking up Terry in his arms. Rolling him over to take his head in his bracing hands.

Where upon three, dark shadows converged on Carl. Not recognizing him over being enthralled in the heat of battle.

Where all three, of them lounged out at the same time, with their swords, stabbing him from all directions. As they gathered up around him instinctively stabbing, and slashing out at him.

Where upon Mickey came charging from out of no-where shouting frantically.

" No...! that's Carl... No...!" Come upon them, as they withdrew their swords, and he went falling face first down onto the ground.

"No...! Look what you've done... It was Carl... You killed Carl..."

" We are sorry Mickey!" Bridget regretfully spoke up. We didn't know. but, it's too late to carry on over him now. Nothing going to bring him back.

We need to get to Connie, now come on! She could be in serious trouble..." Bridget ran off leading the others towards the open door of the Mission.

Where upon entering Bridget saw Virginia laying on the floor in a pool of blood. Where when

Mickey finally caught up to Bridget, and saw Virginia lying dead on the floor.

She sorrowfully dropped to her knees beside her. Picking her dead head in her hands. While morning her death. Picked up her body and held her in her arms, hugging her close against her own body. Crying pathetically over her death insanely shouting out.

" No Virginia you can't die on us... Virginia please come back to us... They killed her...! They killed her...!"

She infuriatingly screamed out at the top of her lungs. Laying her back down. Drawing her sword in defense. Preparing for another onslaught of attackers screaming out hysterically totally distraught by Virginia's death.

When Connie came charging in holding her bloody sword in her hand, still dripping form Clay's blood defensively coming to Mackie's aid.

Rushing up to her standing before Virginia laying on the floor behind her at her feet. Totally in raged blindly ready to fight against her own. So distraught it took all the strength she had to hold herself back from doing so.

As they all just stood not attempting to defend themselves virtually willing to sacrifice their own lives to Connie's rage.

"Connie... My god stop!" Mickey hysterically ranted, and screamed out. Steeping in front of Connie Still pathetically crying out morning Virginia's death. Protecting those who came to stand by Connie's side with her own life. Frantically shouting at Connie.

"No...! Stop... They killed Virginia. No more of our own shall die this night. There has been enough killing this night. We need to leave before more arrive

" I know Mickey. "Connie regained her composure along with her senses. Startlingly realizing what she was on the verge of doing.

Wanting to truly apologize but, realizing now wasn't the time to do it. Where trying to console Mackie's, sorrow was over the tragic loss of losing Virginia.

" Mickey, Virginia's death was not in vain. The one who was responsible meet his fate for doing it. By my hand. Her death has been revenged she is at peace now.

Mickey this is not the time to morn her death, we must keep our head about us. He wasn't linger any longer. There could be a lot more to deal with."

"Connie, Carl's also dead. He was killed unknowingly knowing who he was. While we were acting on instinct."

"You all did what was expected of you. Death is all about us this night. I couldn't have survived without your help. There were far too many outside for me to handle I'm glad you four, came.

I warned Carl not to interfere. There's no disgrace, your honor is pure. However, killing these hoods is one thing. Where killing cops are something else.

We have to remove all the evidence of our being here, and there's only one way to do that. We must burn everything along with all those who died here this night.

Now come all of you, and help me drag them inside the Mission."

"Why?" Bridget asked. They are the ones who started this?"

"Are honor has been satisfied. Where we are going to leave all their weapons where they lie. Where hopefully we will make it appear as if this was a battle between ravel mobs where the cops will hold them who died here. Responsible for what happened here.

We will leave all the dead cops to make it appear if they attempt to prevent it. Where hopefully when the cops that find this place. They will derive at the only logical conclusion about what happened here.

The cops accidently came upon one of the mobs before the other mob got here. Where the first mob killed all the cops and were going to get rid of them. When the other mob showed up and tried to take advantage by attacking them by surprise.

Where it was those who survived who burned everyone except for the cops. What whatever reason. Let the cops figure it out.

That's the best I can come up with for right now. It's better than nothing. Where the cops might think of half of what I just said, and take their minds off what really took place here.

Where those that we burn will be Virginia's benediction from us. So that she'll find peace in the knowledge that her death didn't go without retribution."

We dragged them all inside the Mission. Where Connie went back to the van. Leaving Mickey to set the Mission ablaze. Thinking to climb into the back to remove her armament. Totally forgetting about Art, and that she left him tied up. Just as she opens the side door of the van to climb inside.

When came upon Art and I sitting in the back of the van. Startlingly blurting out.

"What are you two, doing here…? Damn you Art. I forgotten all about you. It's lucky for you that you never stay where I put you. Oh, well what the hell anyway. I'm glad to see you both.

" I spoke out climbing into the van. Closing the door behind me. Beginning to smell something burning. Alarmingly thinking that we best get the hell away from where we were at.

"Sue you drive while I get out of my powers. As for your young man you go sit up front with her. I've to get out of my things, and I don't need you in my way while doing so."

"Where am I driving us to?"

"Home of course. As far as anyone knows we never left now hurry up."

"Connie what are we going to do? Art nervously ask." We couldn't help to hear all the shooting going on. We are in serious trouble again aren't we?"

"No, Art were not. Not if everything goes right, we won't be. Where however you are going to have to trust me, and stay the hell out of it. Especially this time."

Connie decided to lie to Art by blaming what happen on Carl, and those he brought with him. Where she had things all worked out to where everything was going to be forgiven for what they took at his sister's place.

" Honey this time none of this was any of our fault. Everything would have gone just fine if it hadn't had been for Carl and those cops he brought with him.

Where it was they were the ones doing all the shooting. I'm only doing the only thing we could do. To cover up having any involvement in what went on there. Simply put. We, I, or anyone else wasn't ever there. It was between the cops, and the syndicate that made it happen. We know nothing about any of it. Do you understand me?"

"Yes, I understand." Art redundantly answered her.

" Art" I spoke up entering my concerns about what to expect. Knowing that it was obvious that the police had to know what was happening, or they wouldn't have shown up at the mission.

"Now listen up both of you. Sue you are going to drive me the nearest police station closest to are new place.

Where this time we are going to have to play it by. Where neither of you know nothing. We can't afford to have the police take Art here in for questioning.

Where this time it's going to be different than before. This time if things start getting where I feel I'm losing control. I'll send you both to my place in Ohio where I know you'll be safe.

Now drive me to the nearest police station. Where the two are going to drip me off, and head back home.

As for you Art. You better be dressed for company... Now is not the time to let your guard down. There... pull over there I'll walk from here."

I pulled over to the curve to let Connie climb out. Where she ask me to take her things along with me, as she climbed out . Then just continue to walk away without saying a word heading on her own towards the police station a block away.

* * * *

Connie walked into the police station up to the office sitting behind a counter.

"Yes, Miss what can I do for you?" The officer asked.

"Officer I need to talk to someone... It's a matter of life and death. My life...! I've to speak to someone before it's too late to prevent it from happening...!"

"Connie is that you...? Joe the officer she encountered at Pat's apartment approached her coming out from one, of the inner offices asking.

"Oh, Joe..." Connie nervously cried out appearing very unstable to walk as she walked up to him waiting for her to approach him saying.

" Joe I'm so scared... Where's Carl...?! He told me to go to the nearest police station and waiting for him. You Have to call him and tell him where I'm at...! It's imperative that I speak with him now...!"

"Alright Connie now just clam down, and relax. I'll call him he's most likely with his partner Terry.

We know all about it. Carl radioed in telling us how he attempted to talk you out of committing suicide. The way I have been hearing it. He's most likely already out at the Mission waiting for that guy from the syndicate to show up.

You women talk a good fight but, when it comes right down to it. You get frighten to go through with following through.

You should have let us handle it form the very beginning. You sure stirred up a hornet's nest. I'll say that for you."

"Forget you Joe!" She rebelliously replied." That Pat has to be behind all this! She had to have said something to one of her syndicate friends of hers.

If you want my opinion the police have some rotten cops in their barrel of apples. I already told Carl everything what happened while I was there. I've no idea what was being said after I left. So let's not be placing any blame shall we!"

" Just get me to Carl dammit! By the way just how did he find out about where I was supposed to be going?"

" Excuse me I couldn't help put to overhear the conversation going between the two of you. "Captain Rogers walked up to Joe, and Connie, while they were talking.

So you are the women that has his city up in an uproar? I admire your spunk but, you went about it all wrong."

"Look here captain...!" Connie reprimanding him replying." In the first place I didn't think that I was stirring up anything. All I was trying to do was to protect myself, and my rights.

Against Joe here, and that partner of his. Over them barging in on me at Pat's place. Especially where I heard mention of the syndicate being connected to Pat.

I didn't want to wind up in some trash can, just being another unsolved statistic. Those people don't play around. I had to try something.

I didn't realize that I was stirring up anything until Carl came to my door accusing me of being involved with some outrageous criminal activity. That I was supposed to be responsible for.

Besides if it wasn't for me supposedly stirring whatever it was I did. You never might not have discovered the truth. That it was that women Pat who started all this, and her being associated with her hit man husband, and the syndicate.

That's why I'm here at the police station. I don't want any part of them killing us. Where the damn case will just lay around gathering dust, as so many are already. I want to live damn it! Where you have some rotten cops who could careless!"

"I realize that you're upset." Roger replied to the position she felt herself being place in.

However, I hope you realize just how lucky you are that things didn't turn out the way they might have intended it to.

As for Pat we can't comment on knowing for certain, that she was involved with any syndicate. Her husband is calming he was acting independently, so I wouldn't be accusing her as being involved. Without being certain that she's in collusion with corrupt syndicate activities. When we are still in the process of investigating her case.

By the way seeing how we are on the subject about you being at Pat's residence. Where this supposedly all started in the first place.

What's this name she claims you said to her. As being one by the name of Connie Price. When you are being identified as being Connie Stone on your driver's license? Do you've any idea who Connie Price actually is?"

"Yes, I knew I used that name but, I only used it to frighten her. I didn't want to get personally involved with anything she might be involved with.

Where all I was thinking about was, getting the hell out of her apartment. However, after I said it I suddenly realized I made a drastic mistake in judgment. However, I already committed myself.

I told Carl all that already at Pat's place, after the fire was out. What upset me even more is the fact that I had no idea that anyone especially the police.

Was listening in to my phone conversation. Until Carl came to my door accusing me of being involved with the syndicate.

Which told me right off that you all know what was happening. Where you were actually going to let it happen, and were going to let me get myself killed...!

No wonder Carl told me to tell no one, and not get involved. You all have to be all brought, and paid for by the syndicate... To let a naive idiot like myself get myself killed

Where now that we are actually disgusting it. I can see that I came to the wrong police station. If you don't mind, I'll leave now..."

She nervously started walking backwards towards the door. accusing captain Rogers department of being corrupted.

"Now hold on Miss Stone." Captain Roger's spoke out to her." You can relax I can assure you that you are quite safe here. I can assure you that no one is going to harm you here. You have my word on that so just calm down, and relax."

"Captain!" One of his men panicky yelled out for him. Interrupting what was going on between Connie and him. Getting his attention.

" You best come in the radio room and listen to what's coming in over the radio. We have troubles... Real troubles...!"

"You wait here Connie hopefully the captain will be right back." Joe said following the captain into the radio room.

"Yes, this is captain Rogers who am I speaking with, and what's happening?' He spoke into the radio Mic.

"Captain this is lieutenant Randy I'm out at the abandoned Mission. It's a blazing infernal. Where there's no one to be seen. Where there's a hell of a lot of guns lying about everywhere. I tried to get close to the Mission to look inside but, it's totally in gulped in flames.

However I thought you would like to know, that there's five, squad cars still parked off the road about a quarter of a mile away from t the Mission location. Where there's only two, cops standing here beside me right now."

"Alright lieutenant just hold your position. I'll send more officers out to help out, to you I will also be coming out personally as well." Captain Roger's replied back handing the Mic. back over to the radio man.

"Joe something stinks here? It's too much of a coincidence that she should suddenly show up here. Don't let on to her what's happening until we find out ourselves.

I'll send her home with a couple guards to protect her. You gather yourself up some more men and hightail it out to that Mission. We'll get to the bottom of what's going on, now let's move it."

He leads Joe out of the radio room walking up to Connie standing at the railing before the offices.

"Alright Miss Stone you can go home now. We will send a few men along with you for your protection. Just let is handle things now from are end. By the way. Stay inside where we can find you."

"Sure thing captain she reached into her purse pulling out a pad, and pencil. Writing down her home address, and phone number handing it to him.

" I know that you already know where I'll be but, just in case you might forget. When just in case just remember. I'll be there with my closest friend, and her mice."

Connie felt confident that her plan was working. What as much as her being at the station when the fire was discovered. Would exonerate her from having any involvement with what transpired there.

Where her explaining why she mentions the name Price would be significant enough to discredit her, from being her. Where with Mickey and Bridget handling matters with all the dead, and with the cops seeing her with no evidence of being involved in anyone death.

She was pretty sure that she successfully establish not only an alibi but, excluded herself totally from even becoming a suspect in any murders that took place.

As she stood waiting for her escort to take her home. When two, officers approached her leading her out of the station. To drive her home.

Without asking her where to go. Thereby giving her a very uneasy feeling about their credibility as police officers.

Feeling sure that what was going on at the Mission has probably reached the police before they allowed her to leave station.

* * * *

"Art." I spoke out to him as I stood before the balcony door window, looking down towards the street below.

" I don't know what Connie is up to but, as soon as she gets here, we are getting the hell out of Dodge. We both know what happened out at that mission, and like it. or not we are involved. Where no-matter what, or how we look at it. We have no choice but, to rely on Connie."

I walked over to the bed sitting down on the edge of the mattress as Art nervously got up, and took my place. Standing looking out the balcony door window.

"What's with you Art? I'm not going to bite you..."

"It's not that Sue I'm just having trouble getting what I saw out of my head. I never in all my life seen anything so terrifying. As when I found myself with a knife being held to my throat looking up into those death defying eyes of Connie's...

I actually thought that she was going to kill me... That's hold horrified I was. Where the fear of dying literally terrified the hell out of me. Oh, Sue..."

Art nervously spoke out changing the subject. "It's the police, and they are pulling into the driveway...!"

"What...?!" I panicky blurted out. Alarmingly jerking up from the bed running to join Art standing at the window.

Only to gasp out a sighing breath of relief. Seeing Connie getting out the back door. Being lead up to the front door of the house by two, cops.

"Relax honey its only Connie coming back home being escorted by two, cops. We'll talk about what you saw later."

* * * *

"We will stay outside if you don't mine Miss. Just keep the doors, and windows closed and locked, and you will be just fine. We got things covered out here."

"I hope so." Connie replied back entering the house. Closing, and locking the door behind her. Going upstairs into the bedroom. Seeing Art and I standing at the closed balcony doors.

"Connie what in the hell happen...?" I inquisitively asked, the second she entered the bedroom door.

"Nothing yet." She replied. As far as you know I chickened out, and neither of you knew I left the house. As for your young lady get yourself into a pair of slacks I don't want you parading around in a dress, and put a girdle on!

The cops are mad as hell at me for stirring up so much trouble but, so far they are buying that I chickened out, and never went to the Mission."

Connie continue talking walking over turning on the radio searching for someone, reporting the news. Coming upon a commentator broadcasting the news.

* * * *

" Never in my entire career have I even witness such an appalling sight. The very air about me permeated with the stench of burning flesh...

Where there's no telling at this time how many bodies there are inside that abandon burnt down Mission. That's still in gulped in flames behind me.

However, I will attempt to appraise the reports that I have been receiving from the fire department. I'm only quoting some of the statements that I have overheard thus far.

It makes the Saint Valentine's day massacre look like a Turkey shoot to what's been discovered here tonight.

Bodies were reported piled up upon each other. However, all but, a single severed head was all that remained unscathed from the flames...

We have been ordered by the FBI not to divulge any information pertaining to this holocaust of mass slaughter but, I'm sure that it comes as no surprise to the authorities as to who is responsible for all this.

"Hold on just one second... A report on the severed head was just handed to me. It was identified as being that of one belonging to a syndicate hit-man. To which the authorities are withholding his name at this point in time.

Wait...! Another bulletin has just been handed to me. There was a body of a women found amongst the dead.

My God... What could have happened in that horrid place...?! Will it ever be truly known what happened? That brought about the useless deaths of over 26, or more people who might never be identified.

I have been asking to mention. That if anyone seen anything. No-matter how slight. Too be urged to call the Police in their Districts.

I've the captain of precinct 17. Captain Rogers standing beside me right now.

"Captain can you tell us what happened... Is there anything you can report about what took place here...?"

"No, nothing at this time. Other than saying that indications are leading to what we already suspected."

"And what's that captain?"

"I'm not at liberty to divulge that information at this time."

"Captain can we expect those responsible for this to be apprehended within the next 24 hours?"

"No, comment at this time..."

"Connie are you listening to this...?!"

"Yes, Art I'm listening... Art you must believe me I had no other choice... Do you think I like killing? I don't...

I had the situation under control. When they came charging, and shooting at me. There was no way I could have known who they were.

Where because of them, they cost the life of one of my oldest and dearest friend...

I'd to do what I did to protect all those that I called upon to help me, and myself. I want this all behind us, and to place the blame on those who really started all this.

Honey, if you want someone to blame. Blame your sister, she was the one who had to have started all this to begin with.

Hopefully with the civil authorities going after the ones behind it all. Are lives will get back to moral. Where as far as I'm concerned. Its best they loss rather than us."

"Connie how can one, be so loving and gentle but, yet be so deadly...? You came close to killing me tonight."

" Honey I'm sorry that you see me at my worst but, I didn't know it was you. You weren't supposed to be there...

Art I want you to know, what I did is what I had to do this night. Where if I had to do it again. I would without hesitation.

I warned them not to interfere, I'd no other choice but, to go there, or they would have come after us anyway. Where they might have killed all three, of us.

Even If I want to run I couldn't. They had someone that I also loved. Using her to insure that I would.

The one, who had her killed her before my very eyes. Then ran in fear of his own life, when all the shooting started, and was shoot by his own men who he brought with him to kill me."

"Connie I know you say that you love me but, would you ever kill me...?"

"Kill you...? Never... No, honey no... I would kill myself before I would harm a hair on your head." She comfortingly hugged him to her.

"Honey the killing is over. Now we can relax, and plan for our future. Where within a few more mouths. We will be out of sight, and the minds of this ever happing forever. Now that we have room to breathe."

"What makes you so sure its behind us now?"

" Because that's the way I played it would. Didn't I tell you to trust me? Well its working out perfectly just as I figured it would.

No one has anything on us, as long as you continue to be Donna. Now come on and just relax. I'm handling everything just as I said that I would. After a good night sleep you will feel much better about everything."

* * * *

A week passed without any further incidents. The police didn't ever stop by to question any of us. It was as if we ceased to exist.

During which the authorities rounded up every hood, pusher, and pimp in the city. Cracking down on every want to be criminals.

Questioning them for answers, as to who was behind the massacre at the Mission. That the news media was pressuring the authorities for answers, without getting any replies back from them.

I personally felt that we were pretty much out of the picture. The Connie kept her word by doing the impossible.

Even where Pat, and the syndicate were concern. Seeing how we weren't having any contact with either of them including the police as well. Where pretty much back to things a usual. Where we were concerned

With the exception of what was going on between as for Art and Connie. Where it was pretty much touch and go between the two, of them. Where the less exposure we were having on ourselves. From the police the better things were getting between the two, of them. To the point where the atmosphere was getting back to normal as well.

Where getting Donna enrolled in school was helping out one hell of a lot. To get Art's mind off Art feeling being threatened by Connie do to not being able to get what he seen in her eyes.

Where he sorts of favored staying close to me more so than Connie. Where taking everything in account slowly, but surely things were coming back together again. Where us becoming a family again.

Things were going so good in fact. I decided to spend the day at home with Art and Connie to sort of calibrate the just how close the family was coming back together again where Connie, and Art was concern.

By what I have witnessed upon waking up. Connie and Art were more than close than getting back together again. So much so. It wasn't until around 11 AM, that we decided to go out for an early lunch.

Art was upstairs getting dressed I was kicking back on the sofa waiting for her. When the doorbell rang. Where I got up to go answer it to find Joe standing before the front door when I opened it.

"Well hello there... Joe... isn't it? What bring you here?"

"Connie. Is she here? I came to see how she's holding up over Carl's death. Carl gave me the impression that the two, of them were somewhat close"

"Don't ask, she's still considering his death as a tragic lose. No thanks you the police for not telling her that he was one of the victims in that massacre, and was even informed about his funeral.

Where that being all said and done, she's managing to accept the fact that he's dead. Please come in and sit down. I'll let her know that you are here."

I said inviting him inside, closing the door behind him. Leading him into the living room where he sat down in the easy chair next to the sofa.

Where I went to stand at the bottom of the staircase to shout up. " Hey, Connie, Joe one of Carl's best friends at the station is here, wanting to speak with you" Where I then went into the living room to sit down on this sofa, To wait patiently for Connie to come down the stairs, to find out what he wanted to speak to her about. nonchalantly speaking out being congenial. "So you were saying Joe?"

"Sue being a very close friend of Carl for so long I learnt practically all there was to know about him. The one thing I do know is that no one could have gotten close enough to him to kill him. Unless that is it was someone he knew, and trusted."

"Just what are you trying to say?"

"I don't know for certain yet but, I know there's someone out there that got to him, and I want that sucker! I owe Carl that much.

Sue I don't think that Connie was involved personally in his death but, I feel she's only bidding her time to get her revenge on the one could have been.

I can't allow her to do anything that's why I came to talk to her. Hoping that she would tell me who she thought it was. To convince her to let me handle it. Where as if she acts on her own I'll have no recourse but, to arrest her.

Someone had to have walked away from that Mission, and what we also discovered. Was there wasn't a one of those amongst the dead who were shot.

They were all killed with Marshal Art weaponry. It didn't take much reasoning on the police to realize that no one person could have killed some many men.

It had to take an adequate fighting force to do it. Who had to extremely highly experience in the martial arts. To be able to use such weaponry effectively.

Then there was these other incredible thing that we discovered, after searching extensively. Such as there wasn't any other footprints but, those we compared with the burnt boots, and shoes of those found dead amongst those being dispersed about the hill. In the place where a lot of those men fall. Leaving a lot of evidence behind, and those who were brought down the slop of the hill to be piled up inside that mission itself.

Which brought up one very good question. If they were dead above and around the mission. How did they manage to get down to the mission and be place inside it?

Where the fire department didn't even attempt to put out the fire burning it down to the ground. Leaving the total area undisturbed. Where not even a drop of water washed any evidence away?

Sue I know of only one fighting force that could be so awesomely deadly. That in fact could walk in as much blood that literally socked the ground, yet drag dead bodies. Without leaving any trance.

The one I'm referring to is the very same one that appeared some 5 years ago, then after something similar also took place, upped and suddenly disappeared. That until that night at the Mission.

Where legend had it was led by one Connie Price. Who Connie Stone did in fact mention twice. Once at your friend Pat's apartment, and them again over the phone at this very place. Where on that very night another massacre took place.

Who I do believe also had herself ten, demons straight from out of hell against the mobs once before.

All that was ever discovered about her. Was that she was referred to a swamp phantom. Who killed some 25 men involve with the syndicate, without firing a single shoot."

"Joe I can't believe what I'm hearing? You are becoming obsessed over persecuting Connie unjustly. When I have known Connie for over six, years. What you are implying is not only ridiculous, it's utterly absurd."

"Sue hear me out. Thus far all that's came down, is revolving about one very illusive person that goes by the name of Art ----------.

Pat -------- brother I do believe. who is believe to be involved in the deaths of three, people on the night he supposedly runaway from an orphanage.

Where by the way was never heard of again other than by hearsay allegations of being involved in several other deaths.

Where when his name is placed into the puzzle. All the probabilities seem to come together. Leaving only one logical conclusion.

He has to be a connecting link, or one of them that binds everything together. Where I think Connie is connected with him in some way that's being overlooked.

Carl told me about Connie being in the neighborhood of the orphanage that night Pat's brother escaped. Where it was determined that he was believed to have been seriously hurt.

Where again Connie a doctor.

Where again. All hell did break loose when you two, went to visit his sister Pat. Where I can link the two, of you together ever since being seen in the company of a young girl around this boy own age. Where I do believe as you tell it she is your mice.

Sue I want that boy, and the ones behind Carl's death. Where if I don't get them. I'm going to nail your behinds to the wall!"

"Joe just suppose you could be right to some extent. Which by the way you're not. I think that you should be going after the one, really responsible that boy's sister.

With us you have nothing but, conjecture. Where we have nothing to hide. All that you have stated has been explained to everyone's satisfaction. Otherwise you wouldn't be the only one coming here insinuating

If you did as you suspect. We both know that we wouldn't be sitting here right now. We would be behind bars.

I don't have to defend myself to you, nor does Connie. You go right ahead, and do what you feel you have to do but, you won't find what you are looking for here but, circumstantial coincidence

Where I don't know why you keep bringing up some runaway kid. May I empathize kid? Need I remind you that Connie, and I happen to be two, grown adult women.

Now seriously considering that fact. Why would we want to get involved with some kid? Can't you see how ridiculous that sounds?

Where I don't honestly even want to assume what absurd assumption you have going on in the mind of yours. However, being a victim of circumstance doesn't mean that either Connie, or I are in any sense of the word homicidal. Whereas I recall I do believe Connie was at your police department. When what you're accusing her of took place. Where Donna, and myself didn't even know she went out of the house for any reason. Because we were here sleeping I might add."

"I think I best be going now."

You needn't show me out I know the way but, Sue before I go. I would like to say one thing. Congratulations, you pulled it off, this time. Don't be foolish to think your luck will hold.

Get involved in anything like this again and I promise you it will be your last. I don't forget easily."

"Joe I live life I don't run, or hide from it. As long as I know I'm not doing anything wrong. I'll get involved in whatever I want to. It's in my nature, it's also my profession. Have a nice day."

Chapter 21

Five mouths, past. Five, gorgeous happy mouths with nothing but joyous tranquility where we never let ourselves forget, all that it took us to ravel in it.

Both Connie and I were near to competing are internships. Where Art was reading himself through legal volume, and the entire encyclopedia. Plus, taking entry level collage exams while finishing up high school. Wanting to study to become a doctor himself.

It was Saturday morning Connie and I rose early. Leaving Art sleeping as we showered and dressed.

We were sitting on the bench at the foot of the bed in Art's bedroom. The house we brought had 3 bedrooms but, we all slept in Art's. Except when either Connie or I wanted to be alone.

"Well Connie." I turned to her saying brushing my hair." Just a few more mouths, and we will be on our way to a whole new temporary life in California. Where we will be taking Tommy back to his parents, just like we planned all along.

Just think of it. Spending are extend vacation living on 20, glorious acres, in our own cottage, or soon will be having all to ourselves. Where we will be living happily ever after that will soon to be our own place.

Where we will be able to finally hang up our own shingles and begin to practice are well earned professions without having a care in the world.

Connie it's only a couple weeks until Christmas. Let's say we go out shopping for something utterly fantastic for Art? Seeing how he's finally going to get himself out of hat dress, and be himself again."

"I'm all for that." Connie rose up going to sit down beside Art sleeping soundly. "Come on sleepy head..." She called out to him, shaking him into awareness." It's time to open those gorgeous blue eyes of yours and get up. Sue and I are going to take you out shopping."

"Oh, can't it wait...? I just want to sleep a little longer..." He slumberous spoke out nestling his head cuddling back into his pillow.

"No it can't..." I spoke out yanking the pillow out from under his head." You need some fresh air and sunshine besides we have an early Christmas present for you but, of course if you rather sleep. We could make you wait until Christmas to open it...?"

"A Christmas present...?!" Art excitedly jerked up saying." Are you serous...?! For me...?!"

"Yes, honey for you. Connie go get it will you."

"Sure thing. Where is it?"

"Now wasn't that forgetful of me. I have it hidden in my bottom dresser drawer." I rose saying going to the dresser.

"So what is it...?!" Art anxiously asked." You know I can't remember when I last received a Christmas present... At the orphanage they just past toys out, as for at home Ma, never had any extra money to buy presents."

"Well here you go honey." I walked towards the bed saying. Placing a wrapped package down upon it. As I sat down on the edge of the mattress. While he anxiously unwrapping the colorful wrapping paper opening up the box.

"Why it's a purse...?" He removed it from the box saying.

"It's not just a purse honey." I spoke out to him." It's a night bag, go ahead and open it."

Art open the purse to star startlingly at what was inside it.

" Why it's full of money...?" He joyously gasped out." You shouldn't have, and it's all for me to spend on anything I want...?"

"We thought you could use some spending money seeing how Christmas is so close." Connie spoke out saying." It's not much only $500.00 dollars for you to spend frivolously on anything you heart desires."

"Oh, thank you... now I can buy the two, of you something for a change..." He leaped up from the bed jumping off it." Just give me a few minutes...!" He happily shouted back as he ran into the bathroom.

* * * *

For nearly a week all we did was spend money, buying each other Christmas presents until Donna's money ran out.

Connie and I sat watching Donna placing the presents she bought us under the tree. Smiling at each other, anxiously waiting for her to finish before surprising her with still another unexpected present we bought for her.

"Well ladies." Art turned to them leaning back while sitting on her lower legs before the tree.

" I didn't get you all I wanted to but, it's the thought that counts. Let's say that I take you both out for lunch? Your treat of course."

"Well I don't know ...?" Connie skeptically replied." It's sort of windy out, and the glue I applied to you wig might not be dry yet.

" Oh, come on Connie. It's dry, boy I'll be glad when I can have my own hair back again I hate being bold headed... See look..." She pulled up on her hair saying." It's dry..."

"Well you heard her. Come on Connie stop being so skeptical, let's go out and eat." I rose up from the sofa saying. Walking towards the hall closet being followed by Donna going to get are coats. Stopping before opening the door for Connie to come up, and join us to open it.

"Well, my goodness...?" I gasped out." What's this...?" I removed a tan cashmere coat with a fluffy fur collar. From off a coat hanger bringing it out of the closet." Well I know this isn't mine...?" I enviously spoke out. "What about you Connie does it belong to you...?"

"Why no it doesn't..."

"Well then it can only mean that it belongs to Donna here..." I held it open for her to put on." Let's find out if it fits her shall we..."

"That's not my coat...?" Donna stared starry eyes at it saying.

"Now it is honey." I slid it on her say." Happy early Christmas honey from Connie and I with love." I wrapped it close around her.

" My Goodness don't you look ever so gorgeous... If ever a coat was made to bring out your splendor this is it..."

" Sue it's so furry and cuddly..." Art fondly caressed the fur collar cuddly rubbing her cheek against the fur collar.

" Oh.... I just have to see what it looks like on me...!" She gasped out. Ecstatically running up the stairs towards the bedroom.

"Look at her Connie she's so excited..."

"Sue she's a he."

"I know that."

"Do you...? For that matter does he anymore? He's becoming more like a woman than we are, can't you see what happening to him? He's starting to become a woman. Where we can't let that happen."

"It won't Connie, we don't let him forget that he's all man but, let's not talk about that now. Hush now he's coming back down."

We stood watching Art walking down the stairs. Where I never really given much thought to the devastating side effects his becoming a woman could have on him. Startlingly seeing what Connie was saying.

Not being able not to notice his elegance, and gracefulness which left nothing to be desired, or for that matter envied by another woman. She was divinely exquisite, dazzlingly refined, and mysterious alluring.

"My God..." I gasped out from shear jealousy as she stood before us.

"Well ladies shall we be going? I'm dying to show off my new coat. I feel so gorgeous, and extravagantly sexy..."

He spoke out saying walking out the front door towards the van. With us following behind her."

"Connie." I whispered out speaking to her behind Art's back. "I'm beginning to see what you mean Connie." I shut the front door walking towards the van beside her saying, as Donna stood impatiently standing at the van waiting.

" Connie maybe we let it get out of control I hope it's not too late to undo what we have done, is it?"

"Sue you don't know how badly I want to but, we can't. All we need is a couple more mouths. Until them all we can do is procrastinate, and never let him forget that he's all man underneath all the femininity. We still need to prepare him for what lies ahead. We can't risk confusing him anymore than we already have."

"What are you two talking about?" Art asked as we joined him standing beside the van.

"We were only talking about how good that coat looks on you." I answered him." Where we also can't help but, to know how incredible of a man you are that lurking underneath that gorgeous exterior.

Who's even more so handsome, and debonairly spectacular. Art you must never forget that in that house, and out in the world. You are still all man, where I for one, am not about to let you forget who you are."

"I know that. How I could not forget? With the two, most gorgeous ladies in the world never chess to remind me.

Now come on let's go... This is Christmas and I only have a few mouths left to drive men wild... So let's go and have some fun..."

"You are right sugar, come on Sue let's get back into the spirit of Christmas I'm sure Art isn't forgetting his position in life. We will make sure to remind him under the tree when we return back home later. For now, let's go have some fun. I'm driving."

Connie climbed in behind the wheel waiting for Art to climb in the back behind her. While I walked around to get in the back passenger seat beside her. As Connie pulled out of the driveway.

"Where are we going Connie?" Art ask.

"Let's just drive until you spot a place that suits your fancy. How does that sound to you?"

"That sound great, but I only have one complaint. Why is it that I'm always the one, that has to sit in the back seat?"

"We can't trust you up front for one, reason. You have impulsive hands, and we don't have the willpower to say no. Where for another you draw enough attention as it is." Connie pulled to a

stop shopping for a stop light saying. As I slid over closer to Art giving him every opportunity to become impulsive.

"What in the hell...!" I startlingly shouted out. Alarmingly hearing the side door being pulled open. Panicky turning my head. Seeing a derelict looking man jumping inside the van.

Shoving is was passed me placing himself between Art and I. Pointing a gun to Donna's head.

Shouting out at me. "Slam the damn door bitch!"

As another guy looking even worse than the first jerk the front passenger door open. Also holding a gun in his hands pointing it at Connie sitting behind the steering wheel. Slamming the door closed. Shouting out.

"No sudden move...! Move it bitch! Forcing Connie to drive through a red light than through the intersection

As the guy in the back seat got up and forced Donna to move across the seat, to sit next to me. Refusing to remove the guy from her head. While positioning himself against the solid wall of the van.

Making it impossible for me to get at him. Rendering me helpless to protect Donna before he could have shot her in the head.

"Any funning shit. And she's dead...! The guy holding the guy to Donna's head threateningly said.

"Alright you two, get back her in the back of the van. At the next stop light. You first bitch.!" He points the gun at me. saying.

As Connie came to a stop at another stop light. "Alright let's move it!" He demanded shouting out to me. This time chocking back the hammer of the gun he was holding against Donna's head.

"No, Connie...! I yelled out at her. Knowing what was going through her mind as she placed the gear shift in neutral, and was on the verge of rising up out of her seat. The second I was going to move complying to the guys demands to move to the back of the van. "They have Donna, you can't."

"I said get you assess back here, now...!" He angrily shouted out fearfully watching me while looking towards the side window. To see what was happening outside the van.

"Alright mister I'm moving just don't shot..." I spoke out rising to climb over the seat to work my way to the back of the van.

Where I sat against the side wall watching diligently. As he forcefully shoved Donna to climb over. Hold the gun pressing against the back of her head. Holding her by her neck as he climbed over. Forcing her to the back. Where he forced her to sit across from me, against the other wall of the van.

Never once removing the gun from Donna's head. While that other guy holding a gun kept pointing it at Connie.

"Alright dearly now drive or you are dead meat. Now move it and get us the hell out of here!

Now move up behind the wheel and let's get the hell out of here!"

"Hey, Russ what do you want me to do with these two, back here?"

"Damn! Aren't you the fucken idiot! Find something to get one to tie the other. Then tie the other one up. Does that take brains?"

"There isn't anything?" He shouted back.

"Sue their clothes asshole!"

"Here." I alarmingly shouted out at the guy holding the gun. Seeing him looking a Donna to ripe her clothes off. "Use mind." I kicked off my high heels opening my thighs wide open. Showing him my nylons." You can use my nylons. I'll take them off if you want?"

"Yeah, do that. Take them both off, and no funny business or I'll blow her brains out!""

"I removed my nylons holding them up for him to come get from my hand. Making sure to leave my thighs wide open.

Hoping to distract his eyes attention on me for just one second, so that I could make an attempt to get at that gun he was holding against Donna's head.

Knowing that the second I made my move so would Connie.

Where instead of him by having a good look see up under my skirt. He leaned Donna forwards

leaning with her. Having Donna take the nylons from my hand.

Where he them force her to use one, of them to tie my hands behind me. Making sure to check them before he proceeded to tie Donna's hands behind her back.

"Alright Russ their hands are tied. Now what?"

"Don't know just yet. Give me a moment to think dammit! By the was Dave how much did we get?"

"Shit I don't know but, it sure wasn't worth what we had to go through to get it. Where it's getting costlier every fucken minute…!"

" Just stop your damn complaining damn it! And keep a look out those back window I want to know what's coming up behind us…"

"Shit…!" Dave nervously shouted out." It's the fucken cops…! They are right on are ass…!"

"Relax they won't do anything as long as we have these three, as hostages… Listen you rags do exactly what we tell you, and you just might come out of this alive. We have nothing to lose by killing you. When we already killed two, people. Do you understand what I'm saying…?

Dave just kept a close eye on them two. I'll take care of this one.

You, Turn right at the next corner. Then left into the first alley you come onto … Now step on it Bitch! And don't you stop until I tell you too…!"

Connie did as he demanded as we sat helpless at the rear of the van.

Knowing we could get to the one paying more attention to looking out the rear window than he was to us. But, not at the one, holding the gun at Connie

"Dave are those cops still with us?"

"Like flies on shit they are Russ... We are never going to shake them. Least of all not this way... Not the way that cunt is driving were not. We are going to have to make a stand for it. Those cops aren't not going to let us escape."

"I hear you Russ." Dave looked out the front windshield looking around for a place to make a stand spotting an old house with plenty of room to pull the van in front of.

"Your right Dave, this isn't working. Alright bitch pulls over to the curve, before that old house and park this junk heap." He ordered Connie

Connie pulled over to the curve as he demanded. Shutting off the engine.

"Alright scumbag! Get the coat off and cover the windshield with it. Dave get their coats off as well and use them to cover those back and side windows. "

Dave literally yanked Donna's and my coats off to use them to cover all three, of the windows.

Leaving only the two windows on the back door for Dave to peek out of. While Connie used her's to cover the windshield. Hanging it from the vises to cover the windshield.

Leaving only the two front windows to see out of. Where Russ could look through the side view mirrors to spot anyone coming up from his side of the van.

Leaving only Connie's, window where Ross was intending to use Connie as a shield to cover him

"Now sit with you back against that door.".

"Damn it Russ... Those cops are all around us..."

"Back off cops...!" Russ panicky shouted out." Or we'll waste these three, cunts we have inside with us...Back off damn it...!"

"Dammit Russ we have to get the hell out of here...!"

"We are. Now just shut the fuck up! Right now...! Come on you bitch...!" Ross grabbed Connie by her hair pulling her back.

Dave when I tell you to. Open those back doors, and start bringing those two, out ahead of you. Where I'll be standing before them."

"Alight miss hot to trot, we are stepping out. Now very slowly climb out and stand before the open door and wait for me to join you. Any funny crap and your two, friends in the back are dead and you as well.

Hey you cop out there. We coming out. Don't shoot. If anyone tries anything stupid, we are all going to die right here and now! Now back away from the van...!" He demanded.

Alright sweet cheeks now move it very slow. "He let Connie climb out the door. Ordering her to stop so that he could join her. Where he walked her holding his gun to her head to the back of the van. Where he knocked on the door. Speaking out for Dave to come out. As he took up a protective position behind her waiting for Dave to emerge.

"Alright bitch. You are going to be my eyes, and you damn well better tell me the damn trust. Your fucken life depends on it."

He threateningly held his revolver with the hammer cocked back against the back of her head saying." Do you see anyone...?"

"Yes, Connie answered him. Not having no choice but, to comply as long as Donna, and Sue were being held hostage.

"Tell them to move back away from the van..." He demandingly ordered her." Or you will be the first to go out without a head!"

"Please..." Connie nervously spoke out getting the cops attention." Please do what he says... My God. Please...!" She pleadingly bagged.

The officers complied by moving back away from the van.

"They are backing away from the van." Connie informed him as he used her body to cover his.

"Alright... Dave get those two, out here now.!"

"You heard the man get up!" Dave ordered them to get up and stand before the back doors. Using them to stand hunched over as her opened to two, back doors.

"Alright Russ we are here, now what? "

" Remove your belt. As for your cunts, removed your nylons, and hand them to Dave. We are all going to out away from here tied together."

After Donna, and I were forced to climb down. We were force to gather up around the two, of them. Where Connie was force to tie all are hands together. While that Dave guy never let his gun move from Donnas head as they remained inside the inner circle that the three, of us were making around them. .

' Alright Russ their hands are all tied together, now what?"

"Now we are going to grab hold of each other and not letting go, or we are all dead. As we all walk up to that house we are parked in front of.

"Now we are all going to start walking together. Dave I will with the one I got. You keep your two, instep until we make it up to that front door of that house. At the first sign of any trouble. We start shooting back, and let the cops do the rest. Now everyone follows me.

Russ grabbed hold of Connie's waist band of her skirt and shoved. Forcing her to take the first step. To walk towards the house while keeping himself and his partner slouched down in-between them. While shouting out at the cops.

"Listen up cops, make one move towards us and they are dead..."

"Give it up you guys." A loud voice came out over a loudspeaker." There's no place for you to go. Release your hostages, and take your chances in a court.

You are only digging yourselves in deeper, by adding kidnaping to the charges already against you...Give yourselves up... You can't get away..."

"Fuck off cop...!" Dave defiantly shouted back alarmingly shouting out." Russ look out...!"

As he spotted two, people emerging from the front door of the house. He was heading towards. Firing instinctively at the old man, and women as they emerged out of the house onto the front porch. Where they were approaching at the same time. Thrusting them back against the walls of the house, by the impacting bullets hitting them in their chests as.

That impacting bullets repelled them back against the side of the house. Where they slid down against it down onto the deck of the porch. Beside the open door.

As the group shoved their way past the bodies lying upon the porch into the house. With the police walking towards them.

Refraining to fire, pointing their guns directly at all of them bunched up into a human circle entering the house. Where once inside. Russ yelled out for Dave to shut the damn door.

Where he stuck his foot out from the circle to kick out his foot slamming the door shut. After which they continued to walk us into the living room of the house.

"Damn...!" Dave ecstatically shouted out." We made it...! I can't believe it...! We had those cops by their balls...!

I was sure we were dead when you shot those two, coming out the door. Damn...! I could actually feel and taste the bullets of them shooting at me.... Why didn't they shoot us...?

" They haven't as yet but,, that's not saying they will. Unless I can figure out what to do from here to get us the hell out of this fucken mess?!"

Russ released his end of the nylon. Shoving Connie out of his way as he stepped out of the circle. Still aiming his gun at Connie. authoritatively speaking out to Dave.

"Now get those two, cunts back against the wall. Where you young and sexy are staying with me." He grabbed hold of Donna, yanking her right into the gun barrel.

"You miss hot to trot are staying with me. I have taken a liking to you sweet cheeks."

He dragged Donna by her hair towards the large front window. In the living room looking out over the entire street in front of the house. Hold her before him for everyone to see her standing before him.

As Dave walked Connie and I backwards up against the wall. Tossing the nylons at me, shouting. " Tie her up dam nit! Then bring you ass back by me. Any funny business and you are dead bitch!"

I tied Connie's hands behind her back, then walked towards him, and allowed him to tie my hands. Not once taking my eyes off Donna, and her perilous situation. Of him holding that damn gun against the side of her head.

" Now that's what I like an obedient bitch. Just like they should be. Now go sit your ass down against that wall, and you sit too. And don't either of you move or even flinch."

Where he then portended to sit down in a chair facing sideways towards us.

We both sat knowing that we could get to Russ guy but, that other guy wasn't giving either of us an opening to get at him either. Leastways not before he would shoot and killed

at least one of us

As for Donna she was being held at bay facing forwards towards the window, so he could use her as a human shield, to protect himself.

As he drew back the curtains uncovering the other half of the bay picture window. Way across the room from where we were siting. Making are situation virtually hopeless.

"Russ that makes four, now that's been killed... Now what in the hell are we going to do now to get ourselves out of this...?!"

"The only thing we can do. We will make demands that's what, and if they don't come across. We will kill these cunts one at a time until they do. Where we will give them one of the hostages dead until they do or we run out that's the best I can come up with for right now." in exchange until we get where we want to get. As soon as I figure that out."

"What sort of demands...?"

"How the hell do I know? I haven't had much time to think of what we want yet now have I?! Just give me a few minutes to think alright... I'll come up with something we want. Just make sure those two, are tied securely."

"They're. What are they doing out there?"

" Nothing ...They are just sitting there waiting, and watching. Where that's all they can do right now."

"Russ is this it...?"

" It looks like it Dave, that is unless we can come up with a way out before they get tired of waiting, and watching.

Them they will most likely are going to come busting in here but, you can be damn sure that we are going to take some of them along with us but, we're not dead yet."

* * * *

"Captain." Joe spoke out to Page, form their position behind his car." Did you recognize those hostages those two have? They have Connie, Sue and her mice... Of all fucken people for them to latch onto. Jesus who would have ever thought...?"

" I see them... Dammit. Why do they always have to be the ones victimized...? Shit...!" He frustratingly shouted out. I just know that someone is going to die..."

" Capt. they must be holding Sue's mice. Those two, would have done something by now. Capt. they're both kung fu experts. Where Connie goes far beyond that. Carl mentioned that she was some sort of Ninja whatever the hell that is."

"Are you sure about that?"

"Yes, I'm sure. Those nitwits are holding all the aces, where they don't have the vaguest idea what they are holding onto is the devil's demons. Where all those two, would need is a second. It has to be Sue mice that they have to be worried about."

"So what do you suggest we do?"

"Wait it out captain, and hope that they get the chance to get at those guys. Those guys have already killed four, people.

Whereas if we pressure them to make them feel it's hopeless to where they could lose it entirely They might just start shooting. Not giving a shit.

We don't want to attempt to rushing the place. Where just maybe we could get a few men up close enough to analyze their predicament, and formulate a reasonable plan of action where hopefully it won't cost in lives being lost.

There's only two, of them. They can't cover the whole house we could keep them occupied at the front. While we send a couple of men to cover the windows. To reconnoiter what's going on inside the house.

It's my guess that they are in no position to attack them, and won't if the mice are in any immediate danger."

"Alright Joe I'll send some men in with walkie-talkies so that they can keep us informed but, first I want to try something.

Those are desperate men that don't have a damn thing to loss by killing all of them just like you said.

Where the way I surmise it, as their position is hopeless where I might be able to save one if not all of them. However, at the first sign of them starting to shoot I want those men to open fire. Where I'll give you your diversion." He said reaching into his car pulling out a the microphone speaker to amplify his voice over the loud speakers on the squad.

"You go get the men moving out I'll give you five, minutes to get them in position." He rose the mike up to his mouth saying, as Joe left his position behind the car.

"You inside the house. This is captain Page of the police department. We have the house surrounded. There's no way you can get out.

However, I'm in a position to negotiate, and to work out a reasonable compromise that would bring this all to a satisfactory end for all concerned.

I'm sure that you are fully aware of your situation, and so are we. Where killing just for the purpose of just killing serves no purpose, unless you are total lunatics.

Is that why you are. Insane...? If so the law can't touch you. Can you hear me inside that house?"

"Dave did you hear what he just said? That's are way out ... He's telling us to kill them so let's waste them."

"Are you fucken nuts?! Can't you see that it's a set up? You have to be out of your gourds! If we kill them, we have nothing! Where they are the only means of getting out of this alive. If we kill just one of them. They won't hesitate to Strom this place. I'm not all that ready to kill myself just yet. Not when there's a chance of getting out of this alive I'm not. we have to keep them alive if at all possible, dammit!

Hey cop...!" Russ yelled out the window. Your damn right I'm nuts but, not as crazy as you. If you think that we are that stupid to fall for that crap!

You want us to come out. Better yet you come and get us out ... Please do come die with us You have nothing but, what we want to give you. If you don't meet are demands we will send them out to you peace by peace, until you do."

Russ shouted out exposing Donna. Pinning her face against the window holding his gun against the back of her head.

"I'll shoot off her ear then her nose t hen her other ear if you want their lives on your conscience try something stupid cop...!"

"Alright tell me what you want. There's no need for anymore killing. However, if one shot is fired. We are coming in! I need to stress, that as long as no harm comes to your hostages we just might be able to negotiate some sort of terms."

"I hear you cop." Russ shouted out." Just don't rush me. Can't you see we are in conference here. We will let you know when we are ready to discuss terms.

Dave keep your eye on the windows. Those sneaky dastards are up to no damn good I've a gut feeling that our time is about to run out, so let's make it worth are while."

"I'm hearing you Russ . What the hell it was fun while it lasted anyway, and we still have these bitches as hostages. What do you say that we go to hell in style taking them to hell with us sticking it to them?

Let's go out dying like men as are last act. I really do get off on black skinned women. That black hole of inequity and promiscuity is going to be my bottomless pit of damnation... It's inflamed with the fires of passion."

Dave walked over to straddle over Connie out stretched legs. Placing the barrel of his revolver against her forehead. Irately saying

" Hello bitch want to go to hell with me...?" Grabbed himself saying. Emphasizing his intentions of what he was expecting her to do for him." Well, how about it whore...?!"

"Hey. I can go along with that." Russ yelled out. "Alright bitch. Get down on your knees..."

Russ assertively demanded shoving Donna down onto her knees before him." I just love sweet vivacious succulent mouths ... Rub me sweet thing, and do me right, or die right now..." He aggressively demanded placing the barrel of his gun before Donna's mouth.

Donna place her trembling hand upon his manhood. Looking over at us as if telling us not to worry he will get us out of this.

"Hey you cop...!" Russ shouted out getting their attention." I might die this day but, I'm going to do it like a man...Don't you wish you could be so lucky...? My first demand is that you all watch, and appreciate a man willing to die with pride..."

"Hey mister..." I called out to him." Are you so uncertain of your manhood that you would have a mere girl do what only a woman could do for you?

If you are going to die like a man. You are going to want the attention and the affections of a women provocativeness that of a bitch, and I'm all bitch..."

I challenged his selection, hosting up my legs bending them open from my knees, opening my thighs to him.

" This is what a wholesome man wants. You want the heart of passion not the uncertainty of a fearful mouth. If you must die. Do so like a man not a weepy boy...I'm all hot, excited, and dripping wet. Come on big man come and get it..."

I aggressively spoke out, rubbing my tongue about my lips." Come give it to me...Come on big man, and give it to me I want it all. I know you want me ass hole... and I want you to give it to me good. Where maybe I'll give you the sendoff, that will make your death honor you as a man. You have no idea how the thought of tasting you, is making me so hot, and juicy...

Come on if you are the man I think you to be. Why are you wasting time her? Where you can have the time of your life with me.

You can't deny a woman her last request, now can you... Leave her be, and come fulfil your every desire with me.

Look... Look at it..." I invitingly spoke out propping my butt up waving myself before his ogling eyes.

"Yes..., Oh, yes... that is very nice... Real nice I do want it but, you are just going to have to wait your turn, to get yours. I prefer this one..."

"Hey sweet brown sugar..." Dave spoke out to Connie saying pressing his groin region against her mouth.

" I've something for your luscious mouths lips. If you want it, you are going to have to work for it... Come on hot lips do your whorish thing with your teeth. Let me out, and in the luscious month of yours."

* * * *

"Captain this is Tom. I'm in position by the side window. They've the two, women tied sitting with their backs against the wall, just off the living room, directly in front of the front picture window. One of the men is standing before the black women. Rubbing his groin region against her face."

"Tom is there anyway either one of the women could get at those two, without jeopardizing the other one?"

"No, way Capt. There's too much distance between them, and they have their guns cocked back. I might be able to pick off one but, not without preventing him from firing."

"Tom just hold your position, and keep me informed. Sooner or later one, of them has to screw up. All we need is time, and all we can do is wait it out but, don't let them see you.

We can't do anything about the sex thing. Are primary focus being to keep them women alive."

* * * *

"Hey cops...!" Russ yelled out. Standing before the window with the curtains wide open showing everyone what was going on with him and Donna.

" Why don't you come get yours...? There's plenty to go around for everyone ...Come on why don't you, and die like men like we are..."

Connie shoved Dave away from her, using her head." Hey, sugar. I really dig on a man who knows what he wants but, why don't you let me do you right...

Untie my hands so that I can give you the satisfaction you so richly deserve. The way I see it I'm as good as dead anyway. If I'm going to hell I want to do so as the bitch that I am, and go there doing for the man who killed me."

"Say Russ." Dave called out to him." Can I untie her hands...?"

"Why the hell not. Go ahead take your whore but, keep your eye on that other one. I don't trust her one damn bit. She's to dam cool for my liking."

"listen you two." Russ spoke out saying. Hold Donna by her hair. Forcing her to submit to his demands, ghoulishly grinning rambunctiously preforming for the cops being forced to watch the grotesque sight.

" Come on girly don't be jealous. You are going to get your turn. Dave turned his head to look at Sue sitting against the wall behind him. Watching diligently him getting his. While doing so Dave inadvertently aimed his gun directly at Sue.

Arrogantly speaking out." Russ is right about you. You are to cool of a cucumber but, no matter. You are as good as dead already. Don't rush it your time will come soon enough.

Where as long as you are still alive. There's still a chance we might change are minds. Look at her. She's taking advantage of her great opportunity.

Connie looked out of the corner of her eye over at Donna. With Donna looking back at her with enraged anger emanating from her eyes. As if contemplating of bringing an end to our peril. Where Connie desperately cried out to him with her eyes. Trying to tell him not to try anything fearfully saying to herself.' Please my God no... no. don't do anything...'

"Come on my beauty." Russ called out to her getting her eyes attention." Open those luscious lips wider. I want to get it all in...

"Oh, yes... that's it... Nice. Real nice I really like that..." He excitedly gasped out losing his concentration being overcome by the sensationalism he was receiving form Donna.

As Art waited, hoping for that split second. As he could sense the tension building as he hasten for that one, second. Feeling the pressure of the gun lightening against his forehead.

When the second Art waited for came. When Russ could no longer restrain himself form succumbing to Donna's stimulation.

When like a flash of lighting Art jerked up his hand attempting to deflect the gun away from his forehead. When he bit down as hard as he could. Sending such a horrendous mind shattering pain straight up into Russ's brain. That it sent Russ hurtling backwards, causing the gun he was holding to go off in the air.

As Art leaped up and with enraged furry of a charging bull. He charged towards Dave tackling him with such a force. Sending him crashing against the wall beside Connie. Causing his gun to go off.

As Connie jerked herself up from off the floor. Charging for Dave hunched over from being pinned against the wall gasping for air. Struggling to aim his gun to fire at Art as he held him pinned against the wall.

Where Connie leaped up, and hurtled herself feet first thrusting herself against Dave's throat above Art's back has he held him pinned against the wall.

When two, more thundering shots ring out into her ears. As Connie recoiled herself backwards off Dave's throat, and back into a standing position behind Art.

Where both Dave, and Art slid down the wall with Art collapsing down on top of Dave before her. With Art gushing blood out of his head.

Connie's heart stopped as her very being became besieged with panic as her very life ran out of her. As she stood in a petrified state staring down at the out stretched body lying on the floor. With the top of his head half blown away.

"No...!" Connie hysterically screamed out insanely picking up the gun lying on the floor beside Art and insanely squeezed the trigger firing insidiously at Russ, groaning, and moaning while squirming about upon the floor.

paradoxically screaming out at the top of her lungs. The horrifying torment of her heart being torn out of her chest. Not believing that it was Art laying on the floor.

When her finger unconsciously went to the trigger of the gun she was holding, and convulsively kept squeezing on the trigger. aimlessly clicking on the spent casings inside the chambers of the gun. As she looked aimlessly hysterically laughing in a state of total madness.

Where I became stricken with horrified disbelief. Finding myself somehow crawling over to Art so stricken with shock. That I had no conception of what I was doing as I barbarically

attempted to scoop up his blood.

Frantically attempting to pick up his blood to put it back inside his head. As I kneeled beside him with my hands free hysterically trying to save his life. Not even remembering how I managed to get my wrist free.

* * * *

"Holy Jesus...!" Joe shouted out as he came bursting into the house through the front door, leading his men inside the house. Alarmingly seeing me kneeling beside Donna trying desperately to stop the gushing blood from spurting out of the top of her head.

As Connie stood in a rigid state, still squeezing the trigger on an empty gun. Pointing it at the man laying against the wall beside the picture window.

He went to remove the gun from Connie's paralyzed gripping hand. Removing his handcuffs, he handcuffed Connie's wrists behind her back. Then turn to his men standing just inside the front door.

" Dammit! Don't just stand there! Get her away from him, and handcuff her, Dammit! "

"You mean cuff her...?" One of the men ask not knowing if he heard Joe right.

"Yes, dammit! Cuff her... Do it now damn you...!"

"No...!" I paradoxically screamed out at the top of my lungs. As I was being dragged away from Art's body lying on the floor.

" He'll die...1 He'll die without me...! Let me go to him...!" I frantically screamed out. Kicking and struggling hysterically trying to break free.

"Dammit Joe this one is really Waco... As he, along with two, other officers dragged Sue out of the house. As Joe escorted Connie out of the house as she hideously continued to laugh in an insane state of mind.

As she leads aimlessly totally unaware of her state of mind. Oblivious of what happened. With her finger still reacting as if it was squeezing a trigger, while being lead down the steps. Up to a waiting ambulance.

Where she was them handed her over to a medical team waiting to take care of her. As Sue was already being driven off in another ambulance to the hospital.

Tom came walking up to Joe as he stood watching the ambulance driving away calling out to him as he approached him.

" My God, Joe I never seen anything like it. I saw the whole thing through the window. Such heroics with total disregard for life. They all sprung in defense of each other . It all happened so fast there was nothing I could do...

Joe there was no way that mice could have did what she did without not knowing that she wouldn't come out of it alive. She sacrificed her own life so that those other two, might live. Even with her being shoot in the head twice. She still managed to render that bastard helpless..."

"Alright Tom just put it in your report." The captain joined them saying.

'But Captain it was such a waste..."

"Forget it Tom it goes along with the job. Now let's just get this mess wrapped up, and the hell out of here.

Chapter 22

I awakened finding myself lying in bed. Not knowing where I was, or how long I've been where I was.

Finding myself in a room all alone, that was so drab that the only thing one would want to do is to close their eyes, and go back into a deep sleep again.

Shockingly my mind alarmingly recalled the last moments I remembered!" Oh, my God...! Art...! Where's Art...?!" I started frantically screaming out." I want to see Art...! And couldn't stop from hysterically ranting, and raving at the top of my lungs.

When a small slot in the door opened. Getting me to stare diligently at the blinding light that came streaking in through it.

Causing me to jerk up into a sitting position on the bed. Startlingly seeing two, beady eyes appearing in. Followed by a voice saying.

"Who is it that you wish to see?" Barbra the head nurse asked.

"What...?!" I bewilderingly shouted back." Who the hell are you...?! Let me out of here right now...!"

I jerk myself out of bed demanding. Charging towards the door finding it locked." Open this damn door...!"

"Yes, immediately..." Barbara answered. "You just relax I'll be right back." She slid the slot door shut saying.

Where I was left impatiently pacing back and forth about the room waiting for her return. Only to see another pair of eyes peering in the open slot of the door, an eternity later.

"Who the hell are you?! Let me the hell out of here now, damn it!"

"My name is Andy. Now if you would be so kind as to step back away from the door, and calm down I might come inside, where we can talk some."

I disturbingly stepped back away from the door. Hearing a key turning unlocking it. Where upon a pudgy, breaded man entered my room. Wearing a doctor's smock. Where it took me only seconds to recognize him.

"You can't be serous...? I'm not insane...? I know you...?"

"I never said that you were Sue but, I'm happy to see that you have returned back to us." He said closing, and locking the door behind him. Then turning back around to face me.

" Now why don't you go right back to bed, so that we can talk."

"Return...?" I skeptically asked. Doing as he requested. Going to sit on the bed." Just what are you talking about ... Where are my friends...?"

"You friend Connie is just down the hall. As for your other friend Donna. We're going to have to talk, before I can tell you where she is.

"Oh..., My God, No....!" I remorsefully broke down into tears. From the horrifying memory of that terrible horrifying day...

" Andy you've to let me see her... I have to get out of here, and go to her... How long have I been here...?"

" Sue it's too late." He sympathetically replied." That whole nightmare as long since passed. You have been here for almost four, mouths.

Sue, Donna is dead. However, it appears as if you didn't know her as well as you thought you did, or did you know? That Donna was a teenage boy. Who was wanted by the police for murder.

Sue you've been in a comatose state of shock. Totally oblivious of your surroundings since that tragic day.

I didn't want to spring the sorrowful news on you like this but, I just as soon have you find out now, then later where you might suffer an relapses.

Sue you know me. I'm a colleague of yours. I respect and admire you for your accomplishments as well as I do Connie's.

However, you have to come to grips with the reality of all that's happened. You do remember all that transpired that tragic day I take it?"

"Yes, I remember but, I don't want too. I take it that I'm at your sanitarium then?"

"Yes, you're. Sue I can't blame you for not wanting to forget but, you can't close your mind to what happened. You must accept the reality of it, or it will continue to haunt, and repress you from recovering."

" Past" Barbara the head nurse call out to Andy from the slot in the door. Getting his attention.

" Doctor may I speak to you for a second it's important."

"Yes, right away. Excuse me Sue I'll be right back." He went to place his ear up to the open slut in the door.

"Yes, what it is Barbara? He patiently waited listening to what she wanted to tell him. While she was whispering something into his ear.

"Why that's incredible news...And it couldn't have happened at a better time. Thank you, I'll be right there." He walked away from the door anxiously hurrying back towards the bed I was sitting on. As the nurse slid the door slot shout.

" Speaking of a unexpected phenomenon. Your friend Connie also has just came out of her comatose state of mind as well. Now isn't that incredible I must say. Speak of a coincidence..."

"Andy as mush of a miracle as it must appears. It's not a phenomenon. Not when one understands the force behind it. When can I leave?"

"Leave...? Oh, no I'm afraid that you just can't leave just yet... You have been confine here. I just can't release you without authorization form the court."

"Go speak to them then. Just get me the hell out of here...! As you can see my mental fatalities are in order. I'm no longer incapacitate.

I see no reason why Connie and I should be detained here any longer... Andy you could get us out of here if you wanted to."

"Sue there's still the matter of the police wanting to talk to you about your friend Donna. I don't know how I could? Then there's still your mental state of mind to consider. No, I'm sorry what you're asking is impossible."

"Andy I'm a psychiatrist. I'm qualified to ascertain my mental status. I'm as sound as you are. I was only temporary amnesic.

I'm not anymore, nor am I'm a lawyer but. if they are no charges against me. I know that you can't detain me here against my will. There isn't is there?"

"No? but, you have both been placed here under the order of the court. I just can't take your word for being mentally sound.

What if you should suffer a relapse? I have my career to consider… No, I'm sorry Sue. I've to obtain a release not only from the courts, and the police but. from my superiors as well. Then there's all the paper work that's involved.

Sue it's not going to happen because you think you are mentally capable to resume your life. You know as well as I do. That I've no choice but, to follow procedure. It's the same for everyone no, exceptions, That's the rules"

"Andy I know all about procedures. I also know that they can be resolved in less than five, hours. I served my internships in places like this one.

One telephone call could give you a temporary release, to release us for 48 hours on our own reconnaissance.

As for the police. They know where they can find me. I'm not going anyplace but, back home and back to work. Now I want out of here, now get me out."

"I guess it could be done? But, I don't mind telling you that I don't like this one bit. You have only been out of your condition for less than an hour…?"

"You know as well as I do. That five, minutes is ample time to determine if the mind is able to function morally. Where, and as you can see I'm in full control of my mantle facilities.

I can assure you that my mind is as good as it always been. Where the police are my affair not yours. I've nothing to hide, or too feel guilty about."

"Alright Sue I'll see what I can do to get you out. I hope you realize that I'm sticking my neck out a mile on you. If it was anyone else, I wouldn't even be considering doing this... Just remember that I'm only doing this out of admiration for you.

I'll have Connie moved into you room but, only if I feel certain about her mental state of mind as well. Meaning I'm going to have to check her out first."

"Thank you Andy I'll never forget you for what you are doing for us."

"Sue you're going to owe me big time for his. You know I had always had a thing for you. Maybe later we can try to rekindle. That old flame that once burnt brightly between us?" He suggestively implied, unlocking the door walking out it. Forgetting to relock it again.

Leaving me sitting on the bed in a state of remorse. Totally withdrawn sinking deeper and deeper into the depressed state of mind. Also knowing that I had to maintain my composure until I was released.

Nostalgically remembering back though the hardships, and the despairs we went through together. Them the total emptiness that I had left to bare without Art.

When Connie came walking in startlingly bursting out saying." Sue...!" As she came charging towards me, cried out running up to me. Hugging me against her...

" Oh, Connie I'm so happy to see you again... Are you alright...?"

"Yes, I think so, how about you...?"

"I'm fine, now that you are here with me. Come sit down beside me and cry no more. You can't let Art see you like this. He's here you know... He might be dead but, we haven't lost him... He's here with us."

"Sue his body is dead, but his soul lives inside me. I want you to understand that what I feel I must do. Is of my own free will.

Sue from now on you are strictly on your own. You are free to decide for yourself what you want to do.

As for me I could never be happy without being near Art. He gave me life, he made me want to live. My life ended that fatal day…

I want to hold him in my arms again… I want to feel his love inside me… I want the warmth of his compassion and sensitivity ingratiating my soul…"

"Hush Connie someone is coming." I whispered out to her. Hearing the door opening where for the first time. Seeing the women behind the eyes that peer in at me through the slot of the door. appearing as a person.

When she did I instantly recognized her as Andy's wife. The very women that caused Andy and I to break up.

"Well ladies how's everything going? I just stopped by to see if I could do anything for either of you."

"Thank you Barbara." I replied answering her." I can't thank you enough for all you done for us already. Taking care of us all these mouths.

"Well ladies…" Andy entered the room joyously speaking." I have obtained your releases."

"Hi, honey…" He stopped abruptly, coming upon his wife Barbara standing in the middle of the room. Speaking out to him holding out her hand.

"Thank you honey." Barbara impatiently pointed to the release forms he was holding.

"Just give those releases to me, and go tend to your other patients now."

"Yes, dear… right away dear…" He walked back out the door saying.

"Sue if you want my opinion. I think that the both of you should take a couple days to reorient ate yourselves." She stood reading over the release forms.

"Both of you do realize this release is only good for 48 hours. If you don't return back here for further evaluation, an arrest warrant will be posted for your arrest."

"Yes, we understand that, we will be back, where again thank you." I replied answering her. As Connie and I impatiently got dressed in anything we could find.

Only having the clothes, we were wearing on the day Art was killed. Where my dress was still covered with his blood.

Putting on those clothes made our skin crawl, but we had no other choice but, to wear them.

"Don't thank me to soon. It's still going to be an hour, or so yet before you can be released. I'll be back to walk you out.

* * * *

That hour seemed like an eternity that would never end. Before she came walking back into the room, holding the release papers in her hand saying.

"Well I see that you are all dressed, and ready to leave. I've your passes right here. Shall we be going them…" She leads both of us to the front door unlocking it.

Well ladies I'm not going to open it for you. I took the liberty of calling you a cab, its parked right out front. Now don't forget. You have only 48 hours to be back."

"We understand." I spoke up for Connie as we stepped out the front door into freedom once again. Stopping to inhale the fresh air." Just smell that Connie it smells like freedom at long last…"

* * * *

It was 11:30 in the morning when we climbed into the cab. Where upon giving the cab driver the address to take us to.

We sat looking at each other in the backseat. Not knowing what to say for the first time to each other. Really not knowing what was going through the others mind.

"Sue I have a lot to do before this day ends, and I don't know if I have enough time to do all I have to do."

"You mean us don't you? We will make time for whatever it is but, we best get home first and change."

"No, Sue."

"Connie don't say it.... I know what's going through your mind."

"Sue I've been doing some thinking... The first thing we must get done. Is to arrange for Art's body to be exhumed, and re-buried where he should be place to rest. He belongs alongside us in the crypt that my master is resting in."

"Alright Connie we will have it arranged but, what I think we should do. Is make out an itinerary of all that has to be done, that we haven't done already.

We already set everything up in the event of anything happened to either one, of us, so that's covered. Right now all I care about is getting home, and out of these clothes..."

* * * *

A half an hour later we were standing at the front door of our home. Struggling to compose our emotions. As I unlocked the front door and lead Connie inside the house.

Stopping just inside the house at the living room doorway. Not believing what we were seeing...Bewilderingly staring at each other.

"Connie I don't believe it...? Look at this place...? Why it's immaculately clean. What's been going on here...?"

"Hi, there ladies..." Joe emerged from the kitchen door saying." Now don't panic its only me Joe, your friendly neighborhood cop."

"Joe what are you doing here...?" Connie uneasily asked.

"Someone had to take care of the place while you two, were gone. We drew straws and I lost. So tell me how are you to feeling, alright I hope?"

"We will survive." I snapped back saying.

"That's nice to hear. You two, were really put through the ringer. To tell you the truth I didn't think either of you would ever come out of it. As soon as I heard that you were being released I came right over to welcome you home."

"Thanks Joe, and thanks for looking after the place for us but, we are home now. I'm sure we can handle things now." I spoke up hoping that he would get the hint. That we wanted him to leave.

"Sue I don't like to say this but, my visit isn't all social. Some of it is official. It has to do with the teenage boy. Who gave you your lives by sacrificing his own.

The one, that the two, of you have been harboring. Since he first escaped from the orphanage center.

Ladies theses past mouths have been very revealing ones. The two, of you have been making fools out of all of us. The best you two, could hope for is life in prison. You really didn't think that you would actually get away with it, did you?

However, you might have. If it wasn't for the fact of what happened to you. You really had us convinced of your innocence. Even me as well but, it's all over now for the two, of you."

"Joe can't we make some sort of a deal?" Connie asked." No one was hurt, who didn't deserve to be. Let us do what we have too, and we will confess to everything voluntary."

"That won't be necessary. Neither of you are going to confess to anything. I'm the one, who has the reports.

The real reports the ones, that you wouldn't believe all the manipulating I had to do amongst other things to cover all your shit up.

Sue I shouldn't be telling you this but, not more than a month ago I was given the news that you were pregnant."

"What...?!" I startlingly gasped out from utter shock." What... Me...?! I don't believe you! I would have known if I was pregnant...!"

"I have it from very reliable resources that you are. I'm surprised that you weren't informed about your condition before you were released.

Apparently due to the medication they were having you on was inhibiting you from feeling any effects of her being pregnant. Where you obviously aren't showing that you are some five months pregnant. However, whether you like it, or not. You are pregnant.

I also have in my possession the only other two, other copies of the original reports regarding. The young kid that the two, of you have been harboring.

To which I've also withheld that implicates the both of you as accomplices in the three, deaths that brought the three, of you together.

I'm only telling you because I thought that you should know how appreciative you should be to me. Along with how obligated you should feel towards me looking out for your best interests. The rest, as how you could express your application. We will see about later on but, I'm sure we will work out a *culpable restitution that we will all come to agree upon.

I'm not a hard person to get along with but, I've been known to be somewhat difficult to please at times.

Now there's no need to thank me, and it's not going to do you any good to go getting yourselves all uptight. Not when I'm the one holding all the crap on you two."

" Alright Joe it's obvious that you didn't go through all you did for nothing. Just what is it that you want from us?"

"Two, things Connie. The first being the two of you. I'm not such a bad looking guy. That kid had it all, and I mean it all...

A woman I can always get but, I never had what he had. Nothing will change, other than the fact that I will be taking his place.

I know too much for you not to accept me into the family. I know that you two, killed that oriental girl, and that it was Connie, along with at least four, others. Who killed all those men at the mission, cops included. One being my best friend Carl.

I also know about your place in Ohio. I know it all ladies. We could have a great thing going here.

Where for your concern Connie, what you don't know is that I'm black as well. Which is in both of our favor, seeing how you detest white men. So Carl once told me.

I know that you don't love me now but, you'll in time. All I want is what that brat had. Where in return I won't place demands upon either of you. That would undermine you as the undeniably beautiful women that you are.

All I want is the same chance you gave him. Now that isn't asking too much is it? Considering all I've done for the two, of you? Now both of you listen to me."

He nervously spoke out noticing that Connie and I was giving him the impression that we were contemplating some other option.

"I made provision in my will. That if anything should happen to me, out of the line of duty as a police officer. The district attorney will receive a sealed envelope.

Now in the event something should happen. While in the line of duty. The both of you will receive each an envelope.

With the copies of all that I have conceal, and withheld for you to do with whatever you want. As proof of my good faith and sincerity. However, as you can see I'm not stupid enough, not to protect myself.

You Connie are one very dangerous women. Too dangerous to be under estimated. I need assurances that you won't use any of your skills against me. Even though I know that you also trained Sue/ However Sue here has a conscience, where you don't. You wouldn't hesitate to kill anything that got in your way of your freedom."."

"Joe you sure have been working overtime I must say." Connie sarcastically spoke out saying." I would be flattered. If it wasn't for the fact that I'm being forced into a compromising position that I personally am finding repulsive.

I don't like being forced into anything. I don't want to get myself involved in, or with anyone of mot my own chosen. I still have rights, or are they not included in this arrangement of yours? Where I myself want the right, to select freely! The man I care to give myself to?"

"You still have that right. As long as I'm the man you choose. Considering the circumstances, I don't feel that I'm taking unfair advantage of either of you."

"Alright Joe we agree." Connie accepted for the both of them. However, we to have few things that we must do. Where you are going to have to trust us.

Even though it's obvious that we can't go anywhere, not with all that you have on us. Where you are going to have allow us the freedom to come and go as we please."

"Alright Connie you have your freedom but, I want a little reassurance first, of your sincerity I'm the one that's sticking my neck out on this.

Don't make the mistake of underestimating me, by thinking of me some stupid fool. I'm far from it. I've the two, of you where I want you. Just remember that. I'm not here to play games. Besides it's not going to be so bad. All we have to do is break the ice, and everything else will fall into place."

"Joe you don't want us really what you want is the prestige of having yourself two, whore's catering to you. Where now that I think about it. It might be the best thing for the both of us, where it might not be all that bad.

What in the hell difference does it make anyway? Who the hell cares anymore anyway? Leastways where I'm concern. However, I can't speak for Sue here"

"You will Connie. Believe me, after you get to really know me. You will come to realize that I had no choice but, to take the initiative.

Someone has to make you forget about what was, and begin anew. You two, need to start living for a far better future. Where now you have yourselves a man now, not a mere boy.

I'll make you forget your past with him, where he's is now just another has been. That was never meant to be to begin with."

Has been did you say?" Connie walked towards him. Holding back her enragement towards him saying.

" I'm sure that you are all man... I do want to be the first to try you out for size. It's been sometime since I had myself what only was a measure of a man. Let's see what sort of a man you yourself measure up, shall we..."

" Now Connie..." Joe nervously spoke out backing away from her." Just remember I'm holding all the aces..."

"Joe whatever is the matter with you...? You want me don't you..." Connie softy spoke out to him, as he nervously kept stepping back for her saying.

" Yes... You know I do... All I can think about is the two, of you..."

"Well then let me come to you then, and stop acting so childish."

"Connie... You are not going to try to pull anything are you...?"

"Yes, but if you don't want me to... I'm not going to let that discouraged me. When it was you who started this, and we did agree ... You can't start rejecting are advances now..." She stopped advancing towards him. As he stood about three, feet away from her.

"I'm sorry Connie I thought that you were going to pull something... I guess it's going to take time to make the adjustment."

" No, it's not... Not where I've already made it." She spoke out sending a twirling high heel. Crashing into his throat.

Recoiling him back against the wall behind him. Then off of it back onto the side of the palm of her chopping hand. As it came against the bridge of his nose, shoving his nose upwards into his skull rupturing his brain.

Sending him back against the wall again. To be replied back into her thrusting foot crushing into his chest from the impact of his dead body, and the impact of her foot colliding together. Against his rib cage. With Connie disconcertingly shouting out.

"I'll meet you in hell you bastard...!" I infuriatingly stepping back form him, stretched out lifeless upon the floor. With his head being braced up against the wall.

"Come on Sue we have to hide him."

"Connie is he dead...! Did you have to kill him?! Jesus H, Christ...!"

"Yes, dammit! He left me no other option but, to kill him. He pushed his threatening authority to damn far! Beside what difference does it make now anyway?

Let them have their world we don't belong here anymore. Now come on help me put him into the freezer. We've a lot to do."

We put is body into the freezer them showered, and dressed. Leaving the house around 1:30 taking the van that was parked out front.

We headed for are attorney's office. Where from there we went to the bank. Then to the courthouse to the land, and titles office. We appointed my attorney as trustee too Art's child who was going to get all that he, or she was entitled to.

Where unknown to me. Connie snuck out of the house while I was getting dressed, and put her weaponry in the van.

While she also rigged the house to explode into flames using the telephone. Skinning back the wires just enough to set off a spark when it rang. By attaching a dry cell battery to the wires to set off the spark when she called the house. While making sure that all the pilot lights were out and the gas just was left on. All about the house for a few hours waiting for several hours before calling the house.

Chapter 23

It was 5:30 when we finally finished transacting are business. Making certain there weren't any legal loopholes the would prevent Art's child form receiving their inheritance.

"Damn girl I never thought that we could do it I hope that we didn't overlook anything?"

"If we did Connie it couldn't be worth anything." I replied as we stood at a pay phone with me asking her." Who are you calling now?"

" I just have some unfinished business to tend to This won't take but, a second." She replied. Dialing the home number, letting it ring until it suddenly went dead.

" Well I guess no one is home..." She sinisterly said hanging up the phone.

" I'm hungry Sue let's say we go get something to eat, and have ourselves a couple of good stiff drinks? That place across the street looks good enough, come on let's go."

We went in, and ate, and drink whiskey sours, and were going on are forth just sitting back relaxing. Letting are food settle in our stomachs.

"Sue did you ever realize that out of the vast fortune we acquired. That all we have left between us is $400.00 dollars.

That's not much to show for a lifetime of struggling but, it's more that I started out with, so I still came out ahead.

Sue I've been doing so serious thinking about are situation. I think that someone should stay behind to take care of Art's child. Where see that you are going to be the lucky mother of his child it's going to be you. Where you could blame it all on me, and let me go to him. I'm the one that's been doing all the killing where all you done was love him and shared my ever dying love for him.

That way I'll be with him to love, and protect him, and you will be here to give him the chance he never had in this world.

I know I will be able to find him. Due to all that's happened to him, and the way that he dies. By sacrificing his life so that we might live. I know exactly where he will be a "

"Connie you really don't believe that there's a heaven, and a hell do you?"

"No, I don't however I'll tell you what I do believe. I believe there's dimensions that a person goes into when, they can exist according to the way they lived. Where I can to believe in another plateau. To which is just another step of many that one must climb.

Where I know I can find him. Because I told him that I would come for him no matter where he would be if he ever became separated from me.

I gave freely of my heart, and soul, and my body knowing the path I must follow. Being glade that I too didn't get myself pregnant. Like you did. Knowing that would be the only thing keeping me from going after him.

I don't belong here anymore I just couldn't live out the remainder of my life just existing, and not feeling. I have nothing left inside me that would make me want to stay I'm already dead Sue... Sue I've to go to him I can't go on without him. You have to believe me when I say I'll find him.

I honestly believe that it is my destiny to be with him.

Where you were blessing with more than just his memory I was bless in him becoming a part of me that will glide me straight to him.

Sue I'm tired of trying. I haven't felt like living until Art came into my life. Where let's face it,

between the two, of us your place should be right here.

I'll write out a confession exonerating you. Taking the blame for deceiving you, where Art was concern. Saying that it was I who was the one that manipulated you into acknowledging him as your mice. That it was I who created her so that I could have him with me all the time. So that we could share our lives together.

All you will need to do is come up with a convincing story to tell how I manipulated you. Into going along with me where Art's concern, and you will be home free.

I've also seen to it that Joe's death will appear to be in the line of duty. Stating that I alone killed him when he attempted to arrest me.

Here's no court in the land that would keep a child form his rightful mother. Where you will be free to bring the child up the way you want to."

"Connie what about the place in Ohio?"

" Sue it's still are place. You being the child legal mother, everything will revert to you. Both our names are on all the documents we signed.

Believe me Sue where Art and I are concern. We won't be leaving you behind. We will be there with you in spirit."

"Connie you don't have to do this. I know you feel cheated that I got pregnant, and you didn't but, I didn't even know I was. However, in any case Art's child is just as much yours as he, or she is mine.

You know how things were between the three, of us. How many times have we woke up in the middle of the night? Finding him having him having his way. With either one, of us, where afterwards. All we did was roll over and go back to sleep, without any protecting being used.

You could have just as easily gotten pregnant as I did. I was just the one who did.

The child still is ours regardless who the biological mother is. We can bring the child up together and give him, or her a great life.

Connie I don't want you to go. I love you with all my heart and soul but, I know I can't stop you but, don't be expecting me to not to hate you for what you are going to be doing to us…

Alright I'll stay! I just don't want you to think that I didn't love him enough to die for him myself. I would give anything for it to had been me instead of him…"

"Sue you are about to bring forth life where I couldn't. Though my love for him was obsessive. It wasn't strong enough to bless me like he has you biologically. Where I personally know why it was never meant to be.

I've no apprehensions about your love for him, its mine. That's why I must go to him. Where in the other world I might become bless as you have been in this world.

Now let's get out of here, and find us a motel where I can be alone with my thoughts for a while." Connie rose saying walking away from the table.

* * * *

I rented the most expensive one I could fine, and sat hoping, and praying that she would change her mind. Saying nothing just watching her, where she was determined to go through with killing herself. Knowing in my heart that talking and pleading with her was useless. Once she set her mind to doing something she does it.

It was past midnight when Connie rose from the desk she was sitting at. After writing out her confession in the motel room.

I didn't know what was the actually meaning behind why Connie's state of mind was so concentrated on going through with it. Where I discovered later. That it was greatly associated with over the loss of her daughter who she truly loved .

Where even though she was with me. She felt all alone, and made to suffer inhumanely over losing the three, she loved more than life it's, and was just wanting to find peace and harmony at long last with the one who she couldn't bare losing the most.

Convincing herself that by releasing herself from the earthly bonds. That bond that tied her from wanting to be with Art where enduringly hard to break.

Knowing by all she came to believe. That in spirit she would become reunited with him once again. Where nothing could separate them ever again.

"Well that does it." Connie spoke out saying folding the confession. Placing it into an envelope as she rose from the desk. Holding onto the envelope as she walked over to me. To Kiss me good-bye as if she was going to take a walk for herself.

"Connie listen to me. You are wrong in what you're doing... Art died a hero's death with honor and dignity. What you are doing is selfish, and suicidal.

You will not only disgrace yourself but, the memory over why he died for you. You can't go through with this madness...!"

I desperately pleaded hoping to change her mind by attacking her on her pride in herself.

"You are wrong Sue. You are right he did die an honorable death but in life, he had someone who loved him at his side. I just can't let him be alone in death. My dying is not sacrificial but, an honor onto him and my undying love for him.

He once told us that he would rise from hell itself to make it back with us. I'm going to him to insure he can. Believe it or not we will all be together soon.

I could lie to you by letting you believe that you convinced me not to go to him, and go to him anyway.

I'm not looking for you pity, or you despise. My life is my own to live. Where you only want to exist now because you have to for Art's names sake.

Alone, deceiving yourself you are doing so out of your love for him and the child you're going to bare from him.

Where you are concern. You will soon have what you sought from the very beginning. when you first laid your eyes on him. Where he lived in your nephew's memory, and his child will live in his. You haven't really lost anything.

Where I'm concerned even with you, and his child I'll still be alone with only the memory of the haunting nightmare of seeing him dying before my eyes. I must be going now.

Just never forget that I love you with all my heart. You take care of our child now. I'll make sure my confession reached the authorities..."

Then walked out the door closing it behind her.

"Oh, My God... No...!" I cried out wanting to get up to run after her, to stop her. Knowing there was nothing I could say, or do would. As I ran to the door yanking it open. running out to look for her but, she was nowhere in sight.

"Connie... please ... My God I'm so frightened without you...Please don't leave me here alone... Come back... My God. Please come back." I cried out calling out for her. Praying that she would hear me, and come back. Breaking down emotionally in tears of anguish...

* * * *

'Well girl this seems like as good as place as any.' Connie said to herself. Pulling the van to a stop in front of an all-night coffee shop. Picking up her powers before processing to go in. Upon entering going to sit herself down in a booth, waiting to be waited on.

"Yes, what will it be lady?" Alice the waitress on duty approached her booth saying, standing before the table.

"Just coffee please."

"Sure thing." The waitress replied writing down her order.

While Connie waited she sat writing out an additional note to add to her written confession. When her coffee came. While she finished her confession drinking her coffee. Finishing what she had to say. Then placing it an envelope where she planned to leave it sitting on the table.

Nostalgically writing down, going back over her life. Essentially do to struggling with herself hoping to find some reason for her, to want to live where to her there was nothing left for her to want to live for. Knowing what she left behind in the burnt remains of the house. Knowing there was nothing that can't be changed if she would change her mind.

Looking down at the confession she just wrote. Then mentally recalling her life from the time she was life for died on the side of the road, after being raped repeatedly, and brutally brutalized by her attackers.

To when she was adopted by the swamp man who befriended her. Then even nurtured, and cared for her. Who even took it upon himself to train her in how to protect herself using his form of the martial arts.

Where how she in return formed an alliance. With the daughters of the servants working for him at his Southern mansion, and those working on his plantation.

Where due to her they establish a secret league. That she used to reap her revenge on those who brutalize her.

Then remembering her giving birth of a daughter onto her adopted benefactor. Who she fell in love with. Then remembering how he himself was murdered shortly later. Shortly after he taught her everything he knew in his style of fighting.

Where after his death discovering that he left the heiress to his entire estate. Where she turned her home into a refuge center, and medical clinic. For the suppressed black people in the region.

Where she then left abandoning her estate shortly after her daughter died. Deserting her previous life style to make a new life for herself elsewhere. Which came to be Milwaukee and her becoming a nurse. Where she self-promoted herself becoming a MD. And was interning when she met Sue. Where they have been close friends ever since. Accomplishing becoming a surgeon by the age of 26.

Then remembering why, it was she abandoned her Ohio, plantation. Because she went to the aid of a women several black women that the syndicate forced into prostitution. Where they brutally continued to unscrupulously beat, exploited, and even murder them.

Where the authorities kept turning a blind eye to condoning what was happening because they were black. Letting the syndicates reign of terror go unopposed.

Until Connie gathered those she trained to team up. To rid themselves of those who went about openly terrorizing those helpless to rebel against their domination, and tyranny. By eradicating their presence in the region she was living in.

Where she had no choice but, to flee in order to escape being apprehended or killed herself due, to the mayhem, and utter chaos she and her team inflicted upon the syndicate.

Was bringing about drastic changes in law enforcement. That made it extremely uncomfortable doing business in her neck of the woods.

What prompted her to have to leave, and change her name. In order to avoid being arrested, or even murdered. At the age of twenty. Where she was being sought out by both.

Where she diligently applied herself to make a new life for herself. Where met up with Sue and they established a common bond. While going to collage studying their chosen careers. Where they closely netted friendship tuned into a relationship.

Where together they had to comfort constant hardships having to compete for everything they achieved to advance in their chosen profession.

Stopped here

Where it came to Sue's unbearable lose. When Sue loss of her beloved nephew, and couldn't bring herself to believe that he was dead. When Art miraculously came into her life.

Where how Connie was totally against her becoming involved with Art from the very beginning but, went along with her because it was giving Sue something she never had.

An opportunity to morn with peace of mine. By giving Sue motivation over thinking that she could use him get gain her ravage on her Nephews parents.

Where she was blaming them for murdering their own son because he loves Sue, more than he loved his own parents, and they were jealous of her.

Not really caring how Art was going to come out. When Sue came back to her senses, and got rid of him.

Only to once again having to come to gibes with her past life. Dealing with having to come to gibes with accepting that the one she loved more than her own life was murdered right before her eyes. Have to endure seeing him begin force to submit the two atrocities. Of having to perform oral sex on a mental degenerate. While not being able to do anything about it.

After having to deal with the syndicate again resurrecting her true identity. That left some twenty syndicate solders, and eight police officers. One, being a particular officer who she a lot of feeling towards.

Then having to kill again another cop who attempted to blackmail her and Sue into becoming his personal whore's. Where she just lost it over not being able to deal with it anymore

All the while she sat asking herself why? The more she regressed into a deeper depression. The vision of him doing what he was being forced to do, to that derelict, and sacrificing himself. Thinking not of himself but Sue, and I.

Then seeing him lying dead was more that she could bare. Where she was mentally unable to overcome her misery.

In Connie's oblivious state. She was distracted from noticing two, men coming into the restaurant. Who became aware of her. As they sat down at the counter across from her.

Where they instantly developed awareness that she was all alone.

Suggestively developing an obscure conversation about her amongst themselves. Making lewd comments out loud degrading her publicly. Becoming arrogantly obnoxious making their cements known to the other patrons in the restaurant.

Alice the waitress approached Connie's booth, holding a coffee pot in her hand to refill her coffee cup. Snapping Connie out of her train of thought. As she startlingly noticed her pouring her more coffee.

"Excuse me Miss where's the ladies room?"

" It's to your left at the end of the counter."

"Thank you. Excuse me again Miss. I don't mean to be imposing on you but, I was wondering if you wouldn't mind doing me a favor.

They will be some gentlemen coming here soon. Would you mind handing them this envelope" Connie held out her sealed confession to her asking.

"Sure but, how will I know them?" She asked taking it for Connie's hand.

"You'll know then alright. They will be the police. There's some very important information inside, and I want to make sure they'll get it."

"Are your serous lady...?"

" Yes, deadly serious." Connie replied reaching into her purse pulling out a $100.00-dollar bill." And this here is just to show my appreciation. Consider it a tip."

"Well alright lady." She anxiously took the money saying." And thanks, you can count on me to give it to them."

"I knew I could. I'll take that coffee now but, first I must go to the lady's room." Connie slide out of the booth saying. Picking up her things walking towards the lady's room.

Connie was leaving to going change into her powers. Thinking to simply vanish, and go pay a visit on Pat. Blaming her for everything that happened. and for Art's death.

Connie was in the middle of going through her symbolic ritual. When one, of the guys who entered the restaurant came busting into the bathroom, startling Connie.

Connie came springing up slashing out at him with her sword. Just missing him as he went running out of the bathroom. As if the devil himself was chasing after him.

With Connie emerging right behind him. Wearing her powers holding her sword in her hand.

Causing utter chaos to break broke out.

People started to panicky run towards the exit door. The one, who came in with the guy she terrified the hell out of. Rose up to play hero, challenging her.

" Alright what in the hell do you think you're doing...?! He spoke out cautiously approaching her." Just put that damn sword down before someone gets hurt..."

Connie stood excepting his challenge. Thrusting out a shrike, catching him in his right thigh. Her reactions, were totally contrary to her primary function, that was to kill instinctively, without hesitation.

"I'll not die without honor..." She shouted out. Running past her first fatality, towards the door. Then out into the parking lot. Running into, and amongst the people panicky running about trying to keep out of her way.

A police car came to a screeching halt directly in front of Connie. Where Connie Drew her blowgun. Hitting the cops as they emerged from out of the car.

Knowing that she was only at half her strength. Alarmingly discovering that all her weaponry wouldn't hit their target. Where she intended to only wound. Where the darts missed their mark. Hitting one the throat, and another in the forehead instead of their chests.

Knowing she was in serious trouble without being at her fully strength. She fled into the shrub area behind the restaurant. Seeking out a place to complete her ritual. What to be at full strength when she went to join Art.

Where she jumped into a trench. That sort of hid her out of sight. Where she hastily went through her ritual.

After which still not feeling at her fullest she rose up. To see more cops converging all about the restaurant below her.

"There... There she is..." One of the cops yelled out. Pointing at Connie exposing herself purposely.

They came charging up the slop of the hill towards her. Connie herald two, more darts out of her blowgun. Catching one, in the chest and another in his right eye."

"Holy shit...!" Jack alarmingly shouted out." Back off...! Dammit back off...!" He yells out ordering all the officers to retreat back down the hill.

"Dammit Jack.! Steve yelled back at him. Taking cover behind the squad." What in the hell are you doing...?!"

" You dumb Ashlee...!" Jack shouted back at him." That's a fucken Ninja...!"

"What the fuck is a Ninja...?!"

"Death that's what!"

"What in the fuck are you talking about?! That's only one, person that I can see. Let's go get the Asshole, and have done with him... Ninja my ass...! Stop reading those damn comic books..."

" If you do that Steve you better call for reinforcements along with a lot of body bags... I'm telling you that one is the deadliest killer on the face of his earth..."

" What if he hell is it doing here...?!" Steve asked.

Captain Rogers pulled up onto the scene. Climbing out of his car. Running up to take cover beside Jack and Steve.

"Alright what's going down, now many, and is anyone dead...?!"

"We got two, dead cops, and two, more badly wounded. Whoever it is means business." Steve answered him

"Captain one, of the cops came running up to his position behind the car. Calling out to him joining them behind it.

"The waitress just handed me this envelope. She said that a black women gave it to her to give to us, and that she's the one who's up there."

"Holy shit! Capt... Carl told me that he was into that shit! And he studied under some black women. If that's her, it would be suicidal to go up there after her..." Jack related what he learned from Carl to the captain.

"Holy shit...! another officer alarmingly yelled out. Startlingly seeing one, of the officers hitting the ground beside his car. With an arrow lodged in his right eye.

Then another, and another fell, and still another fell, with darts sticking in their necks. Falling all about him.

"Dammit captain...!" Jack yelled out at him." Order the men to back off...! Before she kills us all ... We walked into hell dammit, and we don't stand a chance against her until it gets light... Capt., that has to be that Connie Price that's been doing all he killing around here. If I'm right, she won't fight in the daytime.

Unless that is she want to die, and I think that's exactly what she's here to do. Where to do so she has to do it with honor. We should back off..."

"I don't know what makes you such the authority Jack but, anything is worth a try. At least for the time being. So that I can get a sniper up here. You damn well better be right."

" Capt., Carl told me all about that elite sort of fighters. He's been trying for years to qualify to become one, and wasn't able to make it. I'm deadly serious about the one, who's up there.

As for who I'm sure it is. I don't but, who it is. I damn sure do. You have to get everyone back as far away from her as possible.

Like I said. He has until daylight to do herself honor. Whereas if you don't come to her, she going to come to us, and be gone before daylight where we will never be able to catch her.

Why it is that she came to be here, I don't have the vaguest idea why.

Those damn ninjas are expert assassins. That is what is so damn puzzling. She's not dressed in her invisibility, that's supposed to prevent her from being seen. That's supposed to mean that she was sent here but, to kill who, Then again Why is she exposing herself out in the open like she is.

The fact that we are able to have seen her is weird in itself.

"Alright I heard enough. Everyone back off..." Roger yelled out ordering his men to retreat from their positions. Where those who were still standing all jumping into their cars, and backing out to take up position outside the parking lot, and under overhead lights of the road side.

"Alright we will wait her out here, and see what happens. Jack you best be right about this, if he or she gets away its going to cost you your badge."

"Captain I know I'm right. It's why that comes as a surprise. I should have known this was going to happen, and that it could be who I think it is.

Joe went to speak to those two, who were in that kidnaping, and killing of that kid some five, months back. Where he still hasn't come back to tell me how it went.

Capt., I was at their place earlier today. The place burnt down to ashes earlier. Where they just got out of that nuthouse today.

That has to be that Connie Stone who was with that teenage kid who was killed some months back. I have no damn idea why they released those two, crazy broads.

Carl know all along who she was but, he did nothing about it. He had to have been protecting them."

" Alright Joe let's not go accusing anyone. Especially when they are not around to defend themselves. Besides even if he did know. He wasn't the only one, so don't come down on her. We didn't have a case that would stick against either of them, and the DA had bigger fish to fry, so back off."

Capt. if that his Connie Price up there. We're going to have to kill her, or she'll surely kill all of us."

"Just shut up Jack! We might be here for a while. Let's setup base inside the restaurant I want to read what's inside this envelope. Maybe I'll get a better understanding on what she's up to."

Roger made his way into the restaurants back office. Approaching it from behind using the back door to enter. Where he sits up his base headquarters, and sat down to read the letter. As Jack stood guard covering the back door.

"I just knew it damn it …!" Roger irately blurted out." Dammit! I just knew that she was the one, responsible for all that happened at the mission.

It seems that her girlfriend Sue was also fooled as well. Damn… This is one hell of a confession no wonder she wants to end it all. Well we won't disappoint her."

"Can I read that captain?" Jack asked.

"Sure here." He answered him handing him Connie's signed confession.

Jack stood beside Roger's reading the confession." Capt. I'm reading it but, I'm not believing but, it does explain everything."

"It sure does right up to the kid's death. That we have been waiting to question them both about. That Connie is one kill carved bitch and I'm going to send her where she wants to go! I will deal with that Sue bitch later!"

" Capt. according to this confession she innocent of have any evolvement in any killings, and according to what she dates here. Sue didn't even know about the kid not being a girl. If she was involved in anything Connie was involved in she's been exonerated."

"That's not for you to determine so stay the hell out of it, and get back covering that damn door. Dammit!" Let's get this one's, ass that we are dealing with now.

When that sun starts to come up. She's going to stand out like a sore thumb in that getup of her's. I want three, marksmen here now. With high powered rifles."

" Capt. you best come out, and see this for yourself." Steve came running in through the back door of the restaurant excitedly shouting out.

" You're not going to believe this but, she's making herself visible, and she's wearing a red hood and a belt that has red spots on it. She's making herself out as a human target." We went out to take up positions back behind the car.

"Oh, Jesus…" Jack Disbelievingly spoke out. "Steve's right she's telling us how to kill her... Someone get me a rifle..."

Jack called out. Selecting himself to be her executioner. Having one of the officers come running up carrying a high powered rifle, handing it to Jack.

Jack positioned himself at the rear of the squad. Using the trunk to stabilize his arms while aiming the rifle.

* * * *

"What's going on?" Mickey asked one of the spectators that were congregated up around the barricades blocking access to the restaurant. As the police held the crowds of people back behind them. When she approached the barricade with Bridget following behind her.

"Some dopey board popped her cork. She's running around in black pajamas killing cops. She's really gone Waco..." The guy who went into the bathroom to attack her answered her back.

" Mickey...! Bridget startlingly called out to her spotting Connie hiding behind a clump of bushes." That's Connie up there..."

"Yes, I know. Come on we best be getting home we can't do anything for her. She's wearing the colors of death. She's going to join the one she loves more than life itself. Come on Bridget..." Mickey mournfully said leading her away from the barricade.

* * * *

"Jack are you sure you want to do this?" Roger asked

"No, I don't want to do it but, there's no other way. She'll never find peace if I don't. Where more will die if I don't. She's giving us are one, chance, now move the men back. The last thing I want to do is to miss..."

Connie looked down from the top of ridge as she was hiding on behind a clump of bushes. She could see someone aiming directly at her. Just waiting to get a clear shoot at her.

"Here I come darling..." She rose up from behind the bushes. Yelling out with her sword in hand. As she charging down the hill screaming like a demon from hell. "Dammit …! Damn you shoot…!" Someone yelled out.

Jacks finger squeezed back on the trigger. The rifle recoiled back against his shoulder, as it flashed an echoing sound of thunder. Stopping Connie dead in her tracks. Clutching her chest with her empty hand.

"You got the Bitch…!" One of the excited young rooky cop yelled out. Leading the charge of his fella officers towards the hill. Up to where she fell onto the ground.

Jack rose up onto his feet. Dropping the rifle to the ground beside him remorsefully walking up the hill. Kneeling down beside Connie. Where she was laying on the ground dying to remove her veiling cloak." Why Connie… Why…?"

"Thank you… Now I can go to him with honor and dignity. Did you get my confession?"

"Yes, we got it."

"Believe it, it's the truth. I harbor no regret or remorse for all I did. This world took away from me that which I loved most in life. I'm going to join him now, and to hell with all of you! All I wanted was to be left alone, and to be loved…." Connie died saying.

* * * *

It wasn't until over a year afterwards that I finally got back to Connie's home in Ohio. I walked in the front door carrying Art's child in my arms. Thinking to live out the remainder of my life, bringing him up in the manner which Art, and Connie would have wanted me to bring him up.

Instantly feeling that I wasn't alone. I don't know if it was just wishful hoping on my part but, I definitely felt a very overpowering presence. That made me sight out a relieving breath of relief.

Feeling assured that I wasn't alone. I instinctively I looked up toward the top of the landing, at the door where Art, Connie, and I spent months together living in that room.

Knowing that I wasn't hallucinating when I saw with my own eyes.

Connie leading Art out the door holding onto his hand. To greet us as I stood below holding up Art's son up for them to see.

Only to become startled by suddenly seeing Mickey, and Bridget emerging from the kitchen door coming to greet me.

Followed by another group of black young women. Entering in through the front door. Being followed by several elderly black women also entering. Dispersing about the house entering different rooms with one, women taking Arts son, Arthur the second junior, from my hands to hold him up above her head. Presenting him to all the women gathered up around me.

I stood in a state of bewilderment looking up at the upper stair case still seeing Connie, and Art standing looking down upon what was going on.

As Mickey and Bridget joined me, both hugging me. As the other women all followed their example warmly greeting me. Making me feel more at home, and welcomed.

* * * *

This is my story to which I leave to Arts child. This story that hasn't been told. Where only those who it touched would have never known.

I write this my story so that Art's son will never forget who his father was, and most for all of the others who played a very important part in Art's son being born.

Where Connie Price was, and still is just as much as Art's son mother and I was. Where I brought him up, making sure that I in staled in him her ideals, and conventions, and the moral fibbers that made her the wonderful person she was.

I've often wondered over the years about Pat, and the child she once calmed she was going to have. I never heard from her, or about her ever again.

Where as far as I was concern, they never existed at all, and that included the rest of his family. To which he never really took very much of an interest in. In wanting to find any of them

Art fond more love, and affection just being loved by those he was growing up around. He rarely ever showed any interest in anyone else unrelated, or connected to us.

Where upon I now leave this as my legacy, as I go to join Art and Connie now. Who never really left me. Connie kept her word, and met me with Art, when I arrived bringing Art back with her.

Where I never married because I never felt the need for anyone else. As senile as I must sound I never suffered from the lack of affection, or companionship. I always had Connie, and Art plus all her and now my friends.

Even through Connie and I discussed me giving Art a bother, or sister Art was against it. Besides Art son was more than I could handle as it was.

Now as I'm writing my last word I can feel the pen dropping from my hand slumbering off into a peaceful sleep.... With Art and Connie lying beside me.... Waiting for me to join them.

With are son standing beside us. Holding his loving pregnant wife around her waist. Where her name is also Connie the daughter of the of my house keeper.

THE END

www.ingramcontent.com/pod-product-compliance
Lightning Source LLC
Chambersburg PA
CBHW071425070526
44578CB00001B/10